What God Does When Women Pray

Evelyn Christenson

WORD PUBLISHING

NASHVILLE

A Thomas Nelson Company

Unless otherwise indicated, Scripture quotations used in this book are from the New American Standard Bible (NASB), © 1960, 1977 by the Lockman Foundation.

Other Scripture references are from the following sources:

The King James Version of the Bible (KJV).

The new King James Version (NKJV), copyright 1979, 1980, 1982, Thomas Nelson, Inc., Publishers.

The Holy Bible, New International Version (NIV). Copyright © 1973, 1978, 1984, International Bible Society. Used by permission of Zondervan Bible Publishers.

Library of Congress-in-Publication Data

Christenson, Evelyn.
    What God does when women pray / Evelyn Christenson.
      p. cm.
    ISBN 0-8499-3761-2
    1. Prayer—Christianity. 2. Christian women—Religious life. I. Title.

BV210.5 .C48 2000
248.3'2'082—dc21

00–043268
CIP

Printed in the United States of America

1 2 3 4 5 PC 00 01 02 03 04

Contents

Acknowledgments

THE ONLY REASON this book could be written is because of you who prayed. My heart is overwhelmed at your love and faithfulness. Here are some of you.

My *United Prayer Ministry Board*—praying daily, telephone prayer chains three times a week, and monthly board prayer meetings, consistently and fervently for twenty-seven years.

Gloria Davidson and Jan Mudge—founding U.P.M. officers in 1973.

Jeanne Scott and Marlene Lee— U.P.M. presidents who made their homes and our board meetings holy places of prayer.

Eighty selected intercessors on monthly calendar—praying consistently since the early seventies.

My *extended family*—faithfully praying long before and through this thirty-year journey.

My *mother*—the most powerful pray-er in my life until she went to heaven and found all her prayers in golden bowls up there.

AD2000/Christian Women United Board and participants—praying with me in unity with awesome prayer for nine years.

Kathryn Grant—seeking God's wisdom and guidance and power with me for twenty years—my undying gratitude.

Judy Mbugua, Lorry Lutz, and international leaders of AD2000 Women—praying faithfully for almost ten years.

The original 1968 prayer experimenters from Rockford, Illinois.

My occult prayer chain—praying victoriously for seven years.

Local seminar committees here and abroad—praying sacrificially for twenty-eight years.

International A.D. *2000 leaders*—praying on every continent since 1992.

My twenty-four-hour prayer clock—praying without ceasing when I was overseas, for nineteen years.

Bethel faculty wives prayer group—praying faithfully since 1971.

Twin Cities metropolitan prayer chain, including its *prison chain* and *government chain*—praying since the early seventies.

Nine thousand U.P.M. newsletter recipients—praying since 1973.

Calvary Church of St. Paul friends and staff—praying supportively since 1970.

Calvary Church care group—praying monthly for the last nine years.

Signe Swan and Lorna Johnson—with whom I started praying in 1964.

JoAnne Jankowski, my lawyer and prayer partner—praying personally since the late seventies.

Sally Hanson, Sue Moore, Carri Fadden, and Diane Berggren, faithful administrators—praying while they did all the work I could not do.

The National Prayer Committee—praying for me and with me since 1974, with prisidents Vonette Bright to David Bryant.

Mission America and Lighthouse Committees—praying for nine years.

All the people in the organizations I list in chapter 1.

Plus all of you dear, faithful pray-ers I may have left out of this list or didn't even know were praying! Please insert your name on this list where it fits.

To you, thanks from the depths of my heart; and to God, my deepest gratitude for calling you all to be intercessors, burdening your hearts to pray, and then answering with what He wanted to happen all along! Thanks!

Finally my deep, deep gratitude for my dear Diane Berggren who has been my right hand helper in the producing of the book—in addition to personally accepting God's burden to pray for Him to pour forth His power to and through it to you, dear readers.

Introduction

WHEN I HAD put the manuscript for *What Happens When Women Pray* in the mail to editor Jim Adair in 1975, I panicked. Frantically calling him, I pleaded, "Don't print that thing!"

Jim calmly responded, "Evelyn, what is the matter with you?"

"That book doesn't say anything that every Christian doesn't already know," I exploded—at which Jim laughed out loud and hung up! I was furious—and very serious.

But now, twenty-five years after *What Happens When Women Pray* was first published, I realize how wrong I was. Although we had practiced all of the points of that original book and knew they worked, now there is a quarter of a century of proving that every one of its scriptural principles works far beyond anything we humans could have ever asked or even thought.

If you have been one of the millions who have read, studied, or taught *What Happens When Women Pray*, here is a book that will show you what God has done and taught us since then. If you have not read *What Happens When Women Pray*, you are in for an incredible journey into what God is doing today with the awesome prayer movement He started thirty years ago.

Like an Arctic iceberg, whose tip shows only one-ninth of its ice, the stories you read in this book will be only a little chip off the tip of the gargantuan iceberg of prayer. No human mind could ever comprehend or imagine the extent of God's potential activity in answer to our prayers.

Looking back on thirty years of prayer ministry, here are some of the things we have discovered that God does when we pray:

What God Taught Us about *Himself:*

- He taught us that it is through praying that He reveals His awesome self to us.

- He showed us that He originally initiates all prayer—and that it amazingly comes back full circle to Him with His answering according to His omniscient will.

- God unraveled for us the mystery of the difference between B.C. (before Christ) and A.D. (after Christ) praying.

- He reinforced to us that the privilege of our boldly coming directly to heaven's throne room is because of Jesus' shed blood.

- He showed us that He sends answers to prayer far above anything we could ask or even think about.

- God revealed to us that He worked behind the scenes long before He involved us in prayer.

- He showed us over and over what He had intended to do when He burdened us to pray—and we didn't have a clue why.

- He showed us what of Jesus and the Holy Spirit we may be slighting in our praying for revival.

- He taught us not to be discouraged by His not answering our prayers as fast as the culture whirling around us demands.

- He showed us that little by little He is revealing His overall plan for Planet Earth to us through His answers.

What God Taught Us about *Our Personal Responsibility:*

- He taught us that praying with others bombards heaven with volumes of prayer, but praying all alone in secret also brings incredible results.

- He proved to us that He is holy and that the holiness of our lives determines whether or not He will answer our prayers.

- He taught us to repent of our pride by revealing that He is the most important element of our praying—and thus He gets all the glory.

- He gently yet firmly showed us that He frequently changes the pray-er more than the one for whom we are praying.

- He revealed that our horizontal communication with humans through technological means has all but eclipsed our vertical communication with God.

- God affirmed that He still holds to His original biblical requirements for power in prayer.

- He revealed that He is asking what we Christians have done with His Son, Jesus.

- God affirmed that having Jesus as our own Savior and Lord for praying "in Jesus' name" is His prerequisite for intercessory prayer power.

What God Is Teaching Us about *New Millennium Praying:*

- God is showing us that Christians have the only hope for the rapid moral decline in our country.

- God is revealing to us that there is a surprising hunger among the peoples of the world for supernatural hope and answers.

- God is teaching us what the ultimate new millennium prayer should and must be.

These are some of the topics we will be discussing in this book. As you begin this journey into what God does when women pray, I pray that God will stir your heart to pray with passion and urgency.

Most important, however, I have longed to write a book giving God all the credit in the prayer process. I have personally experienced the awesomeness of God's power, protection, wisdom, and open doors throughout the current thirty-year prayer movement when we prayed. Since 1964, I have not so much as taught a Sunday-school class without organized prayer backing me. So I know the vast difference in the amount of God's power in ministering and living with or without prayer. I have watched God work in incredible ways when people prayed. But I also have seen the dryness, perfunctory speeches, and emotional persuasion of people working for God in the power of the flesh. *I would not dare go without prayer!*

I remember, after accepting the assignment to write *What Happens When Women Pray*, waking on that bitter cold and dark morning of January 1, 1968, knowing I had just six months to find the answer to that question. I did not have the faintest clue how to begin. As I lay in bed, horrified at what I said I would do, God showed me spiritually a door like a large trapdoor over my head. Assuring my racing heart that this was the answer, He said, *This door is the door of prayer. It is praying— not studying about prayer, not analyzing prayer, not even sincerely believing My promises in the Bible about prayer—but actually praying!*

So, dear reader, that is still my dream for you, a dream as fresh and reliable as when God first said it to me so many years ago. My greatest thrill will be to see you—eager young people and mature adults—persistently and fervently using that access to the holy throne room of God as you, too, discover what He is anxiously waiting to do for you—when you pray!

PART ONE

What God Does When We Pray

CHAPTER 1

Who Is This God of Our Prayers?

WE WANT YOU to find the answer to the question, 'What happens when women pray?' We have enough theories. We want you to experiment for six months and, as scientifically as possible, discover what really *does* happen when women pray."

This was my seemingly impossible assignment from The Crusade of the Americas, a national prayer and evangelism two-year event. Their goal was to pray in 1968 and then evangelize all of America in 1969. During the past thirty years, as I have ministered as a full-time prayer teacher in all fifty states and every continent in the world, I have personally seen miraculous answers to that question— "What happens when women pray?"

But now the question has changed. The emphasis then had been on the *praying* itself and on the *pray-ers*, the people doing the praying. While these are essential and vital to the prayer process, the ultimate focus and power of prayer is *the God who answers*. He is the focus of this book.

That original six-months' experimentation of women praying is detailed in my book *What Happens When Women Pray,* which has taught millions to pray and has opened the door to a worldwide prayer ministry. In this book, I will try to capture at least a speck of the awesome things God has done during these last thirty years of praying. In the following chapters, you will catch a glimpse of the awesome prayer movement we have seen expand and almost explode in our country these last three decades—while we prayed. And you will discover what God is showing us in the new millennium—as we continue to pray.

The Power of Prayer

The pastor of a huge Texas church and his wife walked me to the waiting car after a women's prayer seminar in which God had powerfully moved among the more than two thousand women who attended. More than 25 percent had prayed out loud in their little groups, making sure Jesus was their personal Lord and Savior (a percentage we have averaged since 1980). The pastor paused, looked quizzically at me, and asked, "To what do you attribute all that power?"

I answered, "Well, prayer, of course."

"What kind of prayer?" he pushed further.

I began to recount the many avenues of prayer that open up prior to and during our prayer seminars. "First, your own church's seminar committee prayed continually for this day. As we request all host churches do prior to a prayer seminar, they gathered committee members from surrounding churches and met together for six months to pray. They prayed fervently by name for each person registering and for every facet of the seminar. My United Prayer Ministry board and prayer calendar intercessors prayed daily through every aspect of my ministry. And our telephone prayer chain went through to all my board members three times a week, praying for my preparation time for the seminar at your church. In addition, I spent many hours in my own personal preparation in prayer for cleansing, wisdom, and God's power."

The pastor stopped and looked at me. Sweeping his hand toward his huge church building, he asked, "What would happen if I had that kind of prayer when I preached?"

"Sir," I answered, "you wouldn't be able to fit all the new converts into that sanctuary!"

His was the same question I was asked to solve with our women's prayer experiment in 1968. I, too, had fearfully asked, "What will happen?" But not anymore. Now, after more than thirty years of keeping track of God's answers to our prayers, I know what God really does when women pray. And I know what God can do with a church, ministry, family, or a life completely run on prayer.

While writing this book, I pulled out and read years of notes and prayer letters of what God did when women prayed. As I tried to condense the piles into twelve chapters, I suddenly put my head down amidst it all and wept, "Oh, God, I can't do this. There are no human words adequate to record the magnitude of what You have done—and who You really are!"

Oh, the depth of the riches both of the wisdom and knowledge of God! How unsearchable are His judgments and unfathomable His ways! For who has known the mind of the Lord, or who became His counselor? Or who has first given to Him that it might be paid back to Him again? For from Him and through Him and to Him are all things. To Him be the glory forever. Amen. (Rom. 11:33–36 NASB)

Our Awesome God

Traveling alone all over the United States and the world, I have thrilled at the privilege of frequently being completely dependent on God. I should have been somewhat disoriented from jet lag and my internal time clock's being twelve hours off as I arrived alone in Japan, but instead I wrote in the margin of my Bible beside Nehemiah 1:5: "5/23/93. Arriving in Japan. Feeling amazingly good and every need taken care of. Our God is an *awesome* God!"

Only when every human resource has been removed and I have been reduced to total dependence upon Him have I truly known the awesomeness of God. Then I really can say, "My God is an *awesome* God!"

Never once in all these years has He ever failed me. He has always answered the powerful, faithful praying of so many for me.

Knowing who God is has enabled me to put thankfulness in the prayer process where it belongs—*while I'm asking* (see Phil. 4:6). I am to thank God *before* He answers, not because I know the way He is going to answer, but because I know *who* He is. He is the God who never makes a mistake! He is never too soon or too late! He knows the end from the beginning of all things I am praying about! He is working all things for my good because I love Him!

I'm also thankful that I am not responsible for the answers to my prayers—*God is*. He doesn't expect me to be able to figure out the best solutions to my problems. That's His job.

So then, *God's answers are not limited by my ability to ask*. For years I have run my prayer ministry on God's promise to us in Jeremiah 33:3:

> Call unto Me, and I will answer, and show you great and mighty things, which you do not know. (NKJV)

If we call on God, He will not only answer—but then He will go past what we could ask or think.

This is the God who ordained all the laws of space and time. Biological or physical scientists are not inventing anything new; but just God allowing people to think His thoughts after Him. God reveals the power of who He is and His purposes for Planet Earth through His answers to our prayers.

I have been in a perpetual state of surprise—sometimes startled, sometimes shocked, frequently thrilled, and even ecstatic—when I saw what God was waiting to show me when I prayed. But I often was humbled, realizing my human mind has no capacity even to think of the things He wants to give when we pray. As our daughter Jan said, "Prayer is the awesome privilege of humans exchanging their finite for His infinite."

Leaving the tyranny of the urgent and dashing to a plane, I've always used that quiet time en route to let God prepare me personally in prayer and to finalize my speaking notes. But one day on the way to Dallas, my heart was so bursting with who God is that all the way from Minneapolis to Dallas, the only prayer words I could get out were, "Oh, God! Oh, God! Oh, God!"

Who Gets the Glory?

Although this book will show that God has used people and their prayers to unfold incredible, description-defying answers, *it is the One who brought about the answers when people prayed who deserves all the glory—God!*

Millions of people could be sincerely praying to a great tree. But no matter with how much faith they were praying, they still would not receive any answers from the tree. The One to whom we direct our prayers must be powerful enough to be able to supply what is being requested.

In the human charitable-giving process, it is not the helpless beggar or the disaster victim who is praised, but the person able and willing to rescue them and to provide for their needs receives the credit and honor.

So it is with the prayer process. It is not we needy, often desperate humans who get the credit for asking, but our all-loving, all-powerful Father who comes to our rescue by giving us answers to our prayers who gets all the glory:

> Now unto Him who is able to do exceeding abundantly above all that we
> ask or think, according to the power that works in us, to Him be the glory
> in the church and in Christ Jesus to all generations forever and ever,
> amen. (Eph. 3:20–21)

God pointedly brought this to my attention in South Africa in 1987 at the height of apartheid terrorism. From the beginning of my prayer ministry, God had instilled in me a determination to let Him remove the walls between races. Praying together has produced amazing, genuine reconciliation. So I had refused to go to South Africa unless they broke tradition and agreed to include both black and white Christians in the same prayer seminars. (The resulting oneness in Jesus was beautiful—and surprising.)

However, it was very dangerous. The fighting between tribes included necklacing—putting a car tire around the waist of the abducted victim, pinning his arms to his sides. Then the tire was upturned slightly and filled with gasoline. They would then light the fuel, and it would take about twenty minutes for the victim to die a horrendous death.

My pray-ers and family multiplied their prayers, asking God to protect me.

After a seminar in a large port city in South Africa, a handsome young black man said he wanted to tell me his story. "You saved my life," he began. I listened in horror as he told me how he had been taking schoolchildren on retreats telling them of Jesus. (About one thousand of them had accepted Jesus.) However, the then-powerful communists were taking young children off too, giving them small bombs to put in their lunch buckets and teaching them how to blow up their schools. (Several mothers pleaded with me to get their young children out of prison for destroying their schools with those bombs.)

"Not being able to convince an enemy tribe that I was not training children to explode bombs," he continued, "they abducted me. The apartheid government by then had outlawed all black gatherings except funerals, so fifty thousand black people gathered at a funeral during which they were planning to victoriously necklace me. They put the tire around me and filled it with gasoline. But just as they raised the match to light it, the police stormed the funeral, and everybody ran. So," he shrugged, "I ran too." Very solemnly he added, "I am the only person ever to escape while being necklaced."

When he finished his story, he threw his arms around me and said, "It was prayer that saved my life. You see," he explained, "we have seven large telephone prayer chains in this city with both blacks and whites. The minute I was abducted, they were all alerted and started praying for me. They learned to form these chains from your book *What Happens When Women Pray*. You wrote the book, so you saved my life."

"Sir," I smiled at him, "I did not save your life. My book did not save your life. The telephone prayer chains did not save your life. Even the prayers themselves did not save your life. The one who saved your life was God—the One who answered all those prayers and orchestrated your freedom!"

The glory for that miracle does not belong to a prayer training book, an author, or even faithful pray-ers; it belongs to the One who actually accomplished the miracle—God!

In John 15:7, Jesus gave His disciples the New Testament's most powerful promise of prayers being answered, concluding with the *purpose* in verse 8. He said God answers prayers *so that* He would be glorified by their bearing much fruit:

> If you abide in Me, and My words abide in you, ask whatever you wish, and it shall be done for you. By this is My Father glorified, that you bear much fruit, and so prove to be My disciples. (John 15:7–8)

Each January birthday time, instead of making New Year's resolutions, I wait on God to give me a birthday prayer—committing to let Him run my life on that prayer for the next year. On my birthday in 1979, God filled my whole being with just one thought—that He would get all the glory that next year. In prayer, I sought to empty myself of all of me as I handed Him all of my pride and ego. "God, You be glorified this year, not me!" I cried out with all my heart. And it wasn't just for the year 1979. Every year since then it has been my deepest desire: "No glory for me, dear God. Only You!"

Thirty-Year Prayer Movement

My book *What Happens When Women Pray* was published during the beginning of what has become a thirty-year prayer movement. Women's prayer organizations were a foundational part of its beginning, and they are now an integral part of the huge prayer initiative that God has exploded in our country.

As churchwide prayer meetings waned and virtually disappeared or became Wednesday night electives in the seventies, and as prayer was taken out of our schools, God filled the gap by raising up a new army of pray-ers.

In the following chapters, you will read the marvelous things God did when we were not smart enough even to think of, let alone ask for, what He needed to do to rescue our country from its rapid downward moral slide. What has mushroomed into so many prayer organizations, to a large extent started by His calling thousands of women together—just to pray—thirty years ago.

Now God has initiated a hunger in the hearts of millions of Christians of all ages to pray asking Him to intervene in the problems of our country and the world. Without His prompting, there would be no current prayer movement!

Rejoice with me as your mind tries to comprehend the magnitude of men, women, and youth organizing the prayer that is sweeping our country. Here are a few examples:

The National Prayer Committee, started by Vonette Bright, grew from five members in 1974 through more than twenty years of approximately twenty members praying together and sponsoring prayer rallies here and abroad. Now, under our current president David Bryant's leadership, it has grown to 128 prayer leaders of every denomination and race. Under our first president Vonette Bright's tenacious leadership, the U.S. Senate and Congress passed Bill S.1387, which amended the current law establishing the National Day of Prayer (April 17, 1952), to set aside the first Thursday of May as the day on which the National Day of Prayer will be observed annually. It was signed in President Reagan's Oval Office on May 8, 1988.

Since that time, the National Prayer Committee has annually sponsored and produced the National Day of Prayer events in Washington, D.C., on Capitol Hill. Chairperson Shirley Dobson trains state and city leaders, with forty thousand volunteers sponsoring thirty thousand local events attended by more than two million people from Maine to Hawaii. Virtually every state governor annually proclaims that Day of Prayer. Under the leadership of Bob Bakke, the National Prayer Committee also sponsors the nation's largest prayer meeting, which is broadcast live over five hundred television stations, more than five hundred radio stations, on the Internet, and on two different satellite systems across three continents (North America, South America, and Spanish-speaking Europe) the first Thursday night of every May.

The World Prayer Center holds a global prayer complex in Colorado Springs, with Bobbye Byerly organizing continuous, twenty-four-hour prayer for the world. Another astounding statistic is that the "Praying Through the 10/40 Window IV" campaign in October 1999 recorded forty million intercessors around the world praying for the same country each day. Campus Crusade for Christ's Great Commission Prayer Crusade has reached the world since 1972 with millions of pray-ers.

Eddy Smith's "Pray USA" works together with dozens of denominations, hundreds of parachurch organizations, and thousands of churches, mobilizing 15.5 million people to pray each spring. CBN news declared it to be the largest fasting and prayer event in history. And millions of Promise Keepers are being led by Bill McCartney and Gordon England to establish their homes as lighthouses of prayer for Jesus.

Then there are Al VanderGrind's "Houses of Hope Everywhere," Gary Bergel's "Intercessors for America," David Bryant's "Concerts of Prayer," Jon Graf's editing of our *Pray* magazine Dick Eastman's "Every Home for Christ," and Bill Bright's "National Fasting and Prayer" annual conferences, which in 1999 attracted more than two million participants via satellite, radio, and Internet and more than three thousand on-site participants in Houston. The international prayer ministry Aglow has six hundred thousand daily intercessors. Denominations and Christian organizations have launched remarkable prayer movements such as Lydia, Youth with a Mission, Steve Hawthorne and several hundreds more too innumerable to list, but awesomely powerful before the throne of God.

The brightest stars on the prayer scene may be our young people. During the "See You at the Pole" event in September 1999, more than three million junior-high, high-school, and college students gathered at their schools' flagpoles to pray in the United States and in twenty-five other countries on six continents. This is a part of sixty-two national youth organizations, plus individual youth praying and sharing Jesus.

Children are praying too. Esther Elniski has marshaled several million powerful child pray-ers worldwide. Moms in Touch has twenty-five thousand groups of mothers meeting weekly to pray for their children's schools. MOPS (Moms of Pre-Schoolers) join hands nationwide to pray for their little ones. Virginia Patterson is mobilizing the reaching and using children in the Mission America Lighthouse Movement.

The worldwide prayer ministry of the *What Happens When Women Pray* book gave me the opportunity in 1991 to chair the AD2000 North America Women's Track (later called Christian Women United). This open door gave birth to the prayer curriculum *A Study Guide for Evangelism Praying*, used extensively on every continent. In addition, the *Love Your Neighbor* curriculum by Mary Lance Sisk is putting feet to the study guide with the praying, caring, and sharing Jesus Lighthouse program of Mission America.

Mission America, with a goal to reach every man, woman, and child in the United States with prayer and Jesus by the end of the year 2000, is a network of eighty-four denominations, more than three hundred, Christian ministries, and seventy-four national ministry networks.

Headed by Paul Cedar, Mission America's Lighthouse Movement has enlisted three million Christians to pray, care, and then share Jesus in their own neighborhoods, workplaces, schools, or spheres of influence.

Mission America's coalition of 421 national leaders has launched remarkable prayer movements nationwide, producing the largest organized prayer movement in history.

However, the exciting part is that this great prayer movement is made up of *individual* pray-ers, who sometimes pray alone, sometimes in small groups, or sometimes with a large congregation, but always one on one with God. The power of it all comes from:

Praying by common laypeople—and praying by great leaders.

Praying by faltering beginners—and praying by mature spiritual giants.

Praying by lonely intercessors—and praying by organized millions.

A Movement to a Moving

These have been years of agonizing prayers, pleading prayers, and persisting prayers. Prayers for God to sweep across our nation in His convicting and restoring power. Prayers for the world, for our families, and for our churches. Prayers in faith even when the waiting seemed so long. But God was at work. He had His time all planned. He knew how much preparation would be needed before the prayer *movement* could change into His *moving*.

A Christmas card from Lorna Johnson, who was part of my first prayer triplet in 1964, said about the things for which we prayed way back then, "Yes, it is happening!"

At the National Prayer Committee meeting in Houston in November 1999, we were sharing what we thought the national prayer movement we had been such a big part of since the early seventies had accomplished. Committee members told of their excitement and delight at the bursting of a seemingly new involvement and power of God in our country. When it was my turn, I said it felt to me as if we were turning from a prayer *movement* to a *moving* of God in answer to all these years of prayer. Immediately there was virtually 100-percent agreement and praising God. They all said, "Yes, that's it!" Although God had instigated the prayer movement starting in the early seventies and orchestrated its phenomenal growth, it seems now God is initiating the answering of those prayers. We all agreed it was the best National Prayer Committee meeting we had in more than twenty-five years.

So What's Wrong?

Now the question is, *Didn't all that prayer do any good?* Why are we still going downhill morally so rapidly in our country? First, let's honestly look at a sobering fact: What would America be like by now if there hadn't been all that prayer? I shudder to think!

So, after all that praying in the last decades of the twentieth century, do we still need prayer as a new millennium unfolds before us? Does God really need us to pray anymore?

George Barna is founder and president of the respected Barna Research Group. In his book, *The Second Coming of the Church*, he says that his research shows that most Americans admit to not yet having found a compelling, defining purpose for their life; millions are steadfastly probing the spiritual domain to facilitate that discovery . . . Most people believe there is no "right" faith; that all of the world's major faiths teach the same lessons; and that all people pray to the same gods, no matter what names they use for those deities."[1]

Although the statistics of pray-ers seems huge, still only a small percentage of believers and churches are seriously seeking God's help for our country through prayer. Barna said, "At the risk of sounding like an alarmist, I believe the Church in America has no more than five years—perhaps even less—to turn itself around and begin to affect the culture, rather than be affected by it. Because our culture completely reinvents itself every three to five years, and people are intensely seeking spiritual direction, and our central moral and spiritual trends are engulfed in a downward spiral, we have no more than a half-decade to turn things around."[2]

The truth is, as we have left the twentieth century and stepped into a new millennium, *prayer is the only answer.* The battle lines between good and evil, God and Satan, are being drawn ever more tightly. And in this supernatural battle, it will take a supernatural weapon to succeed—prayer—because the only answer is a supernatural Jesus!

Is there hope? Oh, yes. *You, dear Christian reader, have the only hope.* The exciting National Day of Prayer theme for the year 2000 is not Y2K (Year 2000) but *PRAY2K* (Pray 2000). Adding those first three letters can change the whole new millennium from possible chaos to positive faith in God—and faith in His desire and ability to work all things out for His children's good!

Faith

In Hebrews 11:6, God clearly tells us about the role of faith in our praying: "Without faith it is impossible to please Him, for he who comes to God must believe that He is, and that He is a rewarder of those who seek Him."

But it is not faith in the amount of praying we do, faith in our ability to pray long, beautiful, and scripturally accurate prayers, or even faith in the prayers themselves. It is faith in God—faith in who He is and faith that He rewards His children who seek Him in prayer.

As the new millennium begins, I can pray, "Father, my *faith* has turned into unshakable *confidence* in You—because of who You are and so many years of seeing You work so incredibly!"

Here, with the psalmist, is my heart while writing this book for you, my dear reader:

I will give thanks to the LORD with all my heart; I will tell of all Thy wonders; I will be glad and exult in Thee. I will sing praise to Thy name, O Most High. (Ps. 9:1–2)

Reflection Questions

Examine your life:

In the light of the current huge prayer movement that God has initiated, are you longing for more of what He has available to *you* through prayer? How serious are you about the time and energy it might take? Would you consider yourself:

A praying layperson or a prayer leader? _____

A beginner or mature pray-er? _____

One who usually prays alone or in a group? _____

Do you know God well enough to thank Him before He answers because you trust who He is? How much of God's awesome answering power are you experiencing?

Have you already discovered that God's answers aren't limited by your ability to ask? So who gets all the glory for the answer?

Scripture

Turn in your own Bible to Jeremiah 33:3 and read it thoughtfully, opening your heart to what God is saying to you about the third part of the verse. However you identified yourself above, ask Him to show you what He has ready for the next step of your prayer life. Let Him bring to your mind additional prayer methods and the prayer movements or people with whom He wants you to pray. Take time to listen expectantly.

For you to do:

Think back on a specific time you felt God gave you far more in His answer than you had asked for in your prayer request. Whether this Jeremiah 33:3 promise of His to "show you great and mighty things you do not know" usually happens, rarely happens, or never happens to you, sincerely pray the following prayer.

For you to pray:

"Dear Father in Heaven, You are an awesome God. I want to praise You for the time/times You really did give abundantly more than I asked for. I am so grateful. But now please teach me how to pray for all You actually have available for me. Lord, I want to be a part of the awesome prayer movement You have initiated. Help me to take my next step and lead me to those with whom You want me to expand my prayer life—for Your glory. In Jesus' name, amen."

In your own words, record and date your new commitment to God:

_____

_____Date_____.

Start praying on your new level, keeping alert to all the things He is doing in addition to what you were able to ask—for your encouragement and praise to God.

CHAPTER 2

B.C. versus A.D. Praying

IN ORDER to understand what God does when we pray, we need to see what time it really is in His plan for pray-ers. As we look back at what God has done in the past thirty years since my book *What Happens When Women Pray*, we first need to recognize the huge division of time He orchestrated and the incredible new dimensions of prayer He brought into being with it.

For centuries, time has been split in half. In virtually all the business, athletic, and transportation worlds, one method of counting time has emerged—B.C. versus A.D. Although there have been various methods of calculating time through the centuries, the most common method today uses a single point in the history of Planet Earth to date everything before it *back* from it and everything since it *forward* to now.

But it wasn't a geological age or catastrophic event that divided time; *it was a person.*

Who was the only person ever born on earth important enough to split time into two halves?

It was *Jesus!* Time on earth split at His birth. Deity arriving on Planet Earth in fleshly form was momentous enough to become our hinge of time—before and after His birth!

Calendar time is a *Who*, not a *what*. B.C., before Christ, versus A.D., anno Domini, or "the year of our Lord."

It is becoming popular today to replace B.C. and A.D. with B.C.E. ("Before Common Era") and C.E. ("Common Era"). But whatever people choose to rename that division, it is still Jesus' birth they are using to split time.

No matter what religions, governments, or systems of calculating have come and gone, God always has had His unchangeable timetable. Galatians 4:4 tells us what time B.C. versus A.D. was in the Father's eternal calendar: "But when the fullness of [B.C./A.D.] time came, God sent forth His Son."

God split time in half by sending His Son to supernaturally usher in the second half of Planet earth's time with the most important birth the world will ever experience.

Jesus' Perspective of This Time Split

However, Jesus' own view of time splitting was not at His birth—but at His death and resurrection.

This difference in Jesus' view of when B.C. versus A.D. happened totally changed praying by Christians.

My heart was overwhelmed when the reality of Luke 22:44–47 dawned on me. After His resurrection and before His ascension back to heaven, Jesus explained B.C. versus A.D. to the eleven disciples and those with them:

> These are My words which I spoke to you while I was still with you, that all things which are written about Me in the Law of Moses and the Prophets and the Psalms must be fulfilled." Then He opened their minds to understand the [Old Testament] Scriptures, and He said to them, "Thus it is written, that the Christ should suffer and rise again from the dead the third day; and that repentance for forgiveness of sins should be proclaimed in His name to all the nations, beginning from Jerusalem." (Luke 24:44–47)

Jesus opened their minds to understand that all of the things written about Himself in the Law of Moses, the prophets, and the psalms must be fulfilled—in the light of His death and rising again from the dead the third day. Officially A.D. had begun.

After publishing an article on this exciting fact, I went to San Francisco for a Mission America meeting. There for sale were T-shirts asking, "Who split time?" B.C. and A.D. were graphically pictured side by side—split, not by a manger, but by the cross! I got so excited I bought one for every member of my family.

Relationships of people with the Godhead had remained basically B.C. until Jesus' death and resurrection. *Everything changed, including prayer, when Jesus rose from the dead.*

What Happened to Prayer When B.C. Turned A.D.?

What changed so dramatically about prayer at Christ's resurrection? When God the Father gave His Son a human body, Jesus became the only pre-existent person ever to be born on this earth. He was the fulfillment of all of B.C.'s waiting, and He would birth a whole new system of people's relationships with the Father and the Holy Spirit.

After finding in my Bible the following staggering list of differences in B.C. and A.D. praying, I cried out to God, "Oh Lord, I am so grateful you let me live on this side of Jesus. How many of the wonderful things of prayer I would have missed!"

Praying and pondering over each one's affect on our praying, little by little God unfolded it to me. Here are some of the awesome differences Jesus' death and resurrection made in our praying as Christians:

- **Direct access to the holy of holies.** One of the awesome blessings of living in A.D. time is that there is *no veil* in our churches allowing only our leaders access to the holy of holies. We all now have direct access to the Father's holy presence in prayer.

21

Even when Jesus' birth was imminent and God was about to announce Jesus' forerunner, John the Baptist, only his father Zacharias was chosen by Lot to enter the temple of the Lord and burn incense while the whole multitude of people were in prayer outside(see Luke 1:8–10).

Before Jesus was born, only the high priest of Israel had access to the holy of holies, the inner chamber of the temple in which God's presence literally dwelled. One day each year, the Day of Atonement, the high priest would go through the veil into the holy of holies to offer a sacrifice to pay for the sins of the people. All the people had to stay on the outside. Hebrews 9:7 describes this limited access to God:

> Into the [holy of holies] only the high priest enters, once a year, not without taking blood, which he offers for himself and for the sins of the people committed in ignorance.

However, when Jesus died on the cross, the veil was supernaturally torn in two from top to bottom, and suddenly there was access directly to God's throne room for every believer! (see Matt. 27:51). I wrote in the margin of my Bible beside Luke 1:10 with a big exclamation mark and large capital letters, "Jesus' birth and death gave us the right to come directly to God in prayer. We are inside now! Only a priest was permitted inside before Jesus died."

The last time I was in Jerusalem, my guide was an archaeology professor. He told me that archaeologists now think they know the exact place the veil of the temple stood—on what is now an outcropping of solid granite. I knelt, laid my hands on that rock, and wept as my whole being was enwrapped in groaning prayer as I poured out my heart in deep gratitude to my Jesus! Gratitude for suffering and dying and splitting the veil that kept me on the outside—and opening up heaven's throne room personally to me.

- **Confidence through Jesus' blood.** However, more than a split veil, it is by the *blood of Jesus* that we Christians have confidence to enter the holy place of God.

  As Hebrews 10:18–20 explains:

  Now where there is forgiveness of these things, there is no longer any offering for sin. Since therefore, brethren, *we have confidence to enter the holy place by the blood of Jesus,* by a new and living way which He inaugurated for us through the veil, that is, His flesh. (emphasis added)

  Why did the cross change prayer for us in A.D.? It was because forgiveness of sins has always been necessary for sinful humans to come into the presence of a holy God. "And whatever we ask we receive from Him, because we keep His commandments and do the things that are pleasing in His sight" (1 John 3:22).

  But the good news about sin separating us from God is in Revelation 1:5: "Jesus Christ . . . the ruler of the kings of the earth. To Him who loves us, and *released us from our sins by His blood*" (emphasis added).

  There no longer needs to be offering for sin by humans. Jesus' cry, "It is finished!" on the cross closed the door on B.C. sacrifices as He became the A.D. propitiation for our sins (see 1 John 2:2). *Our sins were paid for by Jesus' death, not His birth.*

  As I taught in my book *What Happens When Women Pray,* there are *two classes of sin* that must be forgiven through Jesus' blood in order to have unhindered access to the Father for intercessory prayer.

  The first class of sin is that original state of sin (singular) in which we all are born. This includes every man, woman, and young person who doesn't have Jesus as his or her personal Savior and

Lord (see John 3:18). Jesus said in John 16:8–9 that He would send the Holy Spirit, who would, among other things, "convict the world of sin . . . because they do not believe in Me."

The good news about that kind of sin in all of us originally is that it is forgiven through Jesus' blood when we are redeemed—when we repent and accept Jesus as Savior and Lord.

In Him [Jesus] we have redemption through His blood, the forgiveness of our trespasses. (Eph. 1:7)

I was only nine years old when I cried all afternoon over my sin, repented, and accepted Jesus as my Savior and Lord. That very night, I was completely forgiven through Jesus' blood and became eligible for intercessory prayers for all my neighbors and friends who still didn't know Jesus.

We are cleansed of that original state of sin through Jesus' blood so that we are eligible to enter the holy place of God!

The second class of sin covers those plural sins that we commit after becoming a Christian. Peter, writing to Christians, refers to this class of sin in 1 Peter 3:12:

The eyes of the Lord are upon the righteous, and His ears attend to their prayers, but the face of the Lord is against those who do evil.

I am continuously horrified that some of the seemingly innocent and insignificant little things I do, think, or say are called *sin* by God—and keep Him from listening to my intercessory prayers. It keeps me sending "Please-forgive-me!" prayers heavenward many, many times a day. I'm not taking any chances!

One day, still struggling to forgive a fellow Christian when I had been deeply wronged, I kept asking God to forgive my unforgiving spirit. Then I saw it. The apostle John, writing to Christians, told *us* how *we* can be forgiven of these sins—by the blood of Jesus:

And the blood of Jesus His Son cleanses us [literally, "keeps on cleansing us"] from all sin. . . . If *we* confess our sins, He is faithful and righteous to forgive *us* our sins and to cleanse *us* from all unrighteousness (1 John 1:7–9; emphasis added).

It was the shed blood of Jesus on the cross that keeps on cleansing us Christians in order to have the Lord attend to our intercessory prayers. Although it was the first prerequisite of answered prayer I taught in the *What Happens When Women Pray* book and seminars, I still need it and am still teaching it because it gains for all of us unhindered access to the Father in prayer.

- *Praying in the Name of Jesus.* Jesus gave His followers an incredible privilege of A.D. praying, assuring them it would be their new source of joy.

  Until now you have asked for nothing in My name; ask and you shall receive, that your joy may be full. (John 16:24)

  Who is eligible for this privilege? Only true Christians, those who have accepted Jesus and had their sins forgiven, can pray in Jesus' name.
  Paul says this about the name of Jesus:

  Therefore also God highly exalted Him, and bestowed on Him the name which is above every name, that at the name of Jesus every knee should bow, of those who are in heaven, and on earth, and under the earth, and that every tongue should confess that Jesus Christ is Lord, to the glory of God the Father. (Phil. 2:9–11; emphasis added)

  That name encompasses all that Jesus is: the Lord—with the fullness of the holy, omnipresent, omniscient, omnipotent Godhead dwelling in Him (see Eph. 3:19).

For years I have listened for the name of Jesus in church services and prayer meetings. My heart has broken when so many times recently I have listened in vain. Though not intentionally, I'm sure, many have let the most precious and powerful dimension of A.D. praying gradually slip through the cracks—unnoticed and unmissed.

Included in the name of Jesus is His absolute authority. In His Great Commission in Matthew 28:19, Jesus said, "Go therefore." What was the "therefore" there for? Jesus commands us to go because all authority has been given to Him in heaven and on earth. Therefore with His authority, *we* go in prayer, sharing Jesus to all nations. We do not go in the name of our church or organization—but in the name of Jesus!

Of course, Jesus warned that the opposite is also true since He came to earth saying, "I am the way, and the truth, and the life; *no one* comes to the Father, but through Me" (John 14:6; emphsis added).

Trying to pray in the name of any other god is useless. Since the angel announced to Joseph that His name would be called Jesus and He finished His earthly assignment through death and resurrection, there has been no other name in heaven or on earth by which we can biblically pray.

The most amazing promise by Jesus to us is that, if we ask according to what His name really includes, we will receive answers to our prayers! "And whatever you ask in My name, that will I do, that the Father may be glorified in the Son" (John 14:13).

Victory, power, and answers to our prayers are there for us—because of Jesus' name!

- **Praying with A.D. Doctrine.** How differently the first believers were able to pray with A.D. doctrine after Jesus continuously explained the whole Old Testament to them and then wrapped it all up in Luke 24:44–47 in the light of His death and resurrection! How thrilled they must have been that the mysteries of the Old Testament were revealed first to them! How they must have prayed for understanding as the awesomeness of it all unfolded before their eyes!

They evidently embraced this fulfilled doctrine immediately, for Acts 2:42 tells us that from that time on they continued steadfastly in four things: the apostles' teaching, fellowship, breaking of bread, and prayer. And these prayers progressed as they sought to apply all the things Jesus had taught them and demonstrated for them. It instructed them how to pray effectively to obey their new marching orders from Jesus.

The apostles' doctrine contained what they were to pray for and about—brought up to A.D. by Jesus' teaching. The truths they clung to when imprisoned, scattered, hiding in caves, and martyred were all covered by Jesus—ready to sustain them no matter what. But it also encouraged more and deeper praying as they saw that victory after victory came from their new A.D. prayers.

How often I have wished that somebody had recorded all that Jesus said to His followers that day before He left Planet Earth. But that obviously wasn't God's will. However, we do have the now-written account of all of these truths of Jesus. And now, two thousand years later, they are the foundation of the beliefs in which we confidently put our trust and hope—the whole Bible.

The Holy Spirit and A.D. Praying

When Jesus ascended back to heaven, one of the main reasons He sent the Holy Spirit was because He knew we would need help in our praying.

The well-known reasons for the Holy Spirit's being sent by Jesus—providing supernatural power, giving us boldness, recalling what Jesus had said to us, convicting of sin, and comforting us—would determine the direction and content of our A.D. praying. But needing the Holy Spirit to help in our praying is an often-overlooked reason in our "I-can-do-it-myself,-God" modern culture.

However, when we are confused or devastated by circumstances, not only at a loss as to the answer we desire, but even *what* to pray, it is the Holy Spirit who takes our prayers to the Father—according to His will. This is the omniscient Father, who never makes a mistake, who knows the what-ifs of every possible solution, and who knows how to answer while He works out everything for *our* good.

Romans 8:26–27 explains the Holy Spirit's role in prayer:

And in the same way the Spirit also helps our weakness; for we do not know how to pray as we should, but the Spirit Himself intercedes for us with groanings too deep for words; and He who searches the hearts knows what the mind of the Spirit is, because He intercedes for the saints according to the will of God.

Many times when life has crashed in around me, I have found myself utterly unable to see a light at the end of the dark tunnel. Incapable of even thinking of any possible solution to what had happened, I was not capable of suggesting to God what His remedy might be. It is at those times I have cried out in agony to the Holy Spirit, "Please pray for me. I can't pray!"

The Holy Spirit is the member of the Godhead for whom Jesus told His followers to wait as He was leaving them to go back to heaven. Their waiting for the promised Holy Spirit in their ten-day prayer meeting before Pentecost began their A.D. praying. Jesus kept His word with the Holy Spirit's coming in His new A.D. way to them with the sound of a mighty rushing wind and sitting as tongues of fire on each of them.

And the Holy Spirit remains their prayer helper—and ours—until Jesus comes back in person again.

The Holy Spirit is the in-residence intercessor in my life—and yours—at all times. He helps us to pray when we can't, assuring us that our feeble prayers are reaching the Father in heaven according to His all-knowing will!

Jesus Is Not Replaced in Our Prayer Life

However, Jesus did not *replace* Himself with the Holy Spirit when He told His disciples it was expedient for Him to go away so that He could send the Holy Spirit (see John 16:7).

The Holy Spirit took up His enlarged role in their prayer lives, but Jesus did not turn all of His prayer relationships over to the Holy Spirit in A.D. Jesus used three prepositions to describe His relationship with His followers after He left them:

- *"I am with you."* Jesus closed His Great Commission in Matthew 28:20 with these words:

  Lo, I am with you always, even to the end of the age. (emphasis added)

  When 120 of His followers gathered in Jerusalem in obedience to Jesus in the first ten-day prayer meeting to wait for the promise of the Father, there were actually 121 of them—including Jesus.

  Although they had seen Him float away in the clouds with the angel's announcement that He would come back just as He went, Jesus Himself was *with* them.

  With Jesus' announcement, "Lo, I am with you always," still burning in their minds, what must they have prayed that first prayer meeting? Were they uncomfortable, knowing He knew all their motives? Was Peter still repenting at not heeding Jesus' warning of Satan's wanting to sift him—and his denying his Lord? Was Thomas embarrassed for having doubted?

Were the men sorry they had not believed the women that first Easter morning? And were the women who had seen and talked to the risen Savior still hurt that they hadn't been believed?

Or did they explode in endless praise in that first A.D. prayer meeting, bowing in hours of adoration, willingly submitting to anything Jesus had for them? Knowing Jesus would never break His promise to be with them always, were they overjoyed that they were not alone—and never would be again? How did Mary, Jesus' mother, feel, knowing the end of all her sorrow was that her Son would continue to be with her—something no other mother on earth can ever expect? Was she thrilled to see Jesus' brothers finally all together "in one accord" with their unseen ascended brother? Could the room and their hearts contain all the ecstasy they were feeling?

How about us? Do we blissfully pray in our prayer groups and prayer closets, unaware that Jesus is there with us too? Or are we so in awe of Who is with us—our sinless, pure, loving, victorious Jesus—that we are enwrapped in His divine presence?

While I was on his board, Chuck Colson used to scold me for traveling overseas alone. "But I'm not alone!" I would insist. And I wasn't. When I couldn't eat the food, drink the water, or understand the language, I always had a quiet confidence, knowing Jesus was there. My prayers never were in panic, but in a deep-down peace knowing Jesus was with me and would never abandon me when I was serving Him.

So we, too, after Jesus has been gone almost two thousand years, know Jesus didn't replace or rescind His promise to be with all believers all of the time—especially when we pray!

- **"*I am in their midst.*"** While speaking about what we are asking the Father for in prayer and His doing it, Jesus gave His followers this mind-boggling promise:

> Where two or three have gathered together in My name, there I am *in their midst*. (Matt. 18:20; emphasis added)

The committee on a large military base in England had prayed for six years to have our prayer seminar. The night before, as we were sitting around a huge polished officers' conference table deeply praying for our next day's seminar, suddenly several of us were aware of Jesus. We caught our breath. To our spiritual eyes, He seemed to be almost hovering over our group.

But it wasn't the babe in a manger, the teacher in Galilee, the sacrifice on the cross, or the risen Savior on Easter morning. It was today's Jesus. The same Jesus whom the apostle John saw on the Isle of Patmos—"clothed in a robe reaching to the feet, and girded across His breast with a golden girdle. His head and His hair were white like white wool, like snow; and His eyes were like a flame of fire; and His feet were like burnished bronze, when it has been caused to glow in a furnace, and His voice was like the sound of many waters. . . . And out of His mouth came a sharp two-edged sword; and His face was like the sun shining in its strength" (Rev. 1:13–16).

The A.D. Jesus of today is victorious and all-powerful, yet tender and kind, understanding our infirmities because He, too, suffered. Even if we aren't conscious of Him, Jesus nevertheless is in the midst of us believers every time we gather to pray!

That is what produces the beautiful oneness in Jesus we feel when we pray together—with just one other, in small groups, or in huge concerts of prayer. He *is* in our midst!

- **"*Christ in you.*"** The most wonderful encouragement in prayer is the mystery that was not available to B.C. (Old Testament) pray-ers—that Jesus Himself actually is *in* each of us, including while we are praying. Whether we are praying all alone or with small or large groups, Jesus is living in each intercessor. In Colossians 1:26–27, Paul unraveled that mystery for us:

> The mystery which has been hidden from the past ages . . . but now has been manifested to His saints . . . which is *Christ in you*, the hope of glory. (emphasis added)

The dream of most Jewish little girls in B.C. was to be chosen by God to bear His Son, the promised Messiah, in her body for nine months. But only one could have that highest of high privileges— Mary. She knew, because the angel Gabriel announced to her that the holy Son of God would be *in* her. And the unborn forerunner of Jesus leaped in the womb of Mary's relative Elizabeth when the two mothers-to-be met. Mary was at the foot of the cross when they snuffed out the life of God's Son and hers. But then she was numbered among those who were praying in the first pre-Pentecost prayer meeting with another incredible blessing—her Son once more *in* her. This time He was in Mary spiritually, not physically, just as He was in all the rest of them—and us today.

In our A.D. *prayer meetings, Jesus is not only in our midst, He is also vibrantly, powerfully living in each of us as pray-ers.* Oh, for the spiritual eyes to be able to see the real Jesus throbbing with each heartbeat of our fervent, persistent prayers!

Two-Kingdom Praying

Having been transferred from the kingdom of Satan into which we were born into Jesus' kingdom at salvation enables believers to pray the way Jesus taught His followers to pray, "Father . . . Thy kingdom come" (Matt. 6:9–10).

This transferring is done when God lifts a spiritually lost person out of Satan's kingdom of darkness and places him or her into Jesus' kingdom through repentance and belief in Jesus. As the apostle Paul explained:

> Giving thanks to the Father . . . for He delivered us [Christians] from the domain of darkness, and transferred us to the kingdom of His beloved Son, in whom we have redemption, the forgiveness of sins (Col. 1:12–14).

We who are already in his kingdom, are to pray for the fulfillment of God's kingdom coming here on earth—as the lost are transferred into it one by one. This is evangelism praying for others who are not yet in His kingdom to accept Jesus. Then, once they belong to God's kingdom, they, with us, can become pray-ers with the awesome A.D. prayer power.

The Hope of His Resurrection

As we pray, Christians do not just blindly hope and trust in a prophet who died and stayed dead. We confidently believe in One who actually rose from the dead and is alive today, not like all other world religions, which follow dead prophets. As Peter emphasized:

> [God] has caused us to be born again to a living hope through the resurrection of Jesus Christ from the dead . . . to obtain an inheritance . . . in heaven. (1 Pet. 1:3–4)

While I was teaching prayer in Calcutta, India, a medical doctor told me that several surgeries for an incurable stomach problem had led to preparations to remove the rest of her stomach to save her life. While she was waiting in the hospital, the risen and glorified Jesus appeared at the foot of her bed and healed her instantaneously and completely. She immediately accepted Him as her Savior. She told me that now she asks her patients why "we" Muslims worship a dead prophet, while there is One who is alive forever. And many of them, she smiled, have also put their trust in the resurrected Jesus—and will spend eternity in heaven with us—and with Jesus!

Our Enemy or Mission Field?

All through B.C., God was preparing His chosen nation of Israel to bring forth the Messiah and settling them in a homeland. So throughout that era of history, those who opposed the nation of Israel were *the enemy*. God's children prayed, and rightly so, for Him to defeat the enemy in battle, to bring calamity to them, and to overcome as they fought, killed, and even occasionally plundered. And God answered those prayers.

But then God sent His Son, Jesus. In John 3:17, Jesus said of Himself, "For God did not send the Son into the world to judge the world, but that the world should be saved through Him."

In A.D., these same people are to be our mission field, not our B.C. enemies. Ephesians 2:11–12 tells us that those who were "Gentiles in the flesh . . . excluded from the commonwealth of Israel" had no hope and were without God. But verses 13–22 tell us that Gentiles (non-Jews) "have been brought near by the blood of Christ . . . that in Himself He . . . might reconcile them both in one body to God through the cross, by it having put to death the enmity." God's message to those who once were God's enemies is found in the Gospel of John:

Whoever believes in the Son has eternal life, but whoever rejects the Son will not see life, for God's wrath remains on him. (John 3:36)

Since Jesus came all things are different:

- We no longer are to conquer enemies of God—but to win them to Himself (see Acts 1:8).
- We are not to kill God's enemies—but to bring them the message of eternal life in Jesus (see John 3:36).

- We are to tell everybody in the whole world how they can experience forgiveness of their sins (see 1 John 2:2).

- We are to make disciples—not to keep adversaries (see Matt. 28:19).

God wants all enemies transferred from the kingdom of darkness to His kingdom of light through the forgiveness of their sins. *The* B.C. *enemy is now the harvest field of lost souls.* We are to "beseech the Lord of the harvest to send out workers into His harvest" (Matt. 9:37–38).

Always doing the Father's will, this is the prayer Jesus told us to pray now in A.D. Since Jesus died for the whole world, the prayers for the harvest of lost souls are His will and the ones God answers today!

Regressing

To remain in B.C. praying without bringing it up through Jesus' death and resurrection is to regress to the backside of time's B.C./A.D. hinge—without Jesus.

Are you still operating on B.C. praying? How much of the power of the authority of Jesus' death, blood, redemption, and resurrection have you put into your prayer life? How much of His compassion and urgency for a lost world are in your prayers?

Someday human reckoning of time will be over when "there should be time no longer" (Rev. 10:6 KJV), and our praying will also be over. Eternity will stretch out into an eternity in which there is no longer even the reckoning of time—with Jesus, who split earthly time, reigning forever and ever and ever. *And where you spend eternity will depend on what you have done with Planet Earth's hinge of time, Jesus—whether you accepted or rejected Him while there is still* A.D. *time.*

Make sure you have accepted Jesus—and rejoice with me in triumphal praise and humble adoration of the One who not only split time that first Easter weekend, but also was the hinge of time that supernaturally opened the door to A.D. praying—and eternity—in your life and mine. Jesus!

Reflection Questions

Examine your life:

Up until now, were you aware of the difference in doing A.D. praying with Jesus versus regressing back to b.c. praying without Jesus? What portion of your prayers' content, privileges, and authority are b.c. prayers that could have been prayer before Jesus came, died and arose again?

All_____ Most_____ Some _____ Few _____

Scripture:

Turn in your Bible to Hebrews 10:19. In what one thing can you have confidence to be able to go directly to the Father in A.D. prayer? List the awesome prayer privileges that you have because Jesus shed His blood and arose again Easter morning?

_____

_____

_____

_____

For you to do:

Are you sure you are personally eligible for A.D. praying with Jesus in you, with you, and in the midst of your group? If you are unsure about ever having asked Jesus into your life as your Savior and Lord, 1 John 5:13 affirms you can be sure right now by praying the following prayer.

For you to pray:

1. To accept Jesus: "Dear Father, I admit I am a sinner. I believe that Jesus is the Son of God and that He paid for all of my sins with His blood on the cross. Please forgive all my sins. Jesus come into my heart as my Savior and Lord. I do believe I now have Jesus living in me, that I am forgiven, and that I am now a Christian. Thank You that I now am eligible for all the awesome privileges of praying in Jesus' name. In Jesus' precious name, amen."

2. For all who have accepted Jesus to pray: "Dear Jesus, my heart is exploding with joy at what You did for my prayer life. Thank you that I was born on this side of the b.c./A.D. hinge of time. Keep me practicing all Your privileges of A.D. praying, especially those I may have omitted before. Oh dear Jesus, words cannot describe my gratitude to You!" In Your awesome name, amen."

CHAPTER 3

What God Does Through Solitary Prayer

DOES GOD use one person's prayers, or does He pay more attention to a large group? This is a question frequently asked by those learning to pray. The answer is *both*. The Bible records tremendous power when many prayed together, but it also is filled with amazing answers to one person's prayers.

Our prayer seminar in Manhattan, during which approximately 50 percent prayed to make sure Jesus was their Savior and Lord, had been preceded by fervent and persistent prayer from a relatively small group of wonderful pray-ers who refused to let go of their determined vision of prayer for New York City. All their previous years' prayer gatherings had drawn a relatively small group of dedicated pray-ers. But that day, the tremendous crowd's outburst of cheering, stamping of feet, and praising God that so many accepted Jesus was at least partly a result of *one woman's prayers*—perhaps mostly..

When she came as a Swedish immigrant to America, she became the custodian of that downtown New York church. For thirty years, every single day as she worked, she prayed the same prayer: "God, fill this church building." It never happened—until that day—thirty years later. Then God not only filled the large sanctuary but the downstairs auditorium too. I had her stand, shy yet radiating, while the audience gave her a huge standing ovation. *One person's praying—in secret while she cleaned!*

Jesus emphasized the importance of solitary, secret praying in Matthew 6:6 as He taught His disciples, and us, how to pray:

> But you, when you pray, go into your inner room, and when you have shut your door, pray to your Father who is in *secret*, and your Father who sees in *secret* will repay you. (emphasis added)

The tendency is to think the most important kind of praying is public or corporate praying, which does produce powerful results. However, one of the greatest things God taught us through the years is that *the power of our public praying depends upon the quality and quantity of our secret, private praying!*

How Long?

But Jesus did not tell us *how long* to pray in secret. Often, the solitary prayer that has been prayed for years may need a new direction for God to answer.

With her hair just growing back from cancer treatment, Nancy was excited as she told me how she had been praying for her husband's salvation for years. "Then I prayed to the Lord a year ago that I was willing to do anything for Him to bring my husband to the Lord. God answered my prayer by allowing me to have cancer and to go through chemotherapy for a year. One month ago, he received Christ!" She thanked me for teaching how "God causes all things to work together for good to those who love God, to those who are called according to His purpose" (Rom. 8:28). One year!

Another confirmation of God's answer to persistent, private prayers was recorded in a note from a woman in Austin, Texas: "I was encouraged to pray for my sister after reading your book more than ten years ago. My sister accepted Jesus as her Lord and Savior February 28, 1999. Love, Chrys."

Sometimes one person's prayer by necessity, or perhaps for a witness, is in front of people. Our granddaughter Crista's seventh-grade public-school class was at an environmental learning camp in northern Minnesota. Jan, her mom and our daughter, was along as a chaperone and the medical doctor of the team. The two of them led in worship and praise at the invitation of the other girls in their cabin, and the next day they started out over the rugged, half-frozen, slippery terrain. Suddenly Jan was lying at the bottom of an icy ravine, unable to stand up. Crista came running back, yelling, "Are you all right, Mother?", at which Jan moaned, "Noooooo!"

Jan told us that all at once she was aware of Crista's arms around her neck and the whisper of her prayers. With all the students trying to help, Jan miraculously found herself standing on the level ground above. Then Jan added, "I walked two miles out through the brush and ice on my broken ankle!"

That night Crista led songs, read from her Bible, and answered questions from fifteen of her cabinmates about God and the Christian life. The next night, with Jan at home in a cast, Crista led one of the girls to the Lord! One solitary prayer *does* accomplish much! (See James 5:16.)

Joshua's Solitary Prayer

One person's prayer in the Bible had even greater results. His prayer is perhaps the most outlandish request ever prayed in the Bible or anywhere else. After marching all night with the Lord, confounding the Amorites and giving a great victory to Israel, Joshua said to the Lord in the sight of Israel: "O sun, stand still at Gibeon, and O moon in the valley of Aijalon" (Josh. 10:12).

God incredibly answered Joshua. Verses 13 and 14 tell of God's miraculous answer to Joshua's prayer:

> So the sun stood still, and the moon stopped. . . . The sun stopped in the middle of the sky, and did not hasten to go down for about a whole day.

And there was no day like that before it or after it, *when the Lord listened to the voice of a man*. (emphasis added)

In the margin beside this passage in my Bible, I have drawn a big box with these words in it: "Incredible results of one man's prayer."

In 1994, while ministering at a monastery by the valley of Aijalon in the foothills of Jerusalem, we seemed so close to God as we ate only simple soup and homemade bread with water, fresh fruit, and vegetables and had powerful prayer times together. The moon was going to be full one night, so I read again the account of Joshua right there by that valley. As I read, I noticed my prayer recorded in the margin of my Bible dated four years earlier: "Oh, God, make me eligible for that kind of You listening—to me!"

I took a flashlight and picked my way down the rocky path to the edge of the valley of Aijalon. I watched breathlessly as the moon rose over the far side of the valley, feeling I was almost hanging over the edge as the deep valley stretched between the moon and me. I tried to comprehend that it was the *same moon* Joshua had told to stand still so many centuries ago. I was spellbound. Once again I cried to the Lord, "Make me eligible for that kind of prayer power!"

God is still answering my prayer at Aijalon as He continues to bring His amazing answers to our expanding praying. However, Aijalon was not the first time I had prayed for power in prayer. It was built on *many more that went before it*.

Secret Prayers Before Aijalon

Perhaps the most important ministry prayer I ever prayed in secret was responding to God's call back in 1967 to say yes to the six-month experimenting to find out what happens when women pray. That short prayer turned into a lifelong prayer seminar ministry.

In 1972, while studying Jesus' words in John 15:7—"*Ask whatever you wish, and it shall be done for you*"—I had wept before God as I prayed, "Lord, I want that power in prayer. Teach me and break me until I have it." This was after all the prayer power God gave us in our experimenting in 1968 when He was birthing our "What Happens When Women Pray" ministry—which shaped much of our future teaching.

However, more than ten years earlier, another prayer that had just seemed to explode out of me was, "Lord, I want to teach everybody in the whole world to pray." Then, embarrassed at the audacity of such a prayer, I did not tell anyone about it for many, many years." But that prayer had come from God, and He has fulfilled it with books and extended prayer speaking tours on every continent.

Most corporate praying is organized because of an original call, burden, or vision given to one person. Then God raises up *intercessors* to help fulfill those calls, *other teachers* to expand it, and *people inspired by it* to pass it on to the next generations.

How God Started *What Happens When Women Pray*

It is imperative that Christian leaders first set their goals in their prayer closets with God—and then take them to committees or board meetings. This is how *What Happens When Women Pray* started—alone with God in my prayer closet.

That 1967 assignment from the Crusade of the Americas campaign to find out in six months' time exactly what does happen when women pray was an impossible task. Praying sincerely about it, I had no answer from God. I was stalling.

While reading devotionally in Revelation 3, where Jesus (about fifty years after He had returned to heaven) was instructing the apostle John what to tell His church in Philadelphia, Jesus was speaking directly to me. Nine of Jesus' words about His open door seemed to jump off the page at me from, and I knew I had my answer to accept the assignment:

Behold, I have put before you an open door (Rev. 3:8).

So I accepted the job—and the rest is His-story.

The Door No One Can Shut

After thirty years of going through that open door of prayer full-time, Jesus has shown me the first part of that verse's call—*why* it has stayed open. Through this verse, He showed me that there were three reasons for keeping the door open for our prayer ministry:

Behold, I have put before you an open door which no man can shut **because** *you have a little power, and have kept My Word, and have not denied My name.* (Rev. 3:8; emphasis added)

- **"You have a little power."** The first reason Jesus gave for keeping the door open these past thirty years is, "You have a little power." At first I thought that was demeaning, almost insulting. Why did Jesus call me if He knew I didn't have enough power? But what He has taught me is that it was *because* I didn't have enough power that I would learn where the power would come from. That power would come in two categories: spiritual power and physical power.

    First, God taught me that *spiritual power* would come from God's Holy Spirit working in me. God made this clear to me as I prayed for six months for the First International Prayer Assembly in Seoul, Korea, where I was responsible for the women's teaching sessions. It was timed over Pentecost Sunday, and I had prayed repeatedly for those months, *"Oh, God, send something of Pentecost! Send something of Pentecost!"* (Sometimes I smiled during my praying, wondering what would happen if God really did. Would our delegates from those ninety-six countries run for the first plane home?)

Three thousand women gathered in the sanctuary of the church, and translator booths were set up in the balcony. Each participant had a set of earphones and dialed to her own language, no matter what was being spoken from the pulpit. The sponsoring Lausanne Committee sent bilingual people to check to see if the delegates were hearing adequately. When my former chairperson in Taiwan, Jeanne Swanson, was sent to the Chinese-speaking delegation, she came running to me. She said that when she asked them (in Chinese) what they had heard me teach and how they had responded in prayer, they all understood everything I had said. Jeanne asked them, "You don't speak English, do you? When they all shook their heads saying No, no" in Chinese, a startled Jeanne said, "There wasn't a Chinese translator in the booth! It was empty. He is still on his way on the plane!" Nonplussed, the Chinese women responded, "*Oh, it must have been the Holy Spirit!*"

Arriving in Hong Kong after that prayer assembly in Seoul, I checked with Faye Leung, the Chinese woman who translated my Trans World Radio tapes from English to Chinese. Telling her the story, she calmly replied, "Oh, that doesn't surprise me at all. I was praying that day with a Chinese woman who, although she doesn't understand a word of English, prayed each prayer you asked us to pray!" Then Faye confirmed that all the Chinese she knew there understood every word I said! With no translator—but God!

No, the power was not mine; it was God's Holy Spirit. My bold prayer had been prompted by Acts 2:5–6, in which Jesus' followers were filled with the Holy Spirit, and three thousand men, plus women and children, were saved that day when they spilled out into the streets of Jerusalem—with everybody hearing in their own tongue. I never even imagined God was going to do that! I am never prepared for what power God's Holy Spirit is going to furnish. It is always far above what I could think up— but it is always according to His power working in me.

Now unto Him who is able to do exceeding abundantly beyond all
that we ask or think, according to the power that works within us.
(Eph. 3:20)

I have learned never to leave for a speaking assignment
without waiting in prayer for the Holy Spirit—just as Jesus told
His followers to wait until they were "clothed with power from
on high" (Luke 24:49). While walking to the podium at a
Promise Keepers' "think-tank" meeting, I felt uncomfortable
about being a woman sharing there. So I silently prayed, "Lord,
before I open my mouth, come in power—so it will be You, not
me, getting any glory." Several men came to me afterward, saying that just as I was *walking up* to speak they suddenly felt
God's power surrounding us! His power—not mine!

My opening prayer in front of any audience always includes
asking the Holy Spirit to come in His power. And together we
all feel His awesome power changing the whole atmosphere of
the meeting. Almost never is it as dramatic as Korea, but it is
always what Paul said in Colossians 1:29:

And for this purpose also I labor, striving according to His power,
which mightily works within me.

I have learned I have just "a little power," and I also have
learned Who does have all the power of the universe! Because
it is God's power flowing, as long as He keeps replacing my
"little power," no one will shut the prayer ministry door—until
He decides it is time.

Another kind of power of which I have just "a little" is *physical power*. God taught me in amazing ways that physical power for
ministry would be the power of Christ in me. I could fill this
whole book with incredible examples of how in my weakness the
power of Christ has rested on me.

Paul, praying three times for his thorn in the flesh to be removed, listened to the Lord saying to him that His grace and power would be sufficient for Paul *with* his physical thorn still there. I, too, have learned that when I am weak, then Christ is my strength. Paul wrote:

> Most gladly, therefore, I will rather boast about my weaknesses, *that the power of Christ may dwell in me*. Therefore I am well content with weaknesses . . . for Christ's sake; for when I am weak, then I am strong (2 Cor. 12:9–10; emphasis added)

God has kept open the door of this prayer ministry, not because I have been hale and hearty physically. No, just the opposite. Many major surgeries and now a heart that can pump only about one-third of its blood should have closed my work down years ago.

However, way back in 1965, it was in secret prayer while reading Romans 12:1 that *I gave God my body once and for all as a living sacrifice to Him*. (I have thought many times since it would be easier to be a dead sacrifice than a living one!)

The price never seemed higher than it did in South Africa the morning I was to be videotaped all day before an audience of several thousand, as I shared in my book *A Time to Pray God's Way*. At six o'clock, I woke with a violent intestinal parasite attack. Because of all the resulting symptoms, for two hours I could not get up from lying on my stomach on the bathroom floor. I knew there was no backup speaker. (We always have trusted God, and He always has taken care of us!) So at 8:00 A.M., I struggled to my feet, took a shower, and headed for the auditorium. While the committee prayed fervently and my intercessors all across America were praying (without knowing why), I stood up to speak. And then the miracle happened!

I was on camera from 9:15 A.M. until 4:00 P.M., with only a

break at lunch. (I didn't dare to try any food or water.) But the miracle was that I kept gaining momentum as the day wore on. Instead of crumpling in a heap, I was invigorated with more and more power—until they turned off the cameras at 4:00! As the power kept increasing, I was stunned. I had not "a little," but *no* power on my own. But the power of Christ that was mine that day, and for thousands of other days, was from His omnipotence!

One of the greatest thrills of my life has been completely depending on God when no human help was available or capable of solving the problem. When I bowed to Him in prayer, God either healed me, temporarily lifted the symptoms while I was speaking, or gave me His incredible strength for the long, grueling days. Never once has He ever let me down!

Yes, that first reason in Revelation 3:8 that no one can shut our prayer ministry door is "you have a little power" spiritually and physically. But that was not an *insult*. It not only was a *compliment*; it was a *privilege*! I have had the privilege of experiencing this closeness to God and His awesome power all these years—as He poured out His power!

- **"You have kept My Word."** The second reason Jesus said no one has been able to shut our ministry's door of prayer until now is that we have kept His Word.

  The prayers we pray alone in secret eventually produce our influence on other people—our families, our friends, our coworkers, and especially those we formally teach. This is why it has been so important to make sure that everything we teach in our prayer seminars and books is from the Bible.

  The reason people from all Christian denominations have prayed together in unity during these years is because we use only the prayer principles from God in His Word, not following any one church's persuasions.

However, not only our teachings are not only *based* on God's Word, but also we have kept His Word by *applying* each biblical teaching in small groups in our seminars. More than just reading, studying, memorizing, or sharing Scripture, keeping God's Word is *applying it to our lives.* Keeping His Word is not just digging in our heels, determined that we will obey it or else. That usually ends in failure and frustration. Real, lasting results come from the person praying promising God (usually in secret) that he or she will obey—and asking Him to give the power to do it. Volumes of thank-you letters have told us that readers also have applied the Word of God in their private prayer times.

- *"You have not denied My name."* The third reason Jesus told me why no one could shut our door of prayer was, "You have not denied My name." *This was Jesus Himself talking about His own name.* The name that is above every name. The name at which every knee shall bow.

  This was Jesus talking. The crucified, risen, ascended Jesus at the right hand of the Father in heaven! *His name!*

  As I will discuss further in chapter 11, one of the deepest callings from Jesus to me was to bring His name back to those Christians and churches that have let it, intentionally or by carelessness, slip through the cracks. Denying His name does not have to be denouncing Him as God, as divine, or as immaculately conceived. It is just leaving Him out of our preaching, teaching, our priorities, and our devotion. It is replacing Him with our plans and programs or our church's or organization's name instead of His.

  It has been a constant struggle to keep the praying "in His name" and not to regress to the kind of praying they did before they had Jesus' name, His authority, His cross, His blood, His death, His resurrection, and His ascension to the right hand of the Father in heaven. But we have made a conscious effort in our ministry to include the precious, saving name of Jesus in our prayers.

Amazing Results of Prayer

Because we have constantly tried to rely on God's power, to keep His Word, and to exalt His name, we have seen God do amazing things in the lives of pray-ers. The following are just a tiny sampling of our looking back to see how some of our ministry's teachings turned out.

Praying in God's will has been one of the most important and life-changing aspects of our prayer teaching. Here are some examples from my United Prayer Ministry board members:

Missionary Shirlee Vennerstrom wrote to share how an illustration I had used about her in *What Happens When Women Pray* had turned out. Back in 1972, when they left Ethiopia the first time, she had prayed, begged, and pleaded with God to let them return. The message I had taught in that book and counseled her personally was for her not to pray answers, but requests. (We leave the results to Him.) Her secret praying was for His will, but her heart was breaking over her beloved Ethiopia. Here is an excerpt from her letter:

> Adjusting to life in the States was a long and painful process, but as we look back, we see how God's plan for our lives unfolded. God provided a house with exactly the down payment we had been able to save. It was near Bethel College, and our house provided a home base for many of our former students in Ethiopia. We were able to help our own three kids through their college years, and both our sons found lovely Christian wives at our home church. Also we were able to provide a home for a student while his parents were still in Ethiopia—only to have him become our

son-in-law eleven years later. God, in His timing, permitted us to serve Him in the Philippines, back in Ethiopia, and then in the Cameroons.

Shirley had learned not to pray *her* answer to her prayer, but to pray God's will according to His Word in Jesus' model, the Lord's Prayer!

Teaching the message of praying in God's will had come from my own secret prayers applied to my life. As I mentioned previously, every year I spend as much time as it takes before my January birthday asking God to show me what He wants for me the next year. In 1987, I felt I was emptying myself of all that was me as I prayed, "Father, if there is only one person on earth who wants to do your will completely, let *me* be that person!"

This is the compelling force behind all my decisions—always based on the Bible. It is what God so powerfully told me from His Word in 1990 while I was reading 2 Timothy 1:9: "[God] has saved us, and called us with a holy calling, not according to our works, but *according to His own purpose and grace* which was granted us in Christ Jesus from all eternity" (emphasis added). Sinking deeply into my prayer pouffe, I had cried, "Lord, anoint me afresh for *Your* purpose!"

Mentoring and teaching by example is also important because other people catch our relationship with God not just because they *hear it* from us, but because they *see it* in us. A rule I have kept as I have taught Sunday school, Bible studies, seminars, and conventions is *never to expect somebody else to obey what I am teaching unless I have sincerely tried to apply it to my own life first.*

Marlene Lee, our board chairman, wrote, "The whole twenty-seven years on the board (and as president many years) has been a big learning experience for me. Every month at board meeting, you taught us what God was teaching you right then."

It all started at a 1974 prayer seminar at the church where her sister

Vi Waite's husband was pastor, she prayed for the first time, "All I want is Your perfect will for me and my family."

Marlene, her husband, and their small children had moved in with another sister because of a financial setback, and everything seemed wrong for that young family. When she called me crying to pray that their house would sell, I responded that I would not pray that prayer—because the Lord may have something else for them. His timing is always right. "That is when I learned to pray *requests,* not *answers* to God," she said.

God answered with a job teaching piano for sixteen years at a local Christian college, followed by eight years of teaching children in an early childhood music program with her own daughter. Now in charge of writing and producing the children's Christmas program for her church, she was chosen to be a trainer of teachers for a national organization that demonstrates that the learning pattern of the brain is influenced by repeated music participation from the mother's womb. The exciting part is that the results of doing something—as opposed to the usual "sit-down-and-be-still" approach to children's learning—can be seen in modern brain imaging. "What an awesome threshold of learning for children!" she wrote.

However, Marlene said she should not write for this book because they are still praying about a project that God dropped in the lap of her husband ten years ago. "We don't have the answer yet!" she protested.

"Oh, no," I replied, "that is what we *do* want in the book. Many of our prayers are not all answered yet!"

"I used to sob with every little blow of the wind," Marlene said. "We still don't have all the answers for our future, but I have quiet confidence in the God who never makes a mistake. We hold on to what God wants to have happen, not what *we* want to manipulate!" First John 5:14–15 are her scriptures: "And this is the confidence which we have before Him, that, if we ask anything according to His will, He hears us. And if we know that He hears us [in] whatever we ask, we know that we have the requests which we have asked from Him."

Teaching men also came out of that first seminar of Marlene's. As I shared in *What Happens When Women Pray*, Marlene's sister Vi's husband, who was the pastor, had asked me to share from his pulpit the Sunday morning before the six-week women's seminar, explaining what it would be about. When I discovered he meant for me to preach the morning sermon, I panicked. In our board prayer meeting, Vi prayed, "Lord, we're going to put out a fleece. How the men accept Evelyn next Sunday morning will be our sign if she ever is to open the seminars to men." How dare she pray that prayer for me, I fussed, explaining how uncomfortable I was *preaching* on Sunday mornings (although it was different when I had been *teaching* men for fourteen years in my Sunday school class). "But it was my *husband* who asked you—not me!" Vi insisted. My husband, Chris, also was in favor of the idea.

When the people filed out of the sanctuary that Sunday, my knuckles turned white from all the men so powerfully shaking my hand, smiling, and thanking me! No matter where I am in this prayer learning process—I never have all the answers!

God's timing has been another focus of our teaching. Doreen Mossberg was single and on staff of a church many miles away from home when she read *What Happens When Women Pray*. As she prayed for a much-desired husband, she started understanding about praying for God's will in her life, about God's timing, and how to continue to pray even when an answer isn't imminent. While she waited, she interviewed for a church staff position in the Twin Cities. After three years of praying, her groom was just what she prayed for!

But when she and I met at the prayer meeting for Women of Faith in Minneapolis, she asked me to pray about getting a position closer to her husband's work. "After that prayer," Doreen said, "I just accepted the position I had interviewed for so long ago in the Twin Cities—closer to him! But the amazing thing," she said, "was that I had not even met my husband-to-be when I interviewed for that job." *God's timing is perfect and worth waiting for!*

The need to actually pray is another biblical precept we emphasize during our prayer seminars. It is so true that *it is much easier to attend seminars and read books about prayer than to pray!* I finally started calling our teaching on intercessory prayer a prerequisite to answered prayer. In order for God to give us answers, we must not only be prepared spiritually in our own lives—*we must pray!* The Bible says,

You do not have because you do not ask (James 4:2).

Forgiven for prayer power has been another vital prayer tool in our ministry. We learned that there are conditions in our spiritual lives God expects fulfilled before He answers.

If I regard iniquity in my heart, the Lord will not hear me (Psalm 66:18).

Our board member Peggy Oaks at age thirty-three had asked Jesus to be her Savior, but had no assurance in spite of reading everything in the Bible people suggested. When her pastor told her of his friend's praying "to grow in grace"—and on the way home from church breaking his leg—Peg said she thought if she were assured of salvation she wouldn't mind a broken leg, and she also prayed to "grow in grace."

Ten years after her original prayer for salvation, Peg knelt before God and started confessing her sins, based on 1 John 3:22. She knew she was guilty of murder because she hated her neighbor, was guilty of having taken the Lord's name in vain, and even, she said, her thought life was impure. She knew if she had broken one commandment, she was guilty of all (see James 2:10).

God set her free from her sins. Instead of hatred, God gave love. She learned to thank God from 1 Thessalonians 5:18—even for her son being caught in a robbery. That was an answer to prayer, she said, because she had prayed for him not to take the glory to himself for his acceptance at West Point. "Such peace flooded my soul, I knew God was going to use it for good," Peg said confidently. That son is now a surgeon.

Her other son, for whom Peg prayed unceasingly as he rebelled from God's ways, has opened an extension college in the Empire State Building to train five hundred inner-city young people to love and depend on the Lord and to be trained in leadership. Their main campus encompasses 128 acres located thirty-five miles from the Empire State Building, and it will be used as a flagship for colleges in major cities across the United States and in foreign countries to accomplish this task for Jesus.

Peg's oldest child is a daughter who also walked away from the Lord but is now back walking with Him. "A year ago," Peg said, "a young lady, who had been born to our daughter when she was not married and then put up for adoption, came into our lives. For more than thirty years, I prayed for that grandchild when I prayed for our other children and grandchildren. It is fascinating to know what God allows us to go through so we will seek Him and know Him."

Peg's letter went on and on. Her husband prayed, asking God to remove his desire for cigarettes. God answered one day in April 1990 at 9:30. Peg's husband has had no withdrawal and no cigarettes since then! Also, a young man who had spent twenty-six days high on alcohol and cocaine had stayed with them. His wife and children had left him, and he had given all their furniture away. He finally admitted he was going to hell in a phone call to Peg's husband. Accepting Jesus, God has given him his job back and a lovely house—and his family. He was baptized in the Pacific Ocean last Thanksgiving! Peg said her brother-in-law lived fifteen years after the doctors told him he had three weeks of life—while they prayed he would know Jesus before he died. God answered and gave him the last three years attending Bible study and growing in the Lord.

Reminiscing about being on our telephone prayer chains for so many years, Peg said the answers that stood out most were the cancellation of Shirley McLaine's seminar on the New Age—and our board member Barb's leading so many to the Lord in her inner-city ministry while her husband, Ken, was chaplain at the county jail's workhouse. "But," said Peg, "the biggest answered prayer of all is our seeing many thousands pray to receive Christ in Evelyn's seminars and then go on to live the Christian life as they use her books. I see a humble servant of God who is a great prayer warrior herself accomplishing the impossible for an ordinary woman. The praise goes to our heavenly Father, who is 'all in all.'"

Forgiving others has turned out to be the second most life-changing prayer, next to the one to accept Jesus as Savior and Lord. It has been the prerequisite for answered prayer that has improved relationships with family, friends, neighbors, coworkers, bosses, and others. I have listened to thousands of tearful yet radiating women in autograph lines after every seminar tell me of the victory and lifted burden each experienced when she had forgiven that day. Here is the story of one woman with whom we kept in touch for years. She has experienced one of the most drastic—and most dramatic—transformations:

After many years of counseling by both professionals and her pastor, Mary Lynn (not her real name) came to a seminar. She already had told me her story, but I was not prepared for the drastic change. She came from a Satan-worshiping family. Her brother had raped her almost nightly as a child, and her father—with her mother standing by consenting—frequently had almost smothered her as he repeatedly forced himself sexually on her tied-down body. No counseling could touch her deep trauma, but God could!

When I had asked each attendee to think of one person who had hurt them and whom they really had not forgiven, of course Mary Lynn's family came to her mind immediately. Then when I told them to "pray in silence, forgiving that person," she did! (This prayer is just between God and the pray-er.) It was the first step in her healing process. (Forgiving is mostly for the victim's good. It does not mean they condone the evil action, nor does it free the perpetrator from

responsibility and guilt before God. The offending ones only get forgiven when they ask God to forgive them.)

Immediately Mary Lynn followed up the next step she had prayed
with the rest of us—*promising God to confirm His new love in her toward
her family.* They had not communicated for years, but immediately she
phoned and told her startled parents that she had forgiven them—and
then asked them to forgive her for her unforgiving attitude all those
years. That did it!

Upon being told, her pastor exploded with joy, "That's the fastest
transformation I've ever seen!"

Many years of healing have taken place, and Mary Lynn has now
earned a master's degree in counseling. She has worked for several years
as a nurse in the psychiatric department of a large hospital where
patients clamored to request her—because she understood! Then she
spent several years as a social worker in a large Christian hospital with
people who have depression—while involved in a four-thousand-mem-
ber church. Her last note said she had just led two of her patients to the
Lord. While actually living with her parents at times—she was still witnessing to them and praying for her parents to accept Jesus!

Jesus said it so clearly right after teaching us Christians how to pray
in His model "Lord's Prayer":

> For if you forgive men for their transgressions, your heavenly Father will
> also forgive you. But if you do not forgive men, then your Father will not
> forgive your transgressions (Matt. 6:14–15).

Forgiving us too? When I turned sixty-five, I felt I should throw in
the towel, or at least a little of it. I was tired, and God's power seemed
to lag a little. But when we had our annual board retreat that year, I
found out why. I had argued with God for telling me to assign
Revelation 2–3 for them to read individually and then to pray about in
the group. "With all those *repents*—for my sweet pray-ers? No way!" I
protested to God. But I did—and was in for two big surprises.

The first surprise was that every one of my board members was stopped on a sin in her own life—hindering her power in praying for me. Reassembling to pray together, they each deeply repented—and were on their way to prayer power again.

Now it was *my turn to repent!* I prayed last so I wouldn't influence their praying. I sobbed before God and my board because Jesus had surprised me by stopping me on His words in verse 7, chiding deeply into my heart: *Whose door do you think this is anyway? It is My door, not yours!* His words stung deeply into my heart as I read Revelation 3:7–8 again:

> He who is holy, who is true, who has the key of David, *who opens and no one will shut, and who shuts and no one opens,* says this. . . . I know your deeds. Behold I have set before you an open door.

No, the decision is not mine to close the door He has opened. Nor is it yours to close the door God has opened for you.

It was comforting when I discovered before Jesus said, "I have set before you an open door," He said, "I know your deeds." Is our track record why He can call us to a bigger job? Was it because of a lifelong prayer life that Jesus felt He could trust me with that huge assignment? And to think I almost blew it—when entertaining the thought that it must be time to retire, or that I should throw in at least a part of the towel—way back in a retreat in 1987!

Prayer Power's Prerequisites

The conditions for achieving prayer power that God unfolded and we have taught with *What Happens When Women Pray* through the years have been based on another prayer of one man—Elijah.

James tells us that "the effectual, fervent prayer of a righteous [person] avails much" (James 5:16). He then illustrates this truth by sharing how much one person's prayers really did accomplish: "Elijah was a man with a nature like ours, and he prayed earnestly that it might not rain; and it did not rain on the earth for three years and six months. And he prayed again, and the sky poured rain, and the earth produced its fruit" (vv. 17–18).

God has used this example in the Bible to teach people through the centuries that there is power in one person's prayers. In our seminars and books, hundreds of thousands of people around the world have been motivated by Elijah's example of what that one person—just like them—could do through prayer. *One person's prayers really do work!*

Kathy's Prayer Power

In this recent incident, many of the topics God taught us are all in a package—praying, submitting to God's will, forgiving, and being filled with His love.

I enjoy going to my hairstylist, Kathy, because we talk about such deep spiritual things and occasionally even pray together.

For months, she had shared with me the unbelievable tragedy she was going through. Her mother had been diagnosed in a nursing home as being in the last stages of Alzheimer's disease because she could not swallow. Kathy had taken care of her mother so much that she recognized that symptom as one of the side effects of a medication they were giving her mother. She struggled with doctors and tried to convince her family—especially her sister—that her mother's problem was being unable to swallow her desperately needed medications for so long. (After she died an autopsy at the University of Minnesota proved Kathy was right. There was no sign of Alzheimer's disease.) Then to Kathy's horror, they took all food and water away from her mother for nineteen days. Kathy became almost frantic trying to rescue her mother.

One day she told me she had finally knelt before going to bed and prayed over and over, "Dear Father, Thy will be done. No one else's! Not mine. Not theirs. Yours!" Then she had slipped into bed completely calm after not having slept for three nights. Although she never remembers dreams, Kathy said, she did this one—of her mother sitting straight up in bed and saying, "I'm hungry. I want to see Kathy."

A few days later while shampooing my hair, Kathy almost sobbed as she told me the worst part was that it was breaking the family apart. With her body tense and her face drawn in grief, I talked to her that day about Jesus telling us the only solution was for her to forgive and quoted scriptures for her. She said that she simply could not forgive them. "Evelyn," Kathy reminded me, "then you just looked up at me, took my hand in yours and said, 'Let's pray.' You prayed for my mom, me, my sister, my family, the doctor—and that God would help me forgive them and fill me with love for my sister."

Suddenly, without an explanation, Kathy dropped her comb and said that she had to be alone. Leaving me dripping wet, she dashed upstairs to her home. In about ten minutes, she came back—absolutely transformed! The anger lines that had been on her face for so long were gone. She was radiant! With eyes almost popping with amazement, she said, "I met God up there! I only got to the top of the stairs when suddenly I became empty. All the hatred of my sister and family drained out. I was absolutely empty," she said. "It almost felt physical. Nothing was there. Then," she said slowly, "just as suddenly I was filled—filled with love for my sister and family. Evelyn, God was up there!"

While I was still under the dryer, Kathy's phone rang. It was her sister (who hadn't talked to her for weeks), telling her they put a feeding tube back in their mother. When she asked why, her sister said because her mother had sat up in bed and spoken to her—and she, her sister, had run out to get a nurse. And I heard the beaming Kathy telling her sister on the phone, "I love you! I love you!" Forgiving!

After the reconciliation with that phone call, the sisters got together again a few days later. It was then Kathy heard from her sister the words that her mother actually had said when she sat up—and they were exactly the same words of her dream! Kathy got to go once more to her alert mother, and she and her sister are closest of friends again, she told me. "I have this incredible love for my sister. When I'm with her it just oozes out of me toward her!"

Just one person—alone with God in prayer. Oh, how it works!

Reflection Questions

Examine your life:

Which very private prayer that only you prayed has God answered? Take time to be specific. Or have you thought God would not answer just *your* prayers? Has praying in groups been a substitute for your personally availing yourself of the power and blessing of solitary praying?

Scripture:

In your Bible read James 5:16–18. Also, recalling Joshua's incredible answer from God when just one person prayed, turn to Matthew 6:6 to see what Jesus promised His followers when they shut their doors and prayed in secret. Why does or doesn't this apply to you?

For you to do:

What do you think Jesus is saying to you about the power of *your* individual prayers? What open doors, spiritual powers, and physical power do you think you may have missed by not spending enough time alone with God in prayer? Can you trust His teaching in Matthew 6:6 that your solitary praying will produce rewards? If so list several kinds of things you should and will begin praying about in secret immediately:

_____

_____

_____

_____

For you to pray:

"Holy Father, forgive me for depending too much on the prayers of others and not realizing Your insistence on my spending time alone with You in prayer. Forgive me for thinking my public praying was sufficient when there are so many things I need to hear form You, settle with You, and pray for with You alone. Increase my faith to be able to believe You, Jesus, that my individual prayers really are great in their workings. How I long for this intimate, precious fellowship. I promise You that I will obey You, dear Jesus, by spending time daily alone in my prayer closet. In your precious name, amen."

CHAPTER 4

What God Does Through Corporate Prayer

THE POWER OF GOD was so strong in that room it almost pushed me back as I walked through the door," Mary Lance Sisk gasped.

Having an earlier appointment, she had arrived at a Charlotte, North Carolina, prayer seminar right after approximately half of the attendees had prayed out loud in their little groups to accept Jesus or to make sure Jesus was truly their Savior and Lord.

Not trusting my own judgment, since most attendees were members of fine churches right in America's Bible Belt, I whispered to the pastor of the church on the platform with me when it happened, "Would you estimate what percentage just prayed that prayer?" Stunned, he answered, "At least 50 percent." Mostly church members! Some were his church members!

Organized Corporate Prayer's Power

Why all that power? Because somebody conducted a prayer seminar? Oh, no! It was God answering all the prayers poured out from the hearts of all the intercessors that "availed much," as we are told in James 5:16.

What were these prayers? Organized, corporate, concentrated praying for one specific thing—their prayer seminar! The committee had prayed. The assigned intercessors plus the churches' prayer groups had prayed. Committee members Phil and Jean pleaded with God together for months. Jean often was in prayer constantly all day long, Phil said. My United Prayer Ministry board, telephone prayer chains, and prayer calendar members daily prayed fervently. I prayed. All that prayer! And all that power!

What is organized corporate prayer? It is that deliberate getting together of two or more Christians to pray for a specific need at a specific time.

Billy Graham, who has preached to more people than anyone in history, says the three most important parts of his evangelism campaigns are prayer, prayer, and prayer. A major thing he requires of his campaign committees is organized, extensive, persisting prayer. It is the power of God answering all that prayer that sends thousands of people pouring down stairs and aisles to accept Jesus.

Amazed at Prayer's Power

Looking back while writing this book, I am amazed at the magnitude of what God actually did when people prayed specific, corporate, organized prayers!

The first followers of Jesus also were shocked at how God powerfully answered their prayers. They, too, learned this secret of coming together to pray. When the apostle Peter was imprisoned by Herod, they gathered in Mary's house to pray fervently for him on the very night Peter was to be brought before Herod. Herod had just killed James the brother of John, and they were desperate in their prayers for Peter's life. Acts 12:5 records, "Peter was kept in the prison, but prayer for him was being made fervently by the church to God."

God answered by sending an angel to Peter's prison cell. Miraculously, Peter's chains fell off. He followed the angel past the guards and through the iron gate to the city, and the gate, without human hands, opened for them by itself.

Those pray-ers were astounded at the incredible events, actually thinking it must be Peter's ghost knocking to get in to their prayer meeting.

There is no biblical record of those early Christians' having gathered together to pray for James the brother of John when Herod imprisoned and killed him. So, could we ask, was the difference organized, fervent, persistent praying? God certainly did answer!

Like the early followers of Christ, we frequently cannot imagine that God could answer so powerfully. This is the reason we started in 1968 writing down and dating our prayer requests and God's answers—and still continue to do so today. Recording our requests and God's answers has worked wonders in building our faith in God for new requests and is a marvelous source of praise for what God actually did—when we prayed.

How It Started for Us

In 1973, the organized prayer group that was to sustain and empower my whole ministry until this day was born—my United Prayer Ministry Board. For all these years, these women have persisted in faithful, fervent praying daily and we have met monthly to praise, pray, and plan together. Because of their prayers, God started moving mightily as women were hungry for answers to their problems. When we passed the first one hundred thousand people coming to the seminars, we stopped counting. We started selling cassette tapes of an entire six-day seminar, and I was astounded when Jim Adair at Victor Books listened to those tapes, called me, and told me I had a contract for a book!

At the same time, while we Bethel College faculty wives were praying weekly for our Christian college and seminary, those mature pray-ers frequently included my emerging *What Happens When Women Pray* book. I was surprised last week when one of those original faculty wives beamed that her current pastor had just finished teaching that book, with powerful results—after all these years!

Upon first arriving at our new home in St. Paul, I desperately missed my prayer support. So I had gathered ten friends together to pray for my speaking, especially to young people about the dangers of the occult practices in which many of them were innocently engaging at that time. It became known as my Occult Prayer Chain, but our weekly meetings and telephone communicating also provided powerful praying for the prayer book and new ministry.

The corporate prayer that produced that book was powerful, sending it back to press after the first week on the market. When it had been out just a year and a half, Jeanne Wagner wrote in our United Prayer Ministry newsletter: "As Evelyn wrote *What Happens When Women Pray*, those of us in the prayer ministry prayed specifically over every detail of it, from titles of chapters to particular context words. When Satan was giving Evelyn a struggle, she would call, and we would double our prayer efforts. Now to see the results of those prayers as the book is being used all over the world, not only to teach people to pray but to bring many to Christ, is so exciting and rewarding. God deserves all the glory, for without Him none of this would be happening."

It was only a few years into our United Prayer Ministry praying that we were shocked again to discover the third part of Jeremiah 33:3:

Call to Me, and I will answer you, and show you great and mighty things, which you do not know (NKJV).

Truly God was answering our immediate prayers, but the most incredible part was discovering those great and mighty things we knew not.

How could we have known God's longtime plan for the simple prayers we prayed?

How could we have known He would protect me from bombs, parasites, hurricanes, and a plane running out of gas over the Pacific? How could we know He had intended all along to take our requests to every continent on earth—and to answer them there?

Analyzing His answers, we soon realized that promise from God was in three parts, not two. There were two "ands," telling us that: (1) we call, (2) *and* He answers, (3) *and* then His omniscient plan goes into operation. It was God doing the "exceeding abundantly above all we could ask or think" of Ephesians 3:20. The following are a few of the "so that" things God had planned to do—because of our organized corporate praying.

God's "So That" Plans for Corporate Prayer

God's ultimate plan for all that praying for *What Happens When Women Pray* was "so that" He could use it in the lives of the recipients. It was "so that" they, too, could become powerful pray-ers—and frequently have God birth a prayer ministry for them too.

I do not write books. I listen to God in my prayer closet and then write down the points and the scriptures He recalls. The biblical concepts in that little book have been used by God to teach millions of people around the world—because every precept came directly from Him(see Galatians 6:6).

But the amazing thing is how these different points from God have reached different people in their specific needs and with different degrees of maturity in their prayer lives. It has spawned amazing results, from an individual's renewed prayer life to a large international organization of prayer.

It would take many volumes to tell all the incredible things God did in and through all the lives changed by prayer. It breaks my heart not to be able to tell all of them for your encouragement—and amazement! But here are samples of the precepts taught and how individuals applied them in their lives and ministries.

Teaching others to pray. Not only did Fern Nichols, founding president of the powerful Moms in Touch International, learn to pray specific biblical ways, but also God birthed a whole prayer movement of now twenty-five thousand prayer groups internationally praying weekly for their children in school. My heart was overwhelmed with awe and gratitude at the following "so-that" letter:

Dear Evelyn,

As I was reading through the book by you, *What Happens When Women Pray*, there was a prayer on page 51 that touched my heart; so I stopped and prayed sincerely the prayer that you suggested. It said: "Dear Father: Please give me the privilege of being aware of the presence of Jesus my Savior in a prayer group. Teach me to help others to pray. Teach me to listen to Your speaking to me in the silent periods." That was 1982.

Little did I know how mightily God was going to answer that prayer. In 1984, as I sent my two oldest sons to a public junior-high school, the burden to pray for them was so great that I knew I could not bear it alone. I asked God to give me another mom who felt the same burden and who would be willing to pray with me concerning our children and their school. That was the beginning of a prayer group that God birthed into an international ministry called Moms in Touch International.

My first request was answered as the presence of Jesus was strongly felt in that group.

My second request was that God would use me to teach others to pray. The principles of "one accord" praying, using the 6S method outlined in your book, were exactly what I wanted our one hour of prayer to be modeled after: praying subject by subject, short prayers, simple prayers, specific prayer requests, silent periods, and in small groups. Teaching this method of prayer has been revolutionary. My third request has been answered as each week in Moms in Touch I continue to learn how to listen to the Holy Spirit in those silent periods, allowing Him to guide my thoughts in how He wants me to pray for the children and the school. I am so thankful for you, Evelyn, as you have passed down such a wonderful tool of prayer that literally transforms prayer groups. As a result of this teaching, tens of thousands of moms all over the world are using this method in their Moms in Touch groups. What a legacy!

Evelyn, you are a sweet gift from God in my life as well as a spiritual "mother" whom I will treasure forever. Love, Fern.

In my book *What Happens When Women Pray*, I outlined the 6S method for praying in small groups so that people who never have prayed out loud before are able to join in at their first prayer meeting. For those of you who are not familiar with the 6S prayer method, let me briefly summarize it here:

1. Praying *subject by subject* eliminates the need for silently planning one's own prayer instead of praying with the person whose turn it is.

2. Encouraging *short prayers* eliminates just the mature pray-ers praying.

3. Praying *simple prayers* gives even the newest pray-ers equal time and power before God.

4. Keeping track of *specific prayer requests and answers* is a great source of encouragement and praise to God.

5. Incorporating *silent periods* before starting to pray and during pauses between prayers highlights another side of prayer— God's turn to speak to us while we listen for His next request or even an answer to one we just prayed!

6. *Small groups* break down inhibitions in even the most shy or inexperienced pray-ers and produce an awesome oneness in Jesus.

Learning to put into practice those simple rules worked even on other continents. In Brazil, a university professor sadly reported in a church, "I'll have to have surgery for a kidney stone on Tuesday, and I don't want to give up my Sunday-school teaching on prayer, my university work, or seeing my first grandchild who is coming soon." She said four women met for specific prayer with their prayer teacher, following the six steps. The Lord heard, and the kidney stone was passed that evening. After X-rays the next day, her doctor said, "Impossible. No one could pass a stone that big!" The professor's note concluded with a happy: "The Lord is marvelous when we follow the principles He has given us in His Word!" Another reason God organized us to pray is teaching others what God has taught us!

These simple rules have worked equally well in all cultures and all ages around the world—from people who are not able to read to Dr. Paul Yonggi Cho, pastor of the largest church in the world. He told me when he had been unable to get his own small children to pray with him, he tried my 6S prayer method. The children then loved to pray with him—all praying just alike.

The first use of my prayer material overseas was the simple 6S prayer method used by a missionary friend on a flip chart to teach her Assamese women to pray. God is now using it extensively all over the world—because any Christian can do it—immediately.

Protection from falsehood. One reason God gave us these biblical prayer training principles has come to light through unusual needs of pray-ers. John warned the early Christians about the dangers of listening to false doctrine:

> Beloved, do not believe every spirit, but test the spirits to see whether they are from God; because many false prophets have gone out into the world (1 John 4:1).

The following truth has proved to be desperately needed and extremely valuable through the years: God wants us to pray so that we will communicate with Him in order to be able to discern truth.

Kathy Baarman, a speaker and area representative for Stonecroft Ministries, told me what our organized prayer for that book eventually did for her—protecting her from a false teacher in our free land. She writes:

> After twelve years of living under communism, my family escaped from Hungary and came to live in free America. Fifteen years later, I found true freedom in Jesus Christ. . . . *What Happens When Women Pray* changed our church family. Many of us in this church were new Christians, hungry for the Word of God. The senior pastor of the church was going the path of a cultist-type leader, and we sensed something was wrong. Our husbands didn't want to come to church, but we loved our "family" and did not want to leave. So after reading Evelyn's book *What Happens When Women Pray*, six of us women covenanted to pray together weekly. Within two months God exposed the wrong, and about fifty of us were out of there. About five years later, the rest of our church family saw the truth, and now this man is out of the ministry. Through this, we see God's faithfulness in protecting us from the false leaders His Word warns us about. We didn't even know what was wrong, but our God did. He answered our prayers as we sought His face! Thank you for your wonderful books, Evelyn. They are a big help to the body of Christ. With love, Kathy.

God gave two commands and two promises in James 4:7–8, all of which have proven absolutely true through these years. The first command is to "resist the devil," and God's unequivocal promise is that "he will flee from you." The second command is to "draw near to God," and its accompanying promise is, "and He will draw near to you." That truth worked for Kathy—and it works for us!

Praying without ceasing. Organized corporate prayer sometimes involves a small group, a whole church, or even millions of people around the world praying for a specific thing. *But astonishingly powerful results can come when just two persist in organized, deliberate praying on an ongoing basis.* This is why the apostle Paul, in 1 Thessalonians 5:17, directs us to "pray without ceasing."

Here are a few terrific examples when "praying without ceasing" was really practiced:

Last January, as Martha was driving me to a meeting in San Francisco, she excitedly shared incident after incident about praying without ceasing. "I brought up seventy-two boys, all of whom accepted Jesus and are living for Him yet today." Intrigued, I urged her on. "In 1979," she continued, "I read your book *What Happens When Women Pray,* and my husband and I determined to pray for our six children. We believed that prayer would sustain us, no matter what. We determined to 'pray without ceasing,' and the Holy Spirit taught us how to stay in a spirit of prayer twenty-four hours per day for our family.

"In 1978, we began to take in at-risk boys to give them a good home. In January 1981, Lee arrived. He was twelve and had been in jail off and on for three years. Drug addict. Alcoholic. Thief. As Lee and his brothers had reached age two, instead of turning on the TV, the father shot them up with heroin. As they reached age eight, their father taught them his profession. They were excellent thieves. When Lee arrived, he couldn't read or write and was placed in the local school's special program as he essentially had no schooling.

"By the end of January," Martha continued, "Lee had accepted Jesus Christ as his Savior. That June he finished his first semester completing an equivalent of five years of accelerated learning. He made the honor roll. Eventually Lee returned to his mother, and she called thanking them that she now knew the 'Gentleman' that we had introduced to Lee, the Holy Spirit, and that her husband, who was in jail for manslaughter, had now also received Jesus as his Savior.

"Over the ensuing years, a total of seventy-two boys ages twelve to fourteen came to the ranch and stayed from six months to graduation from high school," Martha said. "Unceasing prayer resulted in all seventy-two boys receiving Jesus as their Savior. They are currently between the ages of twenty-eight and thirty-six, and the majority of them are married with children. Praise God they are in the kingdom of light!"

A note from Wisconsin said, "Evelyn, I read your book *What Happens When Women Pray* in the late seventies. I used it in our small home fellowship for years and with my prayer partner for seven years. It works! So many answered prayers. It changed my life!"

I remember the excitement and enthusiasm at a Long Beach, California, seminar so many years ago. My year 2000 birthday card from one prayer group was signed by all the still-living original pray-ers and all the new ones. Chairman Ardis Ramsey reminded me that they had been praying "without ceasing" for twenty-five consecutive years now. "Our church of three thousand has had a banner year," she wrote. All that prayer—without ceasing!

From North Carolina, a pastor's wife shared that ten years ago their church was really struggling. She and the other deacons' wives began meeting at the same time the men met and just prayed for their husbands and the church. "This began a wonderful ministry as we have moved to other churches," she wrote. "We have used your book almost exclusively with tremendous influence. My husband and I feel that if the spiritual leaders and their spouses are a united body spiritually, praying and yielding to the Holy Spirit, then the church will follow. We have seen His hand working in our midst! Personally, I have been convicted, taught, encouraged, and motivated by your books."

Connie, the first woman to speak at a Promise Keepers rally, wrote to me, "I want to let you know that the group of ladies who were drawn to a deeper prayer life by your prayer conference two years ago are still meeting twice a month in my home. You made a difference in our lives."

Although our prayer seminars have had from hundreds to frequently several thousand attendees, we're not trying to enlist them into an organization. *They are there "so that" they can go to their homes, churches, neighborhoods, or places of business—and pray.*

Specific answers for specific needs. Fran Howard, president of Freedom in the Son, Inc., with a national and international women's prison ministry and a Native-American prayer organization, writes how the 6S prayer method powerfully works in prayer triplets:

> In the women's prison in Oregon, I was teaching *What Happens When Women Pray* to the Christian women inmates to find Jesus. We decided to try the triplet praying method [three Christians each praying for three who do not know Jesus]. Unknown to each other's groups, there was one young lady for whom all the groups were praying—a young Native American who had been involved in a drug-related gang crime and was sentenced to life without parole. After several months of our groups praying in their triplets, we brought in a black choir of girls about her same age. As she listened to them sing and share their testimonies, she realized they seemed so happy, and she wanted to know what they had that she didn't have. That night she gave her heart to Christ—and the praying triplets rejoiced.

> The story is not over yet, but God has done some miraculous things on her behalf. The parole board lifted the sentence of life without parole and gave her just life, which means a twenty-five-year sentence. She has already served more than ten years and may be eligible for parole in a few years. She is hanging in there with the Lord and growing every day—even as she does her time.

Mary from Texas said they began a prayer chain from *What Happens When Women Pray*, and a deacon's wife got saved. "Then two women got under conviction and dropped out, but we are still praying for them! Boy, have we been attacked by Satan. But God is so wonderful. Every time we have been attacked, we just pray harder. In less than a year we have had 561 requests, 174 answered personal prayer requests, 35 people saved, and 409 answers all together!"

Our United Prayer Ministry Board did some multiplying recently to see how many fervent prayers had persistently almost relentlessly approached God's throne room since 1973 by our United Prayer Ministry telephone prayer chain requests alone. The shocking number is hundreds of thousands.

Three mornings a week since 1973, our board's telephone prayer chains are activated at 6:30 A.M., all praying for our specific current needs and opportunities—continuing to uphold those requests as long as needed.

> Ask, and it shall be given to you; seek, and you shall find; knock, and it shall be opened to you (Matt. 7:7).

At the publisher's chapel celebrating the first million copies sold of *What Happens When Women Pray*, I was asked, "What produces a million-copy book?" Surprised, I answered simply, "Prayer. It was about prayer, it was produced by prayer, and every word and production facet was prayed over. Every day an intercessor has been assigned to pray for those who are reading it."

For more than twenty-five years now, this organized corporate prayer has been storming the gates of heaven—for and from our ministry. Overwhelmed at God's power flowing through their prayers, I cried out, "Oh, God, I want You to get *all* the glory!" Then, as tears welled up in my eyes and my overwhelming love for God almost exploded from my innermost being, I cried a new prayer, "Oh, God, I want this book to be my gift to You. I know You don't need anything, but You have poured out so much so unsparingly all these years, I want to give back to You the only thing I can—Your getting all the glory!"

Unexpected oneness in Jesus. However, powerful answers are not the only reward God intended for organized pray-ers. *The personal blessing that the intercessors themselves receive when they join with others in prayer is very precious.*

Seventeen-year-old Rebecca wrote that after I spoke in their city in Iowa, her mom began praying on the phone with a friend. Then she, too, began praying for needs and people's salvation on the phone with her friend, Lisa. She concluded her letter:

> You launched us to get us praying, and we love it. We've grown closer, and it's been such a time of encouragement spiritually! And guess what? My grandma, who we've been praying for, got saved! One month ago! I was so shocked! Oh ye of little faith, right? [smiley face] I could hardly believe it. Zowie! Isn't God great? Thanks so much for coming to speak here.

For adults and young people, one of the greatest rewards of continuous praying with the same group is the oneness, joy, and love that develops between pray-ers. *The world has no club or secret organization that can match it.*

One prayer group in California reported that they started a prayer chain with exciting answers to prayer, distributed the book *What Happens When Women Pray* to their friends, and gave it to their husbands, who started reading it and praying too. But, they said, the greatest result of learning to pray together is the love and oneness that has developed between them. They've become as close as natural sisters; and the fact that they can share their deepest needs with one another, secure in their hearts that their minds are set together in prayer, is so encouraging, they reported.

Jesus prayed to the Father for this oneness among all true believers:

> I ask not in behalf of these alone, but for those also who believe in Me through their word [us]; that they all may be one; even as Thou, Father,

art in Me, and I in Thee, that they also may be in Us; that the world may believe that Thou didst send Me (John 17:20–21).

When the current prayer movement started in the early seventies, one of the main things we, along with thousands of organized women, were praying for was unity in the body of Christ. How thrilling and yet humbling it is to see God answering those prayers *in* all of us.

Yes, it's happening! How many centuries has Jesus been waiting for His prayer in John 17 to be answered? It is now happening all over America—and the world—like never before in history! Unity in the body of Christ—holy, sweet, loving unity as we pray together. This oneness has been true of every praying group I've been a part of through all these years.

Praying in One Accord

After local prayer seminar committees of all denominations have prayed together for six months, I fly in on Friday and just drop into their awesome oneness in Jesus—immediately one with them. We no longer are strangers but incredibly one in Jesus. Then their prayers and mine mingle as the body of Christ beseeches God for the next day's lost souls, prayer power, and cleansing for the task. I am of all women most privileged and most blessed to have undeservedly all this prayer gift from God.

Phil told me about their organizing and praying for the Charlotte, North Carolina, seminar I mentioned previously in which 50 percent of their attendees prayed, making sure Jesus was their Savior and Lord.

"We prayed about everything! Although they were from all different denominations (with more than fifty churches attending)," he said, "there never was even mild dissension. Starting with differing points of view, every decision always was 100-percent unanimous. Even when a scheduling mixup necessitated scrambling with all those churches' schedules to change the date, we all agreed from Jesus' instructions in His Lord's Prayer that we wanted only God's will, not our own."

Phil continued, "The affection and love we felt for each other was amazing. Nobody was trying to outshine anybody else. It was different from any other business, church, or elder board committee I've ever been on." Phil paused and exclaimed, "And all those changed lives! All that power!"

In answer to organized corporate prayers, God has produced amazing reconciliation between different races and churches sponsoring and praying together for their seminars. We always request them to begin by organizing representatives of all possible area churches and to pray together for six months. My heart has rejoiced as thousands of churches, organizations, and whole communities have kept praying together even after their prayer seminar. They don't want to lose the love and oneness in Jesus that praying together gave them!

Vicki of Spokane, Washington, described it as "The symphony of prayer. Striking one chord in prayer. You've spoiled me for any other kind of praying," she smiled.

"Praying in one accord" is how Jesus' 120 followers prayed between His ascension and the Holy Spirit coming on that day of Pentecost— with hearts and minds throbbing as one in their passion for Jesus! This has been a basic biblical truth we have practiced and taught through our whole ministry, naming our small-group praying method "Praying in One Accord," from Acts 1:14:

> These all [the apostles] with one mind were continually devoting themselves to prayer, along with the women, and Mary the mother of Jesus, and with His brother.

A new dimension of pastors praying with pastors of mixed denominations all over America has emerged these past few years—with a surprisingly great side benefit. *They are becoming one in Jesus, not building their own kingdoms, but God's kingdom in their area by putting aside nonessential differences.* Many belong to nationwide pastors' prayer movements, while others just get together in their own towns or cities.

My niece's husband, Sam, pastor of an Episcopal church, participates in two pastors' meetings. One is the local ministerial association that handles the business side, and then, out of that, there is a smaller group of pastors of all different denominations who meet just to pray. "The difference is amazing," Sam told me. "Praying together has given us a beautiful oneness and love for each other. We don't compete, but we truly care for each other. It is an awesome experience every time we get together to pray!"

As the prayer movement has grown all over our country, there are literally thousands, probably millions, of prayer groups meeting regularly to pray for their families, churches, pastors, schools, neighborhoods, and friends. And collectively all that praying is ascending to the Father in His throne room of heaven. *But, even while they are praying together, our omniscient God can and does listen to each individual pray-er— one by one by one by one.*

What Organized Prayer Produces

Keeping all this organized prayer going has taken careful organizing, humbly admitting needs, continuous feeding in prayer requests, and faithfully reporting God's answers to them—"so that" together we could thank and praise God for His answers—always exceeding what we asked for.

However, the most amazing part is that God could take the fervent, faithful praying of my United Prayer Ministry across-the-board little group of ordinary teachers, housewives, nurses, returned missionaries, moms, and singles—and the simple teaching of a plain, ordinary woman—and use them in the lives of now millions of people around the whole world—because they prayed!

To the best of my ability, I have run a ministry on prayer—theirs and mine. A real prayer ministry takes humility—absolutely knowing I don't know, and admitting it to my intercessors. Then the pray-ers take up the responsibility with me, bombard heaven, and God does the rest!

And it works—in innumerable ways we have been able to see. But also works in surprises we cannot yet see that God has stored up for us in heaven. Those great and mighty things that are beyond any human brain's even imagining do come to pass—when we pray.

When my pastor husband built a new church in the fifties, our first guest speaker was Dr. Armin Gesswein, already a renowned prayer leader. "I'm looking for a church that will be built completely on prayer," he challenged our members—and my heart in particular. Meeting him in 1999, I asked him if he remembered saying that. "Oh, yes, I do," he replied.

"Did you ever find that church?" I asked."

"I came close," he smiled. "It was Paul [David] Yonggi Cho's praying church in Seoul, Korea—*the largest church in the world!*"

Reflection Questions

Examine your life:

With what groups are you, or have you been, a part of deliberate and consistent praying? If none, honestly try to identify your reasons such as:

I am too busy,

I never realized the power of corporate prayer,

I thought prayer was for just a select few God gifted and called to be intercessors,

I did not know I could be a powerful pray-er *plus* my other jobs for God,

I thought prayer was for those who couldn't do things for themselves...

Scripture:

Before reading, ask God to open your heart to what He wants to say to you. In your own Bible read Acts 12:1–17. What is your reaction to God's powerful response to organized prayer by sending an angel to rescue Peter? Is this the same God to whom you pray today? Can and does He still answer that powerfully?

For you to do:

When there is an emergency in your sphere of influence, do you automatically join with others to pray? If so, was there some time the praying really made a difference? How?

_____

_____

Record some personal blessings other than God's awesome answers you experience (or could) when praying with others.

_____

Prayerfully ask God to help you select His choice group, or groups, for you. Be open to His surprises.

For you to pray:

"Dear heavenly Father, thank you for teaching me Your awesome response to fervent, desperate praying by a group. Forgive me for neglecting to join with others to pray on a regular basis—and when emergencies arise. Please help me to prioritize my time and choice of activities to include consistent, deliberate, organized praying. I promise I will seek out and begin praying immediately with the group You have suggested to me. In Jesus name, amen."

CHAPTER 5

God's Divine Prayer Plans

WHILE I WAS STILL IN MY THIRTIES and many years before *What Happens When Women Pray* was written, I experienced an overwhelming desire almost bursting within me during my prayer time. "Oh, Father, I want to teach the whole world to pray!" I cried out. Immediately I was taken aback at my audacity. Who did I think I was to pray a prayer like that? "Forgive me, Father," I begged. I was so embarrassed at that prayer that I didn't tell anybody for thirty years. But now, after the miracle of God's using that little book, and me, to teach prayer on every continent in the world, I know that call was from God.

Now I can see a tiny speck of the incredibly intricate plan God has for Planet Earth—and His children's part in it through prayer. This chapter is not my grandiose plan, but a little taste of how God entrusted us with His desire to multiply Christians' prayer power. This chapter is what God did through a ministry run on prayer.

The incredible part of God's plan is that *He raises up intercessors to produce the power through their prayers for what He intends to do.* Even Christian projects and organizations can be run in the flesh, apart from prayer. Here is how He fulfilled our little part of His prayer plan: Not only was every word of *What Happens When Women Pray* prayed through, but to this day every person who reads or teaches it is prayed for by our

United Prayer Ministry board members and intercessors. This is what God did when they prayed.

Distributed by God

Teaching prayer widely on every continent has been a profound privilege, but it took God to distribute that book's prayer teaching to the millions who live where no one person ever could go, or was even allowed to go. Victor Books' vice president of marketing, Jim Lemon, did a wonderful job launching *What Happens When Women Pray* at the Christian Booksellers Association convention in 1975, and his marketing representatives took it to conventions. But distribution of the book has been amazingly God's. Without a magazine ad, a hired promotion company, or a highly organized or financially underwritten ministry, we never once have written a letter or initiated an invitation to teach people to pray.

At first we did not know where most of the invitations came from—or why. But they did come. This has proved to us that God knows exactly what He is doing and that He not only can, but also will fulfill His purpose. All He needs is intercessors!

The first miracle I heard about of God's distributing that book on how to pray was when a missionary returned to his country, in which Christianity was outlawed, with a whole carton of *What Happens When Women Pray* books. He did not try to conceal them as he arrived. "What's this?" the customs official barked. "Books about Jesus?" "Oh, no," the missionary replied, tongue-in-cheek. "They teach women how to be submissive to their husbands!" "Bring them in!" gleefully shouted the inspector.

At a meeting in North Carolina, a woman excitedly explained the note she handed me: "I did my first Bible study on *What Happens When Women Pray* in an underground Bible study—because it is illegal in my country. If caught, we were sent to jail and then exiled from the country. I recognized your voice from the tapes. We also had the books. Our group flourished, and we all grew through your teaching. We were down to two or three during the Gulf War. But by the end of the war two years later, we celebrated Good Friday with 103 people praising God!"

My very first time in Scotland, a couple with a video ministry asked for permission to take their videotaping of that prayer seminar free to people who could not attend big-city events. With my enthusiastic approval, they told me they then took it and portable equipment for showing it to hamlets all over Scotland—and watched revival spring up in each one of them!

"We had telephone prayer chains, but we had to use code words," a young woman attending an international conference from a country in which Christianity was illegal smilingly reported to me. "We chatted nonchalantly about ordinary women's things, but all of us knew we actually were asking for prayer or praising God for an answer on the coded subject."

God tells us why He sends forth His word in Isaiah 55:11:

> It shall not return to Me [God] empty . . . without succeeding in the matter for which I sent it.

In all the thousands of instances that God supernaturally distributed our prayer material, He was fulfilling His purpose of teaching people to pray—so that they would have supernatural power. The words that went forth from God's mouth were not promised to return to *me*, but to *Him*—accomplishing what *He* desired.

I am thankful that I am not responsible for the answers to my prayers—God is. As my board, twenty-four-hour clock, family, friends, and I prayed and prayed, God did not expect us to be able to figure out what He planned to do. He's the One who knows—and even expects us to know that we don't know. That's why He gave us prayer!

The Book Preceded Me

My overseas prayer teaching did not start until September 1980. But God was working out His purpose long before that. Here are just a few examples:

After the prayer seminar in Osaka, Japan, the pastor of a large church said he wanted to drive my husband and me to the next city because he wanted to tell me something. Through his interpreter, he told about being on the committee the times Billy Graham came to Tokyo. "The first one was great," he said, "because we knew we needed lots of prayer. And Billy's next tour had great results in the other cities where he hadn't been before, and they depended on God through their much praying. But," he said, "there was apathy in our committee when Billy came back to Tokyo, because they felt they had done a great job the time before and didn't need so much prayer."

The first two nights, the crowds were small, and nothing much happened. (He said he knew the power of prayer because he had bought thirty *What Happens When Women Pray* books and started prayer chains in his own church.) "Desperate," he said, "I stayed up all night and called two hundred and thirty churches in that one night, with a thirteen-hundred-dollar phone bill, asking them to pray. And they did. The next night, and the rest of the crusade, we had a full house—with many decisions for Christ!"

Teaching prayer in Brazil the first time, I was surprised when they presented me with a copy of each of my books in Brazilian Portuguese. They were being used extensively in that vast country—and I had not even known about those translations. It was strictly God! God's purpose? To be a part of a new utilization of God's power spreading all over that huge country.

It was a shock when I traveled in South Africa and discovered that telephone prayer chains, learned from my book, were already successfully operating all across the country. Just before apartheid came to an end, it was a miracle of God that blacks, whites, and coloreds were praying together on the same prayer chains. "So that" there could be unity and power in the midst of their terrorism.

Without my knowing it, in a part of the world where teaching about Jesus is forbidden, God had distributed that book in twenty-two countries—with women praying in Jesus' name—and still praying. The woman who sacrificially distributed those books during many years is now a precious friend, but I did not even know her during all those years. God's plan? A network of prayer running under those nations—where we could not go.

Dr. John Richards of the Evangelical Fellowship of India wanted prayer training for his country after hearing what had happened in Australia. The tour concluded with a weeklong national prayer assembly for pastors and missionaries, during which God poured out His Spirit upon us as we studied and prayed in one accord.

God had systematically moved from state to state in America and then from country to country—creating a desire to learn to have more power in prayer! Why? So that His children would learn their potential in prayer power—and what in their lives was hindering that power.

God Prepared Hungry Hearts Before the Book

Somehow God had put a longing in Christians for divine intervention in their problems, creating a vacuum they were eager to fill with prayer training.

When I taught prayer in England the first time, it was shocking to find their expectancy exceeded mine. Those women seemed determined to rescue their country from its downward moral slide by prayer, and they jammed the conference halls to find out how to do it.

In the U.S., it was Watergate time, and we had become "ugly Americans" in many countries overseas. So many were ready for something from God; and, with a new reliance on God's help, the prayer movement was taking off. God's timing was absolutely perfect!

During the years I taught only in our country and Canada, the invitations to speak averaged fifty for every one I could take. So we published a leader's guide so Christians could teach and organize prayer for themselves. This turned out to be an awesome plan from God—as women all over the world now have learned to pray—without me!

God distributed that book without our trying! To us, getting *What Happens*

When Women Pray in the hands of Christians around the world was the impossible task that we had not even tried to do. But to God it was as simple as someone sending a birthday or Christmas gift to a missionary, a military family's being transferred, someone whose life had been changed by prayer traveling overseas, or someone who had a similar vision from God and taught the book before moving to another country.

In my deep gratitude, I have prayed so many times: "I am so thankful, God, that You do not limit Your answering to my ability to ask!"

Trans World Radio Opens Prayer Doors

It was after dinner following a prayer seminar with Joan and Bill Mial when Bill pushed back his chair and said, "I have something I would like to propose to you. Trans World Radio has plenty of evangelistic messages and book-by-book Bible studies, but we have nothing for Christians' daily growth. *We would like to translate your tapes of your prayer seminars and broadcast them to all of India.*" I was stunned. While they were stationed in Hong Kong, Joan had taught *What Happens When Women Pray* several times and was excited about its potential. But broadcasting the taped prayer material had never crossed my mind.

India. God had prepared Juliet Thomas for the Trans World Radio ministry by calling her to a prayer ministry during our seminar. We had prayed and "commissioned" her in our hotel room, not knowing that God was preparing her for radio broadcasting. She took my "What Happens When Women Pray" audiotapes and produced weekly broadcasts first in the Kannada language and then in Hindi. We were thrilled when Trans World Radio obtained one of the world's most powerful radio transmitters, located just outside Moscow when the communists fell. Now they broadcast English, Tamil, and Hindi—reaching at least one-sixth of all the people in the world! Since they acquired a large radio transmitter in Russia when communism fell, only God knows where the broadcasts are going now.

In Bombay, India, a young, blind woman was led to me and ran her hands over my face. "Oh," she exclaimed, "You're the voice I have been listening to all these years. I have been blind since birth, and you are my only connection with the outside world."

We have also been broadcasting in the area of India where, for centuries, parents have given their young daughters to religious prostitution. I am amazed at how many have turned from that vile, pagan religion to Jesus. We've received many letters, but many more cannot write or afford a stamp. What an incredible way for God to distribute prayer material!

Juliet has formed the first all-women's organization in India, and she now has organized prayer triplets running in every major city in that country, reaching out to three thousand tribes.

When, by a miracle of God, I got into the restricted states of India, twenty-three million 10/40 window intercessors had just all prayed for India. And we, along with others, were the recipients of all that miraculous prayer power.

China. That first offer from Trans World Radio also included all of China, fulfilling a call from Isaiah 55:5 that a country I did not know would call me. I knew God was saying *China* to my heart, but I thought having my first three books translated into Mandarin would be what He meant. However, it was to be the radio broadcasts received on simple little radio receivers capable of being tuned to just that one station that would reach another one-sixth of the world's population with the power of prayer training.

God knew why He opened that door when China closed its doors to all foreign missionaries in 1950. There were one million believers then, but now it is estimated there are sixty million Christians. Approximately twenty-eight thousand people become believers every day in China![1]

God's plan for our broadcasts for these twenty years has been so that thousands of people could accept Jesus and learn how to pray—where none of us could go. While we pray without knowing their names, one listener explained the power of our prayers in a note: "I am a regular listener of your program. I am very grateful to the Lord Jesus Christ who gave me new life. Indeed had He not come into my life, I would have perished in sin."

On a short trip into China, the spiritual oppression seemed to hang all around us. But a Christian pastor, we encountered had to evade all questions about our broadcast. Later he sent word with a Chinese doctor, "Tell her to keep up the good work. Very, very important!"[1]

Caribbean, Cuba, and Latin America. As I ministered on the island of Bonaire, there was a great hunger for the Word of God and for prayer. When I left, I gave Trans World Radio free copies of my audiotapes and books to use however and wherever God led them. We just learned that they have been broadcasting them to all of the Caribbean, Cuba, and Latin America (all Spanish and Portuguese-speaking countries) since 1989 with their extremely powerful new transmitter.

Prayer's Power for Open Doors

I knew God was saying "go" when I received a call from Taiwan in the early eighties. Four women, including American missionary Jeanne Swanson, felt the desperate need for prayer for their country. With my unhesitating, immediate approval, they organized a committee of thirty-five women. Packing out the large facilities, we felt an amazing power of God. And four years later, there were ten thousand organized pray-ers on that small island!

However, the power for all of it was God answering prayer. I left home absolutely exhausted the day after having Christmas with the whole family at my house and cleaning up. To make matters worse, my clothes dryer broke down as I tried to pack for Taiwan. Dragging my tote bag down the ramp to the plane, I kept moaning, "I can't go, Lord!" And I knew I couldn't.

But suddenly it hit. I felt as if I could fly to Taiwan without a plane, I had so much power. *What happened?* I wondered. Then I remembered, *This is the day the twenty-four-hour prayer clock starts praying for me!*

When I arrived in Taiwan, there still was strife between Chang Kai-shek's people, who had escaped mainland China, and the landowners in Taiwan (Formosans). The two groups of Christians were divided too. The wife of the politically imprisoned head of a major Formosan denomination asked me to come to dinner the very first night. Weary from jet lag, I ate and talked with her in her unheated, meager little house—while we prayed together. Never had the two religious sides worshiped together, but God broke down the barriers as we hugged good-bye. She then called up and down the island telling their follow-ers, "This lady is all right. Come to the seminar." And both sides did—getting together for the first time through prayer!

Flying to south Taiwan following our wonderful seminar in the north, I was shocked to see the fields dotted with pagan worship houses. Being warned that this was one of the most powerful strongholds of Satan in the world did not prepare me for the battle our first night. All the time I spoke, I felt as if I were in heavy chains, hardly able to get my words out.

Back in my room I wrestled many hours in prayer. My missionary hostess, used to such battles, fasted and prayed all night. Asking God the next morning to give me His scripture for the whole day of teach-ing in this awful atmosphere, He said, *Psalm 37:4. "Delight thyself in the* LORD, *and He will give you the desires of your heart."*

"Oh, Lord, my desire is for You to break this oppression and pour out Your power on this prayer seminar," I prayed. Then the very next verse said, "Commit your way unto the LORD. Trust also in Him, and He will do it." I claimed the victory, thanked Him, and dashed out the door—only to run right into my hostess. She had gotten the *same* verses with the same promise from Psalm 37. Together we shed tears of joy, rejoic-ing over what God was going to do that day. And He did. Never once was His power hindered in that all-day teaching on the power of prayer. We had seen it firsthand!

Spiritual warfare! Satan does not care if we study prayer or memorize scriptures about prayer. But when a believer prays fervent, persistent prayers in the name of Jesus, Satan gets very nervous. Rightly so, because we have learned Satan absolutely cannot stand against that kind of praying. Some of our most thrilling—and most difficult—prayer times are battling with him for the victory—that always comes eventually!

It was reported that eleven mission boards in Taiwan were using this prayer material after our seminars.

Stopping over in Los Angeles on the way home for an all-day seminar, I was exhausted and empty. But on my face before the Lord in that hotel, He reminded me of Ephesians 3:20: "Now unto Him who is able to do exceeding abundantly above all we can ask or think, according to the power that works in us."

I quoted it back to Him, but He kept emphasizing the little prepositional phrase "according to." Then I saw it. God is *capable* of everything, but is *able* to do it only according to the power that works in us. And that power is from the Holy Spirit through prayer—my twenty-four-hour prayer clock—and all the others praying!

God's Power Through Prayer

President Reagan had recovered from his would-be assassin's gunshot wound before speaking to us at an annual National Prayer Breakfast when he told us, "Nancy and I want to thank you for praying. *You really can feel the power!*"

Working with Youth for Christ in a nearby city, I was thrilled at the results of their innovative method of praying for their local students. They cut the pictures out of the school's yearbook and distributed them to Christians to pray for a student for the school year. At the end, administrators reported that discipline problems were down 75 percent.

While I was autographing books at a London seminar, a woman, seemingly discouraged, asked me if it did any good to pray for husbands to accept Jesus. A young lady from Nigeria overheard and loudly called out to her, "When women pray, husbands get saved!"

Telephone Prayer Chains

My telephone prayer chains already had prayed for me the Monday morning I was to finish three days' teaching in San Quentin prison, which held the most violent criminals in the U.S. at that time. Most had been convicted of gruesome sex crimes in addition to other crimes. As I prayed, God emphatically said to call my telephone prayer chains. "Hello, Jeanne? I'm almost too embarrassed to ask you to pray again, but I know I must." Assuring me it was all right, she dialed to reactivate the chain. But why?

While they prayed, the chaplain and I went to the room deep in the bowels of that prison for our meeting. It was empty! The chaplain left me momentarily to make a phone call and rushed back, his face ashen. "Follow me. It's a lockdown!" Miraculously every door and gate that had clanged closed with such finality as we entered—opened. Once safe on the outside he explained, "This has been the typical pattern in the history of this prison. First, they get a weapon—in this case, they had a gun—then they wait for a hostage, preferably a female, and make their break. You were the only outside female there today, and you would have been their hostage." The power of telephone prayer chains!

Another powerful result of telephone prayer chains occurred when Jessie McFarlane and her committee in Scotland were too exhausted to do another convention after the Luis Palau campaign. So they had said no to being the planning committee for Scotland during my first United Kingdom tour in 1981. But suddenly they knew God was saying to do the prayer seminar. Quickly gathering 650 people, Jessie was amazed to see 450 signed up for a national telephone prayer chain. Their praying has expanded from local needs to praying for Parliament members and the needs of the entire British Isles—and the world. Since 1989, it has been in operation throughout all the United Kingdom.

Returning just a few years later I was thrilled to find it took the Glasgow Civic Center to hold the intercessors. This time, twelve hundred people committed themselves to the ministry of the prayer chains. Jessie says that they see this as a living organism, not an organization—and only the Holy Spirit could keep more than seventeen hundred women praying together every week. God has broken down denominational barriers, with twelve denominations in Scotland alone. They have just announced their "Prayer Chain Conference 2000" for September 2000.

Recently the chair of the Glasgow telephone prayer chain, after handling all the fabulous answers to their praying, sadly said to me, "I spent forty years of my life as a medical missionary in Napal, but I was too busy to pray. But now I see all the power I missed in my whole adult life!"

While training Air Force chaplains at Randolph Field in Texas about the power and lifestyle prerequisites of prayer, one suddenly raised his hand and asked, "Why weren't we taught this in seminary?"

But It Takes Praying

For years, I taught five biblical prerequisites to prayer power in intercessory prayer from *What Happens When Women Pray:* (1) making sure there is no known sin in the life of the pray-er, (2) being forgiven *as* we forgive, (3) praying in God's will, (4) personal devotional praying, and (5) making sure it is God, not Satan, to whom you have drawn nigh. These were to be obeyed "so that" they would have power in the various methods of intercessory prayer we taught. But I changed that "so that" into a final prerequisite: (6) intercessory praying. *We can attend seminars, memorize scriptures about prayer, even study prayer in seminary or Bible school; but there is no power unless we actually pray!*

Evangelism Study Guide

One of the great things God did was to use the *What Happens When Women Pray* book as a springboard for teaching His ultimate prayer desire for Planet Earth: "God . . . desires all [humans] to be saved" (1 Tim. 2:3–4). The reason I was asked to do the huge project of producing the curriculum for the AD2000 Christian Women United was because of what God had done with the prayer teaching of that book.

Not only has God used *A Study Guide for Evangelism Praying* in North America, but also it has been the international curriculum for this nine-year movement. It has been published in forty-seven languages plus all the tribal languages into which it has spread. Reports from all continents are thrilling. I wish I had a whole book to pass them all on to you. I will share more details of this exciting project in chapter 12.

Triplets

The powerful pre-evangelism triplet praying method taught in the *Study Guide for Evangelism Praying* has taken root all over the world. As I mentioned in chapter 4, a prayer triplet consists of three Christians, each choosing three non-Christians they know, then promising to get together once a week to pray for the salvation of each of their three, making a total of nine.

The three key triplet words are:

Accessibility. Choose partners you live near or ones with whom you worship, work, or study. This eliminates any financial cost and makes praying for just fifteen minutes a week a possibility.

Accountability. If one drops out, even temporarily, it is easy to disband if there are only two praying, but three always leaves two to be accountable to each other.

Specificity. Evangelism triplets are strictly limited to praying for the salvation of their collective nine and their needs. Other prayer requests are handled in other prayer meetings.

Protection

My hostess at the Spokane, Washington, Sunday-school convention was a well-known national radio personality. While we waited for my luggage, she carried on a ridiculous conversation with a man whose eyes kept looking right past both of us. As it turned out, he was part of a six-month government tracking of a huge international drug ring, and the box of drugs had been put on my plane from Minneapolis. The detectives were concealed around the room with guns drawn as the luggage conveyor started. I reached for a box the exact size of my box of gift books—but pulled back muttering, "Oh, no, my box doesn't have that much tape on it." Yes, I almost claimed *the* box of drugs that broke the drug ring! At lunch, my hostess, who had been sworn to secrecy because they enlisted her as part of the cover-up, could envision the local paper's headlines: *Prayer Lady Caught in Drug Bust!* "Thanks, Lord, for prayer protection!"

Twenty-Four-Hour Prayer Clock

When I went to Australia for my first overseas speaking tour in 1980, my administrator, Sally Hanson, was concerned because my husband could not join me for the first three of the six weeks. So she organized one thousand people each to take a period of time, covering the entire day and night with prayer. They even set their alarm clocks if their times were during the night, as the time zones were opposite there. She had no idea how desperately that prayer would be needed, but I am eternally grateful for all their prayers, and others, who have faithfully and fervently prayed every time I went overseas.

I also have learned incredible trust in God, who answers those prayers and mine. All through the following incidents there was peace—knowing our omnipotent God was in charge.

God's protection when the telephone prayer chain prayed was awesome where it really was not safe to go. In Belfast, Ireland, a bomb went off right where I had been standing speaking a few days before, sending the pipes of the wonderful pipe organ flying like matchsticks.

Nobody, including my family and secretary, expected me to return from South Africa where necklacing was so prevalent between the tribes during the apartheid uprisings. But I was safe—even though we did drive unsuspectingly onto a university campus for my meeting about one and a half hours after the tear gas bombs and uprisings settled down. Safe again!

On our way to Sydney, Australia, the pilot spoke on the intercom of our airplane. "Ladies and gentlemen," he intoned, "I have some bad news for you. We are running out of gas and won't be able to make it to Sydney." Scanning the horizons on both sides of the plane, I saw nothing but the Pacific Ocean. After several minutes, he announced, "But we will be able to limp into Brisbane. However, our turnaround paperwork there will make all of you miss your connecting flights." I mentally calculated the time left to get all the way to Perth for my first speaking engagement. After fifty-six hours en route, I was standing up to speak two hours after my plane landed! What would I have done without the Lord answering all of those prayers?

It was from the weather on the way to Brazil that I needed prayer protection—a hurricane to be exact. After hours of delays, we finally sat in a plane in Miami waiting to take off. There was a hurricane between us and Brazil, but the danger to us was the intense lightning storm from its edge pelting Miami. The pilot explained to us that we could not be refueling for the flight, because if lightning struck our gas pump, it most likely would go right down the hose into our plane—and blow us all up. At the end of two hours, he came on the intercom and said quietly, "Ladies and gentlemen, that explosion was to have been our gas pump!"

Another time I needed prayer protection was during my trip to Bombay several years ago. Traveling from Bombay to Puna alone while my husband boarded a plane for America due to illness was incredibly lonely. I could not eat the food, drink the water, or speak the language; nor had I met the person who was to meet me and take me bumping over the dirt roads to Puna, which we could not locate on our map. I would have to do the whole week's National Prayer Assembly of India alone. But I was not alone! As I walked across the blistering runway, peace swept over me. My intercessors were praying—and God not only met my every need, but by the next morning He also gave me a joy that sent my heart soaring in adoration and praise of Him!

As I asked God for my 1980 birthday prayer, suddenly there was suspended before my spiritual eyes a hand holding a globe of the earth. My immediate response was, "Lord, if You send me, I will go." I have never reneged on that promise—no matter how sacrificial or danger- ous. And for more than twenty years, He has sent me to every inhab- ited continent in the world. He not only *sent* me, but He also went *before me* and *with me!*

While faithful intercessors bombarded the gates of heaven night and day—God answered! But more than that, I have learned the incredible joy of the privilege of depending completely on God—when rescuing us was completely beyond all human ability.

Prayer Breaks Down Barriers

It was the first time in India's history, they told me, that women from all castes prayed together. At our prayer seminar in their beautiful white cathedral of Madras, the untouchables in their rags and the titled ladies in their pure silk saris with pure gold and silver threads prayed together in little groups all day. When I reluctantly had to leave before they wanted to stop praying, I turned to see a kaleidoscope of color as they, in their own position of prayer, were lying on the floor in a circle with their heads touching. This was the product of persevering prayer—in their country and ours.

In Poland, God used the "Forgiving As We Forgive" lesson from *What Happens When Women Pray* as the women from the war-torn sur- rounding countries put their arms around each other, wept, forgave, and prayed for each other's horrendous plights—on both sides. One woman even returned to Germany to forgive those who had done such horrible things to her family during World War II.

In Yellowknife, Northwest Territory, Eskimos, Indians, and Caucasians prayed together with much accepting of Jesus. Many were considered renegades, but their dark, hopeless expressions changed to victory as the prayer day wore on.

A story I shared in a previous book is worth repeating because it is such a vivid picture of God's power to overcome years of prejudice with His love. When preregistration for our seminar in war-torn Belfast in 1981 filled, both Catholics and Protestants called, pleading, "But I have to come. Prayer is the only answer to our country's war!" When they engaged the large downtown Presbyterian Hall, they almost filled it—with both sides of their never-ending war. As usual, I put them in little groups with people in back or front of them, mixing both sides. But when I had them praying out loud forgiving someone, there was a trembling all over the room almost like in the Book of Acts. Having been given permission to stay just through the seminar, we dashed for our plane—only to see the "war enemies" with their arms around each other, weeping and singing about Jesus. Seven hundred from both sides formed telephone prayer chains.

But it was two years later that we saw the results of that reconciliation. Charles Colson's Prison Fellowship International was holding a symposium in Queens University, and the large hall was filled with people from both sides of the still-continuing war. Liam had killed many people as a terrorist and had been the last young man on the infamous Bobby Sands hunger strike, already blind and in a coma from malnutrition when his godly mother insisted they feed him intravenously. Upon regaining consciousness, he was immediately thrown into solitary confinement. He was one of the prisoners released that one night to tell us his story.

He stood on the platform next to Jimmy—an inmate on the opposite side of the war. Liam told how Jesus changed his life. Jimmy had seen such a change in Liam that Jimmy wanted his Jesus too. To a thunderous standing ovation, Liam put his arm around Jimmy and said, "Before I accepted Jesus, I would have shot him dead. Now, I would give my life for Jimmy."

Liam told me later, "In solitary confinement, the only book they allowed me to have was a Bible. So while I was reading it, and because of all that prayer, I accepted Jesus." All that prayer? Those prayer chains formed two years earlier had kept praying by name for *every* war prisoner—on both sides!

A woman who had just toured Northern Ireland excitedly told me that she visited a large meeting of those prayer chain people—getting together to praise God for all their wonderful answers. The war still is not completely settled. But what would it be like by now without all of their prayers?

Just before apartheid broke, I was in Durban, South Africa. A lady said, "I was in Belfast in 1981 at your seminar, and I have been praying, 'Lord, send Evelyn to South Africa.'" But after my seminar there, after teaching that Jesus said we should pray for those who despitefully use us, a British lady sniffed at me, "But I can't pray for those terrorists!" "Who said you should?" I responded. "Oh, *Jesus!*" she reluctantly admitted. "But *what* should I pray?" "Lady, pray for them to accept Jesus. Then they won't be terrorists anymore!"

Scripture tells us "there is neither Jew nor Greek, there is neither slave nor free man, there is neither male nor female; for you are all one in Christ Jesus" (Gal. 3:28). I've enforced this rule of all races and Christian persuasions praying together for thirty years in every country in the world, including the United States—and I have yet to encounter my first problem. It's the prayer!

Prayer for Physical Bodies

I urge you, therefore, brethren, by the mercies of God, that you present your bodies a living and holy sacrifice, acceptable to God, which is your spiritual service of worship (Rom. 12:1).

Studying that verse in 1965, I learned that the verb tense for "present your bodies a living and holy sacrifice" implies a once-for-all action, not an ongoing process. So I gave God my body—forever. And it has been His ever since. I never took it back.

A "living" sacrifice? I've said many, many times that it is easier to be a *dead* one. But my promise to God was not for Him to *heal* it, but to *use* it—any way He needed to—for His glory. But the prayer that has taken me through all these years has always been for His will, not mine. This has produced incredible, and surprising, answers.

God, of course, was capable of healing or preventing every physical problem, but, while my pray-ers prayed for it, He has shown me there are several ways He uses a body dedicated to Him.

Healing. The most desired answer to prayer by us humans, of course, is healing. These times have produced some of the most tangible thrills of my life.

When the 1968 experimenting in prayer that produced *What Happens When Women Pray* was done and I was to report on it to the conference that had called me, I woke with a throat so sore I could not speak. Too sick to pray for myself, I cried out to the Lord to have my pray-ers and a great missionary statesman I knew pray for me. All day long I stayed in bed until just time to get ready. I leaned over to brush my teeth—and when I stood up, I was completely healed!

The day before my largest seminar in Australia, the same thing happened. But this time my prayer was different. At the end of a grueling five weeks, I again came down with a throat so sore I could not swallow the bite of apple that was going to be my supper. Then I just knelt at the foot of my hotel bed and prayed, "Oh, Lord, thank You that there is no human being who could heal me by eight o'clock tomorrow morning. Thank You for the privilege of being completely dependent on You. What an awesome privilege, Lord." My heart soared as I was engulfed in gratitude and love for Him.

But then the miracle happened. When I arose from my knees, there was not a trace of the sore throat or any other symptoms. *Healed when I'm not even asking!*

In Bradenton, Florida, I had been down treating a kidney infection, when God performed another miracle. We had kept the telephone prayer chains buzzing long distance for days. But trying to get ready for that 9:00 A.M. to 4:00 P.M. seminar, I kept breaking out in a cold sweat. My husband was with me and reluctantly almost carried me to the church. As he sat in the back pew expecting to rescue me any minute, it happened. I have on tape the faint, weak voice that started to open in prayer. But then, as I said my first words, my voice suddenly became normal—and I was fine all day long.

However, God always has His reasons for healing—or not healing. This healing was because God wanted to teach us all the power of prayer. Mrs. Cam Townsend of Wycliffe Translators was in the audience, and she received the message during our coffee break that their kidnapped missionary in South America had been found murdered. It was just as I was about to teach on "to die is gain" (Phil. 1:21), and I asked her to share so we could pray. But God changed the tone of the whole seminar—and accomplished a much more important miracle than my healing. Many young people, we are told, dedicated their lives to take up the task left undone by the murder—and the women at that seminar learned an awesome depth of prayer and that to die can be a gain.

Temporary relief. Sometimes God temporarily lifts a physical infirmity to get us through what He has called us to do. It was an intestinal parasite attack in South America that ominously threatened just before my final speaking on Sunday night. They filled me with their remedy—room-temperature coconut juice—and I made it that night and through the long international flight home. Barely inside our house, the parasites hit with full force. Yes, God could have healed me, but watching His incredible *timing* taught me, and all of my pray-ers, more about Him than just a simple healing. Over and over through the years I have seen Him turn what would have been a disaster into finishing what He had called me to do.

Strength during illness. Perhaps the most incredible miracle has been God giving me strength while still ill. This, it seems, is the story of my life—and has kept my intercessors busy.

I developed a 103-degree temperature while the only speaker for the weeklong National Prayer Assembly of India. After speaking, I joined a small prayer group and prayed for the salvation of the family of one of us. When I met him in Canada years later, he was ecstatic at how God had answered those prayers. He described to me how God started working one by one in his family members, when each got saved, and how they were serving God in full-time ministries or through wonderful careers. "I've been praying every day since that time in Puna, India!" he assured me.

Women had jammed the Westminster Hall in London (the original home of the United Nations) to the domed ceiling for a prayer seminar when a lower-back problem that had occasionally completely incapacitated me since our first child's birth hit with a vengeance. Mounting the huge curved marble steps to the podium, I had to keep my back rigid while the searing pain persisted—all day. The next day, my husband had to buy a back brace to get me back to America on the plane, but the audience never guessed the awesome miracle God was performing all day!

My intercessors back home rarely knew exactly why they were praying other than the requests I had told them. *But God took their general prayers for me for that day and transformed them into awesome strength to teach all of us His supernatural power.*

Also, God could have prevented whatever happened to my heart to leave it pumping only approximately one-third of my blood through my body, but He chose instead to perform miracle after miracle as I have kept up an incredibly busy schedule. Teaching me how to take short rest times, God has provided.

In Hydrabad, India, I had been taken by a bumpy open jeep back to rest for twenty minutes before starting another prayer topic as an unfriendly parasite raged in my intestinal tract. My husband taught two subjects for me, but in the evening I stepped out on faith for the last two hours. Suddenly I had terrible pains in the pit of my stomach. Seeing me double over, a woman stood and said, "I'm a medical doctor. If I get you a pill, will you take it?" "Will it keep me from thinking straight?" I queried. When she promised that it certainly would not, I took it in front of the whole audience.

Suddenly, all my muscles seemed to turn to jelly. "Oh, no!" she cried out. "I forgot it would do that to you!" The men jumped up and brought in two eight-foot folding tables—one for me to sit on with my legs propped up—and the other at an angle for the rest of me to lean back on. I finished the two hours. No, my brain did not stop working—but the rest of me did! God again? Yes, He is able to transcend every conceivable problem on Planet Earth while the power of Jesus rests upon us.

Since the beginning of my prayer ministry, I have completely rested in, and been amazed at, the power of Jesus resting upon me—whenever it was for Christ's sake, not mine. With the apostle Paul, I can confidently say:

> Therefore I am well content with weaknesses, with insults, with distresses, with persecutions, with difficulties, for Christ's sake; for when I am weak, then I am strong (2 Cor. 12:10).

Demonstrating His power. Sometimes God uses my body to show others the power of their prayers. Called by God to teach prayer, I believe He took me at my word back in 1965 and uses my body, not only to teach others about His power, but also to give them the privilege of watching *their prayers being answered.* As I write thank-you letters to my intercessors, I always conclude God's awesome answers with ". . . because you prayed!" And it is true!

I'm not sure what all God was showing my intercessors as they furiously prayed to keep my knee working in Scotland until I got home to surgery. (It may have been that God has a sense of humor.) The Scottish National Prayer Breakfast was having their first-ever women speakers. The one preceding me was fabulous, but the men didn't know how to respond and kept looking at their menus or out the window.

When it was my turn, I tried to ignore the throbbing knee as I bravely climbed up the high steps to speak—without a handrail, which I desperately needed. At the top step, my knee suddenly gave out, and I flew one way across the platform while my shoes flew another. Aghast, the men (including the one whose office is by the prime minister's) jumped to rescue me. Brushing me off and putting my shoes back on me, they stood me up.

Thank goodness the pray-ers were praying! I felt complete peace, smiled sincerely, and calmed them by saying, "Please don't worry about me. Jessie [my hostess] and I have been trying to keep this knee together for weeks. This is my last speaking assignment until I go home tomorrow for surgery." People said God never had poured more of His power through any of my messages—while He moved mightily upon us. But the surprise came at the end. I was told these dignified leaders, some in their kilts and some reading poetry only in Latin, had never applauded for a speaker in their history. But I got a standing ovation. Why? Because God used a decrepit knee to break old customs—and to give Him all the glory.

Our daughter Jan, while suffering deeply the first night after surgery, called and said, "Oh, Mummy, pray! It hurts so much!" And I did—for the rest of that night while I longed to go to her. The next morning as I was able to go to her room, she slid her hand out from beneath the sheet and took mine, saying, "Mother, prayer is just like somebody holding your hand long distance."

The Worth of a Book

One of the most cherished experiences I have had was in Calcutta when I had an audience with Mother Teresa. Watching patiently while she graciously accepted and thanked people from all over the world delivering monetary gifts, I humbly handed her my little book. "What is this?" she inquired. "It's a book on prayer I've been teaching in India," I said shyly. She gently took it from me, ran her gnarled hand tenderly over its cover, and pressed it to her breast, smiling the most beautiful smile I've ever seen. She understood. Her Nobel Peace Prize for rescu-ing the poor had not come from money—but from the power of God, who answers prayers!

A young woman came to me after a seminar in Indiana, eager to tell me something. "I am on my way to Japan as a missionary. Nobody ever thought I would qualify emotionally as a foreign missionary because of my horrible childhood. My dad dealt drugs, and my mother was a pros-titute. There was a steady stream of men in and out of our home all the time I was a little girl. But not one of them ever harmed me. When I took the battery of psychological tests required for foreign missionaries, everyone was astounded. I came through with wonderful scores. Even with *that* childhood, I'm perfectly normal emotionally.

"Nobody could understand it—until my grandmother died. She was poor, and the thing she left me in her estate was a dog-eared, tear-stained copy of *What Happens When Women Pray*. Although she was helpless to change my parents or my environment, she prayed for me every day! Now we know that it was her powerful prayers putting a hedge around me, not only from physical harm, but also from emotional harm, protecting and preserving me to bring Jesus—and prayer—as a missionary to Japan."

I pray . . . that you may know . . . what is the surpassing greatness of His power toward us who believe (Eph. 1:18–19).

Our son, Kurt, was fourteen when he picked up my first tape on the subject of prayer and made a statement that has proved to be correct through the years. Through all of his short life, he had watched me studying and producing the lessons for teaching my adult Sunday-school class all of the major doctrines, many books of the Bible, and a three-year series on Jesus' life. He had watched as I produced speeches on whatever subjects people requested. But when he read on that first tape label "'Prayer' by Evelyn Christenson," his face brightened. Looking me right in the eye, he paused and solemnly said, "How can you miss, Mom, with a subject like prayer?"

Reflection Questions

Examine your life:
Does it surprise you that God has chosen to raise up intercessors to pray for what He wants to do? How much responsibility have you taken personally for what God will not do because of lack of prayer? How much joy at praying and watching Him work out His plans is currently your lifestyle?

Scripture:
Thoughtfully read Isaiah 55:8–11, letting God speak to you personally. Have you been expecting God's words in answer to your prayers to accomplish what *you* desired, or what God desired? In what ways are God's thoughts toward Planet Earth different than yours? Which will bring forth the most amazing superhuman results?

For you to do:
Record something you have been praying for God to do with your life.

_____

Record what you figured out as to how He should do it—and told Him.

_____

According to Isaiah 55:8–11, are you encouraged, reproved, or instructed as to how God wants you to change your approach to planning for your future?

For you to pray:

"Holy Father, I am in awe at how much higher Your thoughts are than mine. Forgive me for expecting You to answer my prayers only to the extent I'm able to ask. Father, I never would plan to go to restricted places, to have courage to go where humanly it is too dangerous, could never plan to break down barriers humans have erected, or physically make it with my ordinary human body. Father, I am turning over the planning of my life to You. In my praying I will always trust Your answers to accomplish what You desire, not what I want. Only You know Your plans for them to succeed—returning to You for Your glory! In Jesus' name, amen."

PART TWO

What God Does for the Intercessor

CHAPTER 6

Sin in the Intercessor? Surprise!

GOD HAD TWO important surprises for me as He opened two major areas of my prayer life. Amazingly, both surprises dealt with sin in the life of the one sincerely trying to become a better pray-er. These are prayers that can only be prayed by the intercessor for himself or herself.

The First Surprise—That It Was for Me

The first surprise was to me personally, and it came during my first organized prayer group in 1964 when God called Signe, Lorna, and me to "pray for the church." Although our new building was busy every day and night of every week and we had doubled our membership in four years, the three of us unexpectedly put our arms around each other in that new building and wept before God. He was telling each of us that, as good as it was, there was something more for that church.

Promising God we would pray for our church (and keeping that promise weekly for almost four years), we blindly started out. Feeling it would be good to base each prayer meeting on a scripture, we casually (to us) chose Psalm 66:18:

If I regard iniquity in my heart, the Lord will not hear me. (KJV)

Praying "Father, forgive me" had always been an important part of my personal daily prayers, but I never connected it with God's answering our prayers. So my huge surprise was that God would not release us to pray for the church until we got our own lives cleaned up.

Each week was the same. God searched our hearts for every big or tiny thing that displeased Him, and we wept and confessed—for six miserable weeks. How surprised we were when He dug out such "acceptable Christian sins" as subtle pride over the Sunday-school material I was producing, thinking as pray-ers we were spiritually a little above the rest of the church members, poor attitudes toward family members—especially the shocking one toward one's own husband, and wrong priorities. We believed we had been doing everything for God's glory, but He showed us our own egos, self-satisfaction, and desire to build ourselves up in the eyes of other church members. We admitted that we enjoyed the spiritual pedestals some others had put us on. We checked our motives for our prayers. For six weeks we went from embarrassed—to miserable—to devastated—to anguished repentance.

But it turned out that God knew what He was doing those six weeks. After releasing us to pray for the church, the very next Sunday He sent most of its overflow audience surging down the aisle of that new church building to fall on their faces before Him, beginning a revival that for six months would send people down that same aisle accepting or publicly confessing Christ as Savior.

For fifteen years before that I had deeply prayed for revival, in vain it had seemed. Although God may have stirred other pray-ers we didn't know about, He certainly taught three broken, contrite, ordinary women that deep, persistent, agonizing prayer produces not only answered prayer—but revival!

God emphatically taught that learning to pray is more than just practicing "how to ask for something for somebody," which we call intercessory prayer. Confession by the one asking is a huge piece of effective prayer. *A prayer of confession is always just between God and the pray-er—even if others are present.*

My Second Surprise—That It Was for Others

The second major surprise from God about sin came when He started using that "no sin" requirement so powerfully for other people as they came earnestly seeking to learn to pray too. Through the years it has produced the usual startled, almost disbelief, frequent tears, sometimes loud sobbing, an occasional groaning, or even a crying out to God for mercy.

God used it first to convince our original "What Happens When Women Pray" eight gripers, whose experimenting produced the basis of the book, to finally pray the simplest prayer of repentance at our first meeting in 1968: "Cleanse me; use me; forgive me; show me."

As this shocking prayer training by God about sin to the three of us expanded, it formed the basis of the prayer teaching I would do for the next thirty years. God quickly established the first prerequisite to answered prayer: *no known, unconfessed sin in the life of the pray-er.*

God Surprised Them Too

The first ripples of surprise I sensed across the seminar audiences would come as we looked at what kind of a person could claim the Bible's promise in James 5:16: "The effectual, fervent prayer of a *righteous* [person] availeth much" (KJV).

They were surprised to find the Bible says that the pray-er's power in intercessory prayer (praying for other people and things) is dependent upon his or her personal relationship with God.

After learning of the awesome power of intercessory prayer available to them (which itself was a surprise to many of them), discovering that their relationship with God determined their prayer power would at times send shock waves over the audience. Many didn't appreciate discovering that learning to pray was more than just learning new methods of practicing how to ask for, and get, what they wanted.

Seminar attendees have almost always been surprised by what sin is, according to the Bible. James 4:17 tells us, "To him [or her] who knows to do good and does it not, to him [or her] it is sin" (NKJV). Not a personality trait, character weakness, or environmental deprivation—this failure to obey God is sin!

It was a devastating eye-opener to realize that every sermon they had heard, every Sunday-school lesson they had taught or heard, every Bible study they had attended or presented, and every word they had read out of the Bible—and were not obeying—to God it actually was sin.

The two conditions of prayers being answered in John 15:7 became the basis of our seminar after a few years. In Jesus' perhaps most powerful promise of prayers' being answered in the New Testament, He gave two conditions: "*If* you abide in Me, and [*if*] My words abide in you, [then and only then] ask whatever you wish, and it shall be done for you" (emphasis added).

I was horrified to receive in the mail a beautifully packaged cassette tape of my teaching an hour on only the promise of that verse. Although I had recorded every example of prayer power on that tape, presenting just "ask whatever you wish, and it shall be done unto you" without the two conditions was a lie. I had not authorized that tape's reproduction or distribution, nor did I even know about it. We finally stopped production on it because it absolutely was not what Jesus said. But we never could gather up all those lies that had been sold.

I wondered how many of us want just the promises about prayer in the Bible, ignoring the conditions.

Our own adolescent daughter Nancy was very perturbed one day. "Mother, are the things that were sin when you were a girl still sin today?" When I asked her where she was reading devotionally in her Bible, she replied, "Ephesians." To hear what God had to say two thousand years ago about it, each of us was reading the first chapter of Ephesians silently when she suddenly exploded, "Oh, yeah! It's still sin!" I may never know what God used in His Word to convince her—but she knew!

Almost all, both leaders and laypeople, coming to learn to pray are surprised to learn that *God says all sins are not alike to Him*. In chapter 2, I discussed the two classes of sin: (1) the original state of sin (singular) into which every person is born and that is removed by the blood of Jesus when a person becomes a Christian, and (2) the sins (plural) committed by Christians after they have accepted Jesus as their Savior and Lord. This is one point at which Bible teachers and pastors frequently take notes furiously, making me realize this is a new or overlooked point for them.

Repentance from sin was the message that Jesus proclaimed, from his first sermon in Mark 1:15 to His last advice from heaven to His churches in Revelation 2 and 3. "Repent!" Jesus cried. The emphasis the Bible puts on the impact of sin on our power in intercessory prayer is sobering.

Both classes of sin are described in 1 John 3:23–24. The apostle John addresses the second class of sin—sins (plural)—when he states that Christians who keep God's commandments get answers to their prayers:

> Whatever we ask [prayer] we receive from Him because we keep His commandments and do the things that are pleasing in His sight . . . and love one another, just as He commanded us.

Christians who do not obey God's commands and do not do what is pleasing to Him are, of course, committing sins. They have already been forgiven of the original state of sin—sin (singular)—by believing in Jesus. But they are committing sins (plural).

Verse 23 addresses the first class of sin—the original state of sin into which all humans are born since the Garden of Eden and that is removed only by faith in Jesus Christ (see John 3:18 and Rom. 5:18). John says that non-Christians do not get answers to their prayers because they have not kept His commandment of believing in the name of Jesus:

And this is His commandment, that we believe in the name of His Son, Jesus Christ (1 John 3:23).

Amazingly, the personal handling of both classes of sin is crucial to being eligible for God's "hearing" intercessory prayers for other people or things. He always hears the cry of the penitent sinner coming to Him, even if the seeking takes years. However, this is not human hearing since, being God, He is aware of everything said or done. This means He "gives attention to" intercessory prayers according to the pray-er's personal spiritual condition and lifestyle (see 1 Pet. 3:12).

But the most convicting surprise of all comes when we read our list of sins. Consistently reading the Bible and listening to God in prayer will show us all the sins He wants us to confess. But God has something more concise for us to use in our prayer training.

In the early seventies, someone handed me a typed list of sins from the Bible that he felt needed to be confessed. Impressed, I now had a suggestion for the most powerful tool I ever have used—because it is simply God's words from the Bible.

Each scripture is followed by a couple of questions, worded so that every "yes" answer reveals a sin in the life of the pray-er that needs to be confessed. In our meetings, we read through the entire list aloud, keeping mental and spiritual note of the "yes" answers in our lives. Over and over I hear, "I didn't know *that* was sin!"

As I was reading the list of sins aloud before their confession praying in a seminar, one young woman suddenly put her hands over her ears and cried out, "Stop! I can't take any more!"

In a prison prayer seminar, one dear inmate dropped her face in her hands, shuddered, and moaned aloud, "Oh, my God, I've committed every one of these!"

So often someone prays like Peter, devastated at her or his having denied the Lord Jesus by some word or action, weeping bitterly.

Having used this list for more than twenty-five years now, I've never gotten through it without having to confess something either!

(See end of the chapter for the complete list of sins.)

Applying What We Learn

The great part of prayer seminars is that we don't just talk about a topic; we practice praying about it. And attendees' simple, sincere prayers of confession (using discretion) are all God needed to forgive them! I've watched them almost always hug each other in their groups, beam as they daub dry their tears, and then stream out of the seminars—changed! They have been set free from the load of sin they have been struggling with—forgiven!

Since there are two different classes of sin, there are two different reasons for the changes produced by confessing and being forgiven by God.

Those who are already Christians are freed from the guilt some have been carrying for years. They are cleansed. Their unbroken communion with God has been restored, and they are ready to pray with power. Many can't wait to make restitution or to be reconciled to the perpetrator of an evil against them. They have discovered the liberating truth of 1 John 1:8–9: "If we say that we have no sin, we are deceiving ourselves, and the truth is not in us. If we confess our sins, He is faithful and righteous to forgive us our sins and to cleanse us from all unrighteousness."

In contrast, those who initially attended the seminar as unbelievers and then repented and accepted Jesus are forgiven of all of the sin of their entire lives. They have experienced the promise of Acts 10:43: "Everyone who believes in Him [Jesus] receives forgiveness of sins."

Yes, God is always there to provide forgiveness of original sin and to continuously rid us of any and all of our sin blocking our effective communication with Him—forgiveness through His Son Jesus' blood on the cross.

There are no sinless Christians, only forgiven Christians. First John 1:8–9 (written to Christians) tells us clearly that if we say we have no sin, we deceive ourselves (and sometimes other people), but we never deceive God.

Sin actually is a unique concept. Only Christianity, not psychology or the world's religions, has that word. Our uniqueness isn't that we are given the right to sin; but, when we do, we have the only absolute provision for getting rid of that sin immediately. Forgiveness is available to you right now!

No wonder they throw their arms around each other in their prayer groups—hugging, crying, laughing, and praising God. No wonder we all lift our voices celebrating what the angels in heaven celebrate—a lost soul saved! Many souls! No wonder I wipe tears of joy!

Continuous Surprises for Me

The response of seminar attendees learning to pray and respond to God's convicting almost shocked me at first. Although expecting it now, I still am surprised and thrilled when it happens over and over. God truly has brought about what no human ever could do. Here are a few of my surprises:

One surprise that always thrills me is that virtually 100 percent of prayer-seminar attendees pray out loud the first time I ask them. A rough estimate is that approximately half of the people who have come to learn to pray these thirty years never had prayed out loud in front of anybody before. But they do—en masse!

A famous Christian women's leader had to miss her fall kickoff session because of being out of the country. When asking me to substitute for her, she said, "But don't ask them to pray out loud. I know my women, and they won't!" When I asked her if she would trust me enough to let me try if God so led, she hesitantly agreed. The day came, and I knew all I would teach them about getting prayer power would be futile if God wasn't even listening to their prayers. Remembering my London publisher's warning about British people's being private during my first teaching tour there and then watching them almost explode in prayer when I asked, undaunted, I asked the women to pray. And, as I knew God would, He unleashed their inhibitions and forgave them all over the room—of both classes of sins.

Also astounding to me is the subject of that first prayer they pray aloud—confession of sins! I make it so easy for them. They say aloud with me, "Father, forgive me for . . . " and all at once they go on to confess as many sins as God has shown them from the list of sins—or wherever. Sometimes they hesitate, shyly waiting for the encouragement of others' voices. But frequently they just explode like a gun, anxious to get rid of those sins.

At a seminar across the street from Bill Cosby's Manhattan brown house, I gasped, wondering if I needed to put a lid on the praying. The church and lower auditorium were jammed (for the first time in its history) with every ethnic group in New York City. When about 50 percent of them prayed making sure Jesus was their Savior and Lord, they stamped their feet, whistled, hugged, and cried. They were celebrating and praising God in every language and culture imaginable!

God's Hidden Mission Field

That God would let me discover His "hidden mission field" was a surprise I certainly didn't expect—or even know was there. Where is God's hidden mission field? In some lost forest on Planet Earth, among an unheard of tribe? Oh no. *It is right in the Lord's church* (see Matt. 7:21–23).

Teaching my first overseas prayer seminars in Australia in 1980, I learned that most attending already belonged to well-respected churches and regularly attended a great international Bible study. To my amazement, never fewer than 25 percent and up to 50 percent prayed at each seminar, making sure Jesus was their Savior and Lord. The writer of that Bible study told me she was aghast and was going to add "accepting Jesus" to each series.

I remember years ago refusing to write a foreword for a Bible study on the Gospel of John because it didn't include accepting Jesus—even with John 3:16 in it. The astounded publisher asked, "Don't all people who study the Bible know Jesus?" My "no" answer has proved true as I have traveled around the world.

However, when the same pattern started to emerge in our seminars in America, for some reason I found it much more incredible. It somehow shook my image of our then "fine Christian" America. At first, the 5 percent to 10 percent of respondents didn't surprise me too much, but when the percentage suddenly soared to the current average of 25 percent, I was stunned. Most incredible, of course, is that almost everyone who comes to learn to pray is already a member of a respectable church in the U.S.

With the pastor of a megachurch sitting in the front row with about two thousand of mostly his members, about two-thirds prayed out loud, making sure they knew Jesus as Savior and Lord. He dashed out the door, and we never saw him again that day. Aghast, I wondered what I had done to prompt that action. I asked my husband later what he would have done if some little seminar speaker had asked that question and two-thirds of his congregation would have prayed aloud making sure of Jesus as their Savior. He responded, "I would have fallen on my knees and cried out to God, 'Oh, Lord, where did I go wrong?'"

When I met that pastor and his wife six months later by an elevator in Washington, D.C., they both threw their arms around me and gushed, "You'll never know what you did for our church. It's an absolutely transformed church since you were there!" I firmly explained that I didn't do anything; God did. That pastor now has a church full of genuine, born-again Christians!

In a California seminar, a lady marked her signup card: (1) that she had been on a telephone prayer chain two years, and (2) that day she had accepted Christ as her Savior and Lord. She had been praying those two years without access to the Father through the atoning work of Jesus!

Before God showed me His hidden mission field, I was praying one morning in March 1980, asking God for the usual strength, outpouring of His Spirit, and wisdom for the day. Suddenly I changed my prayer: "Father, what is Your number-one priority for me? What do You want me to do?" Immediately suspended in mid-air before my spiritual eyes in big box letters was:

W-I-N S-O-U-L-S

Asking if He wanted me to give up my prayer ministry to go into evangelism, He kept saying no. It was the next September that I began discovering His hidden mission field right in His own churches. God's immense surprise for me!

What Cleansing Did for Them

One of my greatest thrills is seeing what confession of sin does in the future life of the pray-er. Here is Vicky's story of how biblical repentance made such a big difference in her life:

Dear Eve,

About ten years ago, out of concern about the downward spiral of the moral and political climate of our nation, a group of about twelve women got together to pray fervently—our own ideas of what God should do to straighten things up in our land. We begged God not to let certain people stay or get in office because they were immoral or liberal, to get rid of the school principal who is against teaching abstinence in sex education, to help our pastors to become more spiritual, and *pleeease* to do something to make our husbands the spiritual leaders in our homes.

God says, "If you seek Me you will find Me when you search for Me with all your heart." Well, one day God showed up at our prayer meeting, and we were stunned to discover that the real problem in our nation was with God's own people, i.e., us. We began to repent, and for the next year, whenever we got together, we spent most of our time repenting. We desperately wanted to be right with God, and each of us desired that God would use us to the maximum for His purposes.

Then we used your *Study Guide for Evangelism Praying* to prepare us for praying for those who didn't know Jesus. When I got to chapter 2, entitled "Our Personal Preparation," I spent three days looking up every verse in my Bible and asking God to examine my heart and deal with every area in my life that grieves Him.

I will never forget the joy I experienced after that time with the Lord, knowing that now to the best of my knowledge, I was clean before my God. I have renamed this chapter in the study guide "My Spiritual Enema."

What is so amazing is that eight years later, as each one of us who prayed together looks back, we realize that through repentance God has done amazing things in each one of our lives to prepare us for ministry. God needed to show us what He saw when He looked at our lives in order to humble us and release the compassion of Christ in us for those who are without the Savior. We can all say that *God trained us in His ways through repentance of our ways*. Love, Vicky.

Vicky is now an officer of my board, in charge of future planning for the national Christian Women United network, a trustee of a large Christian college, and being used by God to help steer innumerable national organizations. Cleansing really works!

Can God Use Me?

"Father," I called out to God on January 1, 1991, "make me righteous before You so You can use me in 1991."

It was while I was studying the Christmas story during the holidays that God had shown me that all the people He chose for the first Christmas events already were called righteous by Him. Elizabeth and Zacharias, future parents of Jesus' forerunner John the Baptist, "were both righteous before God, walking blamelessly in all the commandments and requirements of the Lord" (Luke 1:6). Then, before taking the pregnant Mary to be his wife, Joseph is described as "a righteous man" (Matt. 1:19). And to the Virgin Mary, the angel Gabriel said, "Hail, favored one. The Lord is with you" (Luke 1:28). She was the young virgin God could use to enfold in her body His Son for nine months!

Although I had been cleansed by Jesus' blood when I accepted Jesus sixty years earlier, I wanted to be righteous, cleansed of anything that would hinder the Lord from using me to the fullest. Later that same month, I received an invitation from Lorry Lutz, coordinator of AD2000 International Women's Track, to be the North American women's director. It was a ten-year job with the goal of helping reach every man, woman, and child in the world with prayer and sharing Jesus by the end of the year 2000. I wrote these words in the margin of my Bible beside Matthew 1:19: "How God answered!" I accepted the job.

In January 1999, eight years later, I wrote beside that same Bible note, "Although I have not been able to *live* a totally righteous life these eight years, God knew my heart's desire to be righteous. It takes so much of 1 John 1:7–10's confessing!" This is the story of my life. Sinless? Oh no! Cleansed? Constantly!

Who's Hindering the Holy Spirit?

Being one of the intercessors for Promise Keepers Pastors' Conference in the Atlanta Omni Arena was an awesome privilege.

My prayer partner, Kay Hammer, and I were assigned to one of those press boxes high above the whole arena, and we fervently interceded for the forty-three thousand pastors below us—one-tenth of all the pastors in America!

One night, Dr. Charles Swindoll divided these men and had them call antiphonally back and forth to each other "Holy, Holy, Holy!" I held on to the railing as the power of those thousands of trained speaking voices vibrated up to us, filling that vast room. Then someone else was asking for those pastors to pray intermittently for the Holy Spirit to come in a special way, which He did. (The pastors I have talked to since then all agree that the Holy Spirit came in a powerful way the next afternoon, but not necessarily in an outstanding way that night.)

As Kay and I prayed for an outpouring of the power of the Holy Spirit on those pastors, my heart got heavier and heavier. Suddenly I bowed low and cried out to the Lord one of the most anguished prayers I ever have prayed: *"Father, if I am the one who is hindering the Holy Spirit tonight, strike me dead!"*

Yes, I have learned through the years that I can be the one hindering an answer to prayer—mine or others'. I can be grieving the Holy Spirit by sin in my life. My sins!

"Do not grieve the Holy Spirit of God" is right in the middle of a list of things in Ephesians 4:25–32 that Christians should and should not do to keep from sinning.

At our pre-seminar prayer meetings, as committee members are sharing their prayer requests for the seminar, I almost always share my number-one request. Those pray-ers who have been praying for me for six months are surprised when I share: "Please pray tonight, and through the night if God wakes you, that He will bring to my mind every unknown sin that will hinder His Holy Spirit from flowing tomorrow. I can confess the ones I know about, but I desperately need to be completely clean, or God's power will not be here. I will be the one hindering the Holy Spirit." Many through the years have shared how seriously they took that challenge and how deeply they prayed for me—some all night. I am so grateful!

Why All the Fuss About Sin?

God taught us why confession prayers are His means of our getting the attention of His listening ear. It is His holiness!

Through the years God has revealed to us the Person with whom we are trying to communicate—Himself. And when we sin, no matter how little the sin seems to us, we violate His holiness. Our sinning breaks the communion between us—always beginning with ourselves, not God.

My key to answered prayer is a simple word—*holy*. There is none holy but the triune Godhead.

The only attribute of God recorded in triplicate in the Bible is His holiness. The first word I usually say when I begin to pray is *holy*, and most of the time it is in triplicate: "Holy, Holy, Holy Father." The minute I say that word, God brings to my mind any unrecognized sins I need to confess for absolutely clear communication with Him. I confess, He sweeps away the sin hindrance, and I'm in His holy presence.

God has also shown us the environment of heaven we were trying to invade coming to Him in prayer. The word describing it is also *holy*.

After being interviewed on one of America's largest Christian television stations, I was asked to go to the staff lunchroom and lead them in their noon prayer time. The staff was praying for revival and had a large pile of wood ready to light that coming Saturday night to start it. (I wish igniting a revival were that easy!) With no time to prepare, I shot an SOS prayer to God in the hall on the way up. He quickly reminded me of Psalm 24:3–4:

Who may ascend unto the hill of the Lord? And who may stand in His holy place? He who has clean hands and a pure heart.

For several minutes, they worshiped God in praise songs, most holding up hands to Him. My turn was next. I asked them to look at their hands. "Where have your hands been this last week?" I asked. "Where did they click to on the television or slow up just to get a peek at something you knew you shouldn't be looking at? Did they turn to the lingerie section when that catalog came? What little touching innuendoes were there at work or church—of course, never dreaming of actually committing a sexual sin? Or worse? Look at your hands!"

"What have your hands done this week?" I pushed. "And then you had the audacity to wave all that garbage in the face of a holy God! And you thought He was smiling at how sweet you were to be praising Him? God probably was holding His nose at the stench!"

After I reminded them that all revivals since Christ's time have started when one to eleven Christians got completely right with God, we went immediately to repentance prayers and many tears. Most were late back to their desks that noon, but nobody cared. They were on their way to that Saturday-night revival.

Both Isaiah and John heard the awesome sound of heaven's holiness.

In Revelation 4, the apostle John describes the sounds in the environment he saw that surrounds God. He wrote that there was One sitting on a throne appearing like jasper stone and sardius, with a rainbow around the throne like an emerald. Around the throne were twenty-four elders with white garments and golden crowns. And from the throne proceed flashes of lightning and sounds and peals of thunder, with the seven Spirits of God like lamps, and a sea of glass like crystal was before the throne.

John continued that in the center and around the throne were four living creatures, who day and night do not cease to say, "Holy, Holy, Holy is the Lord God, the Almighty, who was and who is and who is to come" (v. 8).

This is the sound Isaiah heard when he saw the Lord sitting on a throne, lofty and exalted, with the train of His robe filling the temple.

And seraphim stood above Him, and one called to the other and said, "Holy, Holy, Holy is the Lord of Hosts" (Isa. 6:3).

There is none holy but God!

When God opens the door of prayer to us, He ushers us into this heavenly environment—reverberating with His holiness. His throne room is filled with His absolutely pure, sinless, permeating, and engulfing presence—His holy presence.

So, as we struggled to learn to pray His way, God affirmed deeper and deeper His provision to make us eligible to enter that awesome presence—His Son, Jesus. As Hebrews 10:19 says:

We have confidence to enter the holy place by the blood of Jesus.

And once we have been cleansed, we enter to pray with unbroken communication with the holy God of the universe, who listens to—and answers—our prayers according to His holy, omniscient will.

Cleansed! Eligible to bring our prayers into His holy presence! Oh, the release, the privilege, and the potential power of those prayers!

A Sample List of Scriptural Sins to Read Before Confessing Sins in Prayer

Every "yes" answer is a sin in your life that needs to be confessed. *"Therefore, to him that knoweth to do good and doeth it not, to him it is sin"* (James 4:17). (References on this list are from the KJV.)

1. 1 Thessalonians 5:18 *"In everything give thanks; for this is the will of God in Christ Jesus concerning you."*

   Do you worry about anything? Have you failed to thank God for all things, the seemingly bad as well as the good? Do you neglect to give thanks at mealtime?

2. Ephesians 3:20 *"Now unto him who is able to do exceeding abundantly above all that we ask or think, according to the power that worketh in us."*

   Do you fail to attempt things for God because you are not talented enough? Do feelings of inferiority keep you from trying to serve God? When you do accomplish something for Christ, do you fail to give Him all the glory?

3. Acts 1:8 *"But ye shall receive power, after that the Holy Ghost is come upon you; and ye shall be witnesses unto me both in Jerusalem, and in all Judea, and in Samaria, and unto the uttermost part of the earth."*

   Have you failed to be a witness with your life for Christ? Have you felt it was enough to just live your Christianity and not witness with your mouth to the lost?

4. Romans 12:3 *"For I say . . . to every man that is among you, not to think of himself more highly than he ought to think."*

   Are you proud of your accomplishments, your talents, your family? Do you fail to see others as better than yourself, more important than yourself in the body of Christ? Do you insist on your own rights? Do you think as a Christian you are doing quite well? Do you rebel at God's wanting to change you?

5. Ephesians 4:31 *"Let all bitterness, and wrath, and anger, and clamor, and evil speaking, be put away from you, with all malice."*

128

Do you complain, find fault, argue? Do you have a critical spirit? Do you carry a grudge against Christians of another group because they don't see eye-to-eye with you on all things? Do you speak unkindly about people when they are not present? Are you angry with yourself? Others? God?

6. 1 Corinthians 6:19 *"What? Know ye not that your body is the temple of the Holy Ghost which is in you, which ye have of God, and ye are not your own."*

Are you careless with your body? Are you guilty of not caring for it as the temple of the Holy Spirit in eating and exercise habits? Do you defile your body with unholy sex acts?

7. Ephesians 4:29 *"Let no corrupt communication proceed out of your mouth."*

Do you ever use filthy language, tell slightly off-color jokes? Do you condone others' doing so in your presence, in your home?

8. Ephesians 4:27 *"Neither give place to the devil."*

Do you fail to see you are a "landing strip" for Satan when you open your mind to him through T.M., yoga, séances, psychic predictions, occult literature and movies? Do you get advice for daily living from horoscopes rather than from God? Do you let Satan use you to thwart the cause of Christ in your church through criticism, gossip, non-support?

9. Romans 12:11 *"Not slothful in business."*

Do you fail to pay your debts on time? Avoid paying them altogether? Do you charge more on credit cards than you can pay when due? Do you neglect to keep honest income tax records? Do you engage in any shady business deals whether as an employer or employee?

10. 1 Corinthians 8:9 *"But take heed lest by any means this liberty of yours become a stumblingblock to them that are weak."*

Do you feel you can do anything you want to do because the Bible says you are free in Christ? Even though you were strong enough not to fall, do you fail to take responsibility for a weaker Christian who has fallen because of following your example?

11. **Hebrews 10:25** *"Not forsaking the assembling of ourselves together."*

Are you irregular or spasmodic in church attendance? Do you attend preaching services in body only, whispering, reading, or planning while God's Word is being preached? Are you skipping prayer meetings? Have you neglected family devotions?

12. **Colossians 3:9** *"Lie not one to another, seeing that ye have put off the old man with his deeds."*

Do you ever lie? Exaggerate? Do you fail to see "little white lies" as sins? Do you tell things the way you want them rather than the way they really are?

13. **1 Peter 2:11** *"Dearly beloved . . . abstain from fleshly lusts, which war against the soul."*

Are you guilty of a lustful eye toward the opposite sex? Do you fill your mind with sex-oriented TV programs, movies, books, magazines? Their covers? Centerfolds? Do you indulge in any lustful activity God's Word condemns—fornication, adultery, perversion?

14. **John 13:35** *"By this shall all men know that ye are my disciples, if ye have love one to another."*

Are you guilty of being a part of factions and divisions in your church? Would you rather add fuel to a misunderstanding than help correct it? Have you loved only the ones in your own church, feeling those of other denominations are not the body of Christ? Are you secretly pleased over the misfortunes of another? Annoyed by their successes?

15. **Colossians 3:13** *"Forbearing one another, and forgiving one another, if any man have a quarrel against any: even as Christ forgave you, so also do ye."*

Have you failed to forgive anybody anything that person might have said or done against you? Have you turned certain people off? Are you holding grudges?

16. Ephesians 4:28 *"Let him that stole steal no more: but rather let him labor."*

Do you steal from your employer by doing less work, staying on the job less time than you are paid for? Do you underpay?

17. Ephesians 5:16 *"Redeeming the time, because the days are evil."*

Do you waste time? The time of others? Do you spend time watching TV trash, reading cheap books, procrastinating?

18. Matthew 6:24 *"No man can serve two masters . . . ye cannot serve God and mammon."*

Is your goal in life to make as much money as possible? Accumulate things? Have you withheld God's share of your income from Him? Is money your God?

19. Matthew 23:28 *"Even so ye also outwardly appear righteous unto men, but within ye are full of hypocrisy and iniquity."*

Do you know in your heart you are a fake, just pretending to be a real Christian? Are you hiding behind church membership to cover a life still full of sin? Are you faking Christianity for social status, acceptance in your church, community? Do you smile piously during the Sunday sermon but live in your sin all week? Are you the person in your home you are trying to impress people you are?

20. Philippians 4:8 *"Finally brethren, whatsoever things are true, whatsoever things are honest, whatsoever things are just, whatsoever things are pure, whatsoever things are lovely, whatsoever things are of good report; if there be any virtue, and if there be any praise, think on these things."*

Do you enjoy listening to gossip? Passing it on? Do you believe rumors or partial truths, especially about an enemy or your competitor? Do you fail to spend time every day reading the Bible? Do you fail to think on the things of God—only good and true and pure things—always?

Examine your lifestyle:

As you have read the scriptures in this chapter, were you surprised that there are conditions for God hearing and answering your intercessory prayers? Did you know that the Bible says your lifestyle determines whether or not your prayers will be heard and answered by God? Do you feel you have hands consistently clean enough to expect God to welcome your prayers? What attribute of God may you have been violating while you were seeking to have you intercessory prayers accepted by Him?

Scripture:

In your Bible, read Isaiah 6:1–4, letting God show you what His dwelling place is really like. Which is the only word, which describes in triplicate the Lord God of heaven? Now, read Revelation 4:1–8 to find what environment surrounds the Father. What words reverberate around Him? From Revelation 5:8, how do you know your prayers go to and are being preserved in that holy environment?

For you to do:

List of Sins. According to James 4:17, which of your evil deeds, thoughts, attitudes, and actions actually are sin? Prayerfully read through the list of sins, honestly letting God convict you of any not already confessed. **Check each one that applies to you.** Now how ready do you feel you are for access to God's holy environment with your prayers? Record from Hebrews 10:19 how you can have confidence to enter that holy place.

Why? _____

For you to pray:

"Holy, holy, holy Father in heaven, I am unworthy to come with my sins into Your holy presence. I confess each of the biblical sins I have just read and all others You are bringing to my mind. Forgive me for: **(Identify and confess each separately.)** Thank You for Jesus' blood that cleanses me. I believe Your Word that I am forgiven-and worthy to come to Your holy presence. Thank You, most holy, holy, holy Father for the potential power of my prayers! In Jesus' matchless name, amen."

*If you are not sure you have repented and believed in Jesus yet, sincerely pray through #19 on The List of Sins being the fake of Matthew 23:28, confessing and accepting Jesus as your Savior and Lord.

CHAPTER 7

Intercessors Need Prayer Too

PRAYER MINISTRIES usually are organized to pray for something specific. This was true when United Prayer Ministry was formed to be the prayer/advisory board for my then-fledgling prayer ministry. But we soon discovered that those so faithfully praying for me also needed prayer themselves. Why? Because Christians are in a spiritual battle, and prayer is the way we obtain God's power against the evil on earth. Intercessors actually are threatening Satan with their praying, and he is desperately trying to stop them. It is not that he is our enemy; we are his enemy! So we found the answer—praying for each other. We followed the command of Galatians 6:2: "Bear one another's burdens, and thus fulfill the law of Christ."

Praying for the intercessors became our gift to each other—and my gift to them.

My Gift to My Pray-ers

Marlene, our board president for many years, took leadership in maintaining continuous prayer for me, deeply and faithfully interceding herself. But life had some ups and downs for her and her family. Through the years, it has been our privilege to pray for her through those difficult times. Marlene said it so well about this beautiful process we have kept going all these years: "There are times I cannot pray for myself. That's when the process reverses."

Edith was so infirm we had to help her into a chair while she could still attend board meetings. How we prayed for this precious former school principal—while she herself was an awesome intercessor. She not only prayed for us, but she had a special mission field in the coal mining hills of a Southern state. Her missionaries would send her a list of those they were trying to win to Jesus right then, and Edith would pray by name for them—sometimes all night because her pain would not let her sleep.

Every board meeting, Edith would sit with a pile of pictures in her lap of those who had accepted Jesus that week, eagerly awaiting her turn to tell us about who it was. I can still see her eyes sparkling behind her incredibly thick glasses, praising God for what He did when she prayed—and while we were praying for her.

Board member Dorothy sat down at my kitchen table the other day. "Pray for my brother!" she pleaded with desperation in her eyes. "He's dying and in a coma. He doesn't have any friends or family who will come to his funeral." "Why not?" I asked. "Because of the horrible life he has lived," she replied.

Raping her when she was a little girl and going to prison for doing the same thing to his daughters, his list of misdeeds went on. She still shuddered at the sound of his almost animal-like angry growling, reminding her of his attack. "I've tried and tried to bring him to Jesus, but now it's too late! He's in a coma!" she lamented.

I told Dorothy about my brother Bud, who was kept alive by pumps after being hit by a car going fifty miles an hour. Desperate, knowing he was entering eternity still saying that there is no God, I bent over him and slowly intoned, "Bud, God loves you. Can you trust Jesus today?" And he heard! Bud trusted Jesus and remained with us for two years before cancer took him to heaven.

After hearing Bud's story, Dorothy apprehensively left to visit her brother. She came back a few days later. She had repeated slowly, several times, the words for him to pray to ask God to forgive him and to accept Jesus as his Savior. "I was thrilled that the director of the nursing home told me she had done the same thing. So now I'll just have to wait," she sighed resignedly. Had he heard? Had he responded to Jesus? Only eternity in heaven will reveal it.

For twenty years while Dorothy had prayed almost daily for my ministry, we had prayed for her through the death in a fire of her son, the death of her husband, constant struggles with children of their blended family, and recovering from the takeover of their lucrative business by a crooked partner.

But now, to hold her hand in mine, to weep with her, and to pray for her was an unspeakable privilege for me. Bearing one another's burdens!

The deep love I feel for those who have cared enough to give of their time and energy to uphold me in prayer has poured out of me—to them—as I pray for them. *This is a dimension of love only the body of Christ can experience.*

Families

As we have prayed for each other's families, we have become an unbelievably close-knit spiritual family. We have prayed for each other on our telephone prayer chains whenever a need suddenly surfaced or became desperate. We have listened as they shared, and we have prayed at board meetings and retreats. Our monthly prayer calendar has one or more intercessors assigned to pray specifically for whoever uses our books and tapes that day, and the rest of us pray for that intercessor.

For six years, Betty and her husband did not know the location of their daughter and her two young children. Through those long years, Betty sat at board meetings with a mother's broken heart and amazing faith in God, and we prayed. We joined hundreds of fervent prayers of family and friends ascending to the throne of God on their behalf.

"God answered!" Betty wrote to me. "They were found in good health in a caring Christian community. God had kept them safely in His care and had provided for their needs above and beyond our expectations. She is now happily married to a Christian college professor. Her two children are with them and very happy in their lovely new home. They'll be in Russia this fall on a Fulbright teaching opportunity. Ephesians 3:20–21!"

Not all problems were that serious. Most of them were the normal things that happen to all humans on our fallen planet—surgeries, wayward children, financial setbacks, broken relationships, and health problems. But all needed bearing one another's burdens.

Not all ended in glorious victory. Many did, several are still ongoing, and a few were disappointments to our way of thinking—but not God's. *God never promised to make all our problems disappear or to give instant answers. But He did promise to give that awesome peace that the world cannot give and the assurance that He is in control and doing all things for our good.* We learned the incredible joy of fitting into His perfect will for us and seeing how He was making finer gold of all of us, knowing what disaster would happen if we had our own seemingly good way we were asking for. And He has kept His promises!

A Pattern Emerged

However, after just a few years of concentrated praying by my board, we began to see a pattern. There were not just the usual problems of living on a fallen planet, but an escalation of their personal and family problems at certain times. Sometimes it would be all of us at once. Analyzing it, we discovered *an increase of personal difficulties would occur when God was about to do something important in our ministry*—such as opening a new continent to our teaching or writing a new book on prayer.

God little by little showed us some of the reasons behind this strange pattern. There was a much deeper reason for this pattern than just our bearing one another's burdens in prayer. *We had an enemy—a supernatural, evil enemy.*

It was obvious that Satan was angry at the prayer power God would send when the intercessors prayed. *Satan can stand all of our planning and programs, but he can't withstand all of that prayer!* Prayer is getting supernatural help to solve problems that were brought about by Satan—when he brought sin to the Garden of Eden. And Satan's way of counteracting the power of prayer was to keep us so enmeshed struggling with problems that we could not think about praying for God's desires for Planet Earth.

But the best part of discovering the source of the pattern was experiencing the scriptural victory that was ours over this enemy. This led to a new reason to pray for each other as Christian intercessors.

After he describes the spiritual armor for battling the schemes of the devil in Ephesians 6, the apostle Paul gave these words of admonition about praying for saints (people who have been redeemed and cleansed of our original state of sin). He gave it to us saints—to whom he wrote the book:

> With all prayer and petition pray at all times in the Spirit, and with this in view, be on the alert with all perseverance and petition for all the saints. (v. 18)

We started diligently *staying alert* to each others' needs—then making sure it was *prayer* and not just us talking about our needs with each other. Our sporadic praying became more of the biblical praying "at all times." We learned to lean more heavily on the Holy Spirit in us and to take our prayers to the Father according to His will.

My own children at differing times have sensed this pattern too. Our daughter Nancy and her husband, Dan, have called to ask, "Did God move in an awesome way in a meeting today?" or "Where were you this weekend?" They, too, sense the source of the battle. We've had several serious talks about this, with me asking if they wanted me to give up my ministry so life would be smoother for them. But their answer always has been a resounding, "No! We'll pay any price needed for God to accomplish what He has called you to do, Mother." My intercessors have consistently prayed for them—while Dan and Nancy prayed for me.

After much speaking in youth groups and schools on the dangers of students' widespread dabbling in occult games and practices, it was our own college son, Kurt, who whistled a soft sigh of relief when he saw my first published tapes on prayer. "Now maybe I can sleep nights."

As my own children pray for me in this battle, my intercessors and I are praying for them too. In Aberdeen, Scotland, where we started one of my tours, there was a terrific spiritual battle. An oppressive cloud hung over our committee's prayer meeting, and it didn't seem to break completely with our praying. It was our daughter Jan's turn to receive a phone call back in America, and she said to me, "Mother, God gave me some scripture for you—the last verses of Romans 8." (This happened frequently when I was overseas.)

It didn't mean much to me until the next morning when the oppression was still there as I awoke. As I reread that section of Scripture, almost jumping off the page at me was:

We are more than conquerors through Jesus who loved us (Rom. 8:37 KJV)!

I knew immediately it was God's answer. We weren't going to barely eke out a little victory that day! And we didn't. The heavy cloud vanished immediately—and a tremendous freedom and moving of God were there all day.

No wonder we need to pray for each other—with God sending such victory against our enemy!

Secret

Taking the sword of the Spirit—the Word of God—was a secret of praying against our enemy Satan that we learned from the description of spiritual armor in Ephesians 6. It is the only *offensive* weapon against him from that list of weapons for defeating the devil; all the rest are defensive weapons. Our telephone prayer chain chairperson, Ruth, includes a scripture with each day's prayer requests. The pray-ers are thrilled, saying how much that Word of God helps in their praying. And they marvel at how she always gets the right scripture from God every time. Satan might quote Scripture, but he cannot stand against us when we are praying it.

Paul added his own need for prayer in his spiritual battle of standing for Jesus. As the last part of the spiritual armor for battling the schemes of the devil, he not only told the saints to pray for each other, but for himself too: "And pray on my behalf, that utterance may be given to me in the opening of my mouth, to make known with boldness the mystery of the gospel, for which I am an ambassador in chains; that in proclaiming it I may speak boldly, as I ought to speak" (Eph. 6:19–20).

These are the verses Jan sent to me when I was struggling with being bold enough to write what God was telling me to in my book *Battling the Prince of Darkness* (an evangelism book about rescuing captives from Satan's kingdom). I keep it Scotch-taped on my computer to this day and reread it while writing this chapter!

Thank You to the Pray-ers

Our intercessors needed lots of prayer for themselves during the times God knew there was going to be an unusually huge spiritual battle. Here are excerpts from what I reported to them in one "thank-you-for-praying" letter after my Protestant Women of the Chapel convention in Europe:

> While you and their local leadership prayed, I headed for Germany to conduct a weeklong prayer training convention for the military women from the whole continent, including some of their chaplains. Gail Wright, their president, had registrants of

leadership from every country in Europe, from Iceland to Turkey.

Obviously Satan was very nervous about their starting organized prayer on military bases in every European country. And on Halloween night, God answered the prayers of the intercessors and kept the whole convention from collapsing. It was the first time in my life I had a meeting interrupted by satanic forces and had to bring back order out of the chaos that erupted.

I was speaking on shepherds and all the things that make the New Testament shepherd, Jesus, different than the Old Testament shepherds who gave their lives for their sheep. My topic, "The New Testament Shepherd Takes Up His Life Again," happened to fall on Halloween night. I explained from 1 John 3:8 that Jesus died to defeat the works of the devil and taught "that through death He [Jesus] might render powerless him who had the power of death, that is, the devil" (Heb. 2:14).

Then I gave them the awesome biblical list of the wonderful things that happen to a believer through Jesus' death: eternal life for His sheep, redemption and the forgiveness of sins through His blood, being transferred out of Satan's kingdom into Jesus' kingdom, power over Satan through Jesus' blood, having their Savior seated at the Father's right hand in heavenly places, and God putting all things in subjection under His feet! . . .

With witchcraft, the occult, and Satan worship exploding then in Europe, I explained their only hope was in the *name* of the risen Savior, Jesus, and His *blood* shed on the cross.

After they had prayed that night all over the auditorium, making sure Jesus was their personal Savior, they sang praises and thanked Jesus in small prayer groups for dying and providing forgiveness. When I asked each of them to pick one person or thing (their church, school, etc.) and in prayer to claim the blood of Jesus over it for God to deliver it from the evil one that Halloween night, they prayed fervent, powerful, persisting, and victorious prayers!

But suddenly that Halloween night the atmosphere changed. With 135 different denominations and many languages represented, we expected variety. But, sitting near my husband, a young Asian woman who had been praying passionately in her native language suddenly arched her whole body and abruptly changed into loud, almost snarling praying. An evil presence engulfed us. Many reported a cold chill sweeping through the room, one saying it was like needles pricking into her whole body. I calmly stepped to the microphone, raised my voice above the din, and firmly claimed the blood of Jesus. The confusion subsided, and rejoicing victory was ours!

It seemed Satan had won by almost breaking up the retreat, but God turned it to good. Most of them went to their rooms to read the Bible and pray together about what had happened. No doctrinal teaching ever could have accomplished what God did in allowing that one incident of the real thing. What a fantastic experience!

But what would have happened if you had not been praying? I shudder to think! Thanks, pray-ers!

JoAnne, a board member who is a lawyer, published a Christian newspaper for years. When she wrote and ran a biweekly series on the evils of pornography, everything in her life started to fall apart. She wisely observed, "In anything where you are directly confronting evil, especially when you take any overt action to confront it, you put yourself and your intercessory pray-ers at risk."

No wonder we need to pray for each other!

Praise?

That this is the time to praise was one of the greatest, and hardest, lessons we learned. God showed us that anything getting that much attention from Satan meant we were doing something to make Satan nervous—or terrified.

This fact is hard to catch, especially at the time we are in the midst of the attacks. All we can think of is an immediate solution to the problem.

But the more we have practiced praising God and focusing on His eternal perspective, the more we have been in awe at His working out all things for our good according to His knowing the beginning and the end of everything we are praying about. This has changed our whole perspective—not just on how we pray, but on our whole relationship with the Lord.

Spiritual Warfare

A ministry that is actively reaching those without Jesus through prayer and asking them to accept Jesus is especially vulnerable to Satan's attacks. Why? Because that praying is part of the rescuing captives from Satan's kingdom. Satan is tenaciously hanging on to those who already belong to him in his kingdom, and he is desperate to get us off our knees.

The winning of souls to Jesus is getting involved in the battle between the rulers of the two spiritual kingdoms on Planet Earth: Satan's domain of darkness and Jesus' kingdom of light.

But we are on the winning side! Jesus came to secure the victory for us so that we could have authority and power over Satan. As Scripture states:

The Son of God appeared for this purpose, that He might destroy the works of the devil (1 John 3:8).

And when Jesus cried, "It is finished!" on the cross, it was finished—for then and for now. And Satan knows it!

I have a silent routine before giving an invitation to accept Christ at every seminar. While seminar attendees are praying and confessing their sins in little groups of four, I silently address Satan. (I always make sure I have confessed *my* sins before I begin teaching so I'll be free to do this.) This is not praying *to* him, as only Satan worshipers do that. I pan the whole audience visually, *telling* Satan that Jesus died for every one of them and that he no longer has any right to hang on, keeping them in his kingdom. Then I pray silently, asking God to woo the attendees to new life in Jesus. This, along with all the intercession, I'm sure, is one reason why we have averaged 25 percent, and twice about 80 percent, praying out loud making sure of Jesus being their personal Savior. So it is obvious *why* Satan is nervous!

> For He [the Father] delivered us from the domain of darkness, and transferred us to the kingdom of His beloved Son [Jesus], in whom we have redemption, the forgiveness of sins. (Col. 1:13–14)

Incredible amounts of prayer have gone into this salvation process by the seminar committee and board pray-ers, beseeching heaven for those eternally lost ones. *One of the main reasons Christians work so hard with so little harvest of souls is that we have failed to sufficiently enlist the power of God through pre-evangelism prayer.* But those intercessors desperately need multiplied prayers for themselves, too, to keep them faithful, persistent, and protected.

And it works! Awesome results have been ours—as intercessors and those praying for them together march confidently forward anchored on 1 John 4:4: "Greater is He who is in you [Jesus], than he that is in the world [Satan]."

Priorities

However, it is a constant struggle to stay alert and not to spend all of our time on each other. Physical and material needs are so obvious and pressing, we sometimes lose our perspective of why we are organized— to pray for God's direction, protection, wisdom, and power to accomplish His will through our ministry.

When the former chaplain of the U.S. Senate asked me to do some prayer teaching at his church's Wednesday night prayer meeting, I included keeping balance in what they pray for. I asked them this question: "Why is it that at most church prayer meetings, and even Sunday-school and Bible-study prayer meetings, at least 90 percent of the prayers are for Christians who, when they die, will go to be with their Lord in heaven—while there are almost no prayers for those non-Christians who, when they die, will go to a Christless eternity?"

An assistant pastor in charge that night was embarrassed as he got up to lead the church's prayer time. "I hardly dare to pass out these prayer request sheets for your praying," he stammered. "Every request is for a sick Christian, except one for wisdom in purchasing some new property."

Intercessors' Temporary Absences

Jeanne, a nurse, started as an original intercessor on our board in 1973. Jeanne left us for several years while she went with her surgeon husband to Bangladesh to build a mission hospital and minister there. When the task was finished, she came back to become our board president and hostess for our monthly meetings. She also put out the telephone prayer chain several times a week for years. Jeanne's leadership was influential in organizing prayer on many fronts while with us. But then God called them back to an unfinished hospital project in Bangladesh.

Returning home to us again, Jeanne was aglow with the difference that organized prayers had made in that mission trip. Here is what she reported to those of us who had supported her financially and in intercession:

For the first trip, we had the fine church prayer support most missionaries get. But this time, prayer support increased dramatically with you all on the board praying for us. Our church and our daughter's church in Iowa by then were more involved in prayer, and Lutheran Aid to Medicine in Bangladesh was organized to pray and support the mission. With all that prayer, we saw God answer with miracle after miracle. There was no comparison in the power of God in those two mission trips!

Our mission was to complete and staff a hospital that had been started ten years previously but had endured many struggles. Through prayer, the community, including the magistrate, many AIDS organizations, and even women from the Dutch embassy became involved helping with road construction, equipment, etc. One of the Canadians working nearby said it was a miracle so much was accomplished in twenty months.

Although there were many challenges, the united prayer effort enabled us to complete the hospital, build staff quarters, and fill it with doctors. We were also able to build a chapel with memorial money. . . .

Coming home, I have seen an increased emphasis on prayer in my church—in small groups and the search committees for replacing our retiring pastoral staff. The first thing our new pastor did was to seek men to serve as prayer warriors—and more than one hundred people volunteered. They meet with all the pastors Sundays about 7:30 A.M., lay hands on them, and pray for all the services. Then they pray over the sanctuary and other areas. During our four services some are praying the entire time, and all receive monthly prayer requests.

Being on our board personally has taught me the importance of prayer; the prerequisites, the power of prayer, and the need for perseverance in prayer. To God be the glory!

When God Moves Intercessors On

Instead of selfishly counting it our loss when God occasionally has called one of our board members to another job for Him, there is a wonderful kind of praying we have practiced. Gathering around her as she kneels, we lay hands on her and commission her to the new venture.

Rather than fretting about the cost of our loss, we've been amazed at how God has given us the joy of seeing Him take our practical prayer learning out to a mission field, into a new pastorate, or begin a teaching ministry through them. We have learned never to question a true call of God away from us. *It has been His way of multiplying His prayer training through the years.*

Barb seemed to have a special "hotline to heaven," and I highly prized her words from the Lord for me and the ministry. There was a powerful presence of God about her—when she entered a room, everything else stopped. Her downtown street ministry, prison meetings, and preaching were fantastic.

But the prayer was two ways. She had an incredibly hard life and needed our support too. She was mixed Jewish and Afro American, and though she had led her mother to the Lord, none of their other relatives had accepted Jesus as Messiah. As we have prayed for Barb, we have seen God start to break through in that awesome family—continuing to this day.

Barb's prayers for us and our prayers for her continue—while she is now ministering with her husband full-time at a powerful inner city ministry. And the circle of love has never broken. There are hugs of delight whenever we meet.

One of my greatest joys is to be needed by God to pray for those who are praying for me.

And we have continued to pray for each other—Liz to a great ministry in Alabama, Doreen to start prayer in her sphere of influence in a Western state, Peg to Iowa to become an extension of us, Mary to become a Bible Study Fellowship leader, Jeanne to multiple ministries, and Shirlee to Ethiopia, the Philippines, and West Africa. And the list goes on through our twenty-seven years.

No Longer Active

As one by one the original intercessors have aged or gone into assisted-care homes, our prayers for them have not ceased. But, more amazing, their prayers have not stopped for us either.

Viola was brought in a wheelchair to our last Christmas party. How wonderful for us to hug her now-frail body and listen to her pray. I have missed her insightful wisdom at board meetings. She would sit quietly listening to all the rest of us, and then, in a few words, she would sum it all up with profound wisdom that often seemed right from God Himself.

As I stooped over her wheelchair to give her a good-bye hug, she said, "Evelyn, every day I pray over and over for you. Three times one day last month the Lord said, *Pray for Evelyn*, and I prayed!"

Ninety-five-year-old Esther sent these words on her Christmas card, "I am sending a small check for Trans World Radio. It goes with my prayers for extension of God's kingdom. Am thinking of you, loving you, and praying for you and your ministry."

Julia was on the committee of my first prayer seminar, and she has been an unbelievably faithful pray-er and active board member ever since. Now that she can't get to every board meeting, especially in Minnesota's snow, she remains on the telephone prayer chain, undergirding the ministry with her powerful prayers.

God has shown us that the greatest untapped prayer potential for the Christian church is our "golden agers." They have awesome spiritual maturity, but, most of all, they have that fast-disappearing and desperately needed commodity—time.

God's Perspective on an Intercessor's Death

A few of our members have died through these long years. Our praying for those faithful intercessors is over. As deeply as we missed their seasoned advice and mature prayer power, God taught us a wonderful dimension to their years of prayers: *He keeps on answering as long as He needs to in order to accomplish all He desires with those prayers.*

Several board members' husbands have prayed faithfully with their wives. Retired Mary Lou and her husband used to spend a couple of hours a day in prayer—much of it for our ministry. Asked to speak at her husband's funeral, I looked at the grieving family in front of me and shared with them the wonderful secret He had taught us. "Your grand-father/father/husband was a tremendous prayer warrior. You will miss him greatly. But you won't miss the prayers he prayed for you, for God will keep on answering those prayers through the years. It doesn't matter to God if the one who prayed the prayer is now living in heaven with Him or still on earth with us." I was comforting them—and myself—in the loss of a great intercessor, but not a loss of God's answers.

When my own mother died at age ninety-one, I had just concluded a new book about how our prayers are kept by God in golden bowls in heaven (see Rev. 5:8). Since she had been my best prayer partner and by far for the longest time, I couldn't wait for her to read about where her prayers were. But just before getting that far in her reading of that book, God suddenly called her home with a massive stroke. My heart grieved that she had missed my tribute to her in the book—until God turned my sorrow into ecstasy. She was *seeing* the golden bowls of all her seventy years of awesome praying. *Intercessors' prayers are cumulative!*

My sister Maxine and her husband, Rudy, picked up Mother's mantle of prayer for me. They already had spent sometimes hours in prayer for me overseas and here, so they were adding this new dimension. A daughter also called to tell me she was taking up my mother's mantle of prayer God had laid on her. So the cycle goes on and on.

How Long, Lord Jesus, How Long?

How long must we struggle in prayer and pay the price to have victory over Satan?

Shouldn't becoming one of God's choice servants as an intercessor ensure smooth sailing—or at least most of the bumps of life being smoothed out? Didn't Jesus defeat Satan once and for all on the cross? *Why do we still need to pray—and to pray for those who are praying?*

Perhaps you have heard me share the following incident, but it is worth hearing again.

In Bangalore, India, my hostess's husband, who had been the United Nations' chief adviser on technology levels, energy systems, and productivity of their country, told me this true story at dinner one night. During the British colonial rule of India in the early 1900s, his father had been a senior officer for them and traveled extensively with his entourage of servants. The British had built houses in the jungles for them where there were no hotels.

Just south of Calcutta, a servant readying one of the houses rushed to his father, white as a sheet and mumbling incoherently. A huge python, capable of swallowing a whole goat or sheep—or human—was coiled under the table. Terrified, they quietly closed all the doors and windows while his father, he said, went to check his ammunition box. There was only one bullet powerful enough to kill a python of that size—if you struck the snake squarely in the head!

His father took very careful aim, fired, and hit the snake right in the head. But, to their amazement, the snake did not die. Crazed with that bullet in its head, the python violently coiled and uncoiled in powerful convulsions, completely smashing every piece of furniture and light fixture in the room. Then suddenly, after an hour and a half of terror, it crumpled to the floor—dead.

My host's father was quite a preacher, becoming the chancellor of a theological university upon retirement, and he explained it this way:

Just as we had only one bullet to kill the snake, so God also had just one bullet to kill the snake, Satan. God's single bullet was His own Son, Jesus Christ. According to Genesis 3:14–15, Satan's head was crushed when Christ conquered him on the cross: "And the LORD God said to the serpent, 'Because you have done this, cursed are you more than all cattle. . . . And I will put enmity between you and the woman, and between your seed and her seed [Jesus]; He shall bruise you on the head.'"

The fatal blow, said my host's father, has been dealt to the snake, Satan. At the cross, Satan was mortally wounded, and all the havoc and sorrow Satan is now causing on earth are only his convulsive death throes. The final end of Satan will come when Jesus comes back. It will take the second advent of Jesus for us to see the final end of Satan. The first advent accomplished all God intended. The fatal blow was struck. But not until Jesus comes back will all of Satan's thrashing and attacking cease!

Yes, we are living in that "hour and a half" when praying still is God's method of gaining daily victory over Satan. How exciting and encouraging to remember that this battle is only temporary—and that we already are on the winning side!

Reflection Questions

Examine your life:

What added hassles did you notice in your life when you became an intercessor in earnest? Did this surprise you since Jesus defeated Satan once and for all on the cross? Have fellow intercessors been praying for you during these times? Who?

Scripture:

Read Ephesians 6:10–20 prayerfully. Why do you think God had Paul put the admonition to pray for each other at the end of the spiritual battle with Satan's kingdom? Is there any indication of us falling instead of standing against Satan? Why not?

Did God commend your heart with "well done"—or reprove you while you read verses 19 through 20? Read those three again, asking God to speak to you about each word.

For you to do:

List the intercessors you have enlisted to pray for you—or those who are voluntarily praying because they support you. (Start list or add names as you now see necessary.)

Enlisted:_____

Voluntary: _____

For which of *them* have you prayed persistently and fervently?

_____

_____

Ask God which intercessors He wants you to pray for. Commit to Him that you will pray faithfully for the following people:

_____

_____

For You to pray:

"Holy Father, I praise You that our intercessory prayers are important enough to make Satan nervous. Thanks, too, that our prayers for each other are powerful enough to stand against his attacks. Lord, I promise to be faithful in my fervent praying for the intercessors You have put on my heart. Keep me alert to their needs. Fill me with the joy of bearing their burdens by praying for them. Thanks for the victory over Satan today and until Jesus comes back to reign. In Jesus' name, amen."

PART 3:

How God Tells Us What to Pray

CHAPTER 8

Listening to God Through His Word

ARE WE IN DANGER of replacing the most important method of communicating in the universe?

My head whirls trying to assimilate all the new communicating words—*Internet, e-mail, on-line, Web site*, and on and on and on. Are you, too, feeling drowned in this "Information Age"? Pitney Bowes, Inc. and the Institute for the Future found that the average U.S. office worker sends or receives 201 messages of all kinds each day.[1] Is what you are trying to get done constantly interrupted by electronic junk mail, voice mail, fax machines, cell phones, and pagers—that were supposed to make your life easier?

Both medical doctors, our daughter Jan and her husband, Skip, just talk into a computer, and it spits out their day's charts all printed. (I'm waiting to simply talk into my computer and watch it spit out books without all this hassle!)

My mother told us children how excited she was when around the turn of the century they installed a clumsy telephone receiver attached to a big box on their kitchen wall—and they could call their neighbors and the doctor.

Yes, we have learned to communicate since the Gutenberg printing press multiplied available knowledge twentyfold. The almost daily advertising for the new gadgets makes us know we are barely seeing the tip of the iceberg. But is our wisdom keeping up with our technology?

I have a deep concern. *With all this technology, we are absorbing only what other humans want us to know.* It can be true and beneficial information, or it can be hard-core pornography or outright lies. It can be honest financial help or a scam skimming off the life savings of the elderly. It can be somebody truly trying to be helpful or a child molester seducing a gullible adolescent. It is very frightening to think that the content of all this communicating is what people already know on a human level.

So how can we get wisdom to keep up with the technology? Fresh, absolutely reliable truth?

A Different Kind of Communicating Skill

There is another realm of information transfer that requires a different kind of communicating skill that is by far the most important in the universe: *listening to God.*

Why most important? Because what God says to us contains the answers to life's problems, the difference between right and wrong, and the safe steps into an unknown future. *The Person communicating with us is the omniscient, all-knowing, all-loving God—with specific instructions of information we never could hear from another human.*

"Oh, the depth of the riches both of the wisdom and knowledge of God! How unsearchable are His judgments and unfathomable His ways" (Rom. 11:33).

I shocked the students at a prestigious Christian college by telling them in their chapel that I had a secret of getting wisdom that not one of their professors could know. (I had their attention—and the raised eyebrows of their professors.) Then I told them that the great part of my secret was that it was transferable to them—because it was in the Bible, available to all of God's children.

Then I told them the secret that God told the prophet Jeremiah. If we use this kind of communicating with Him by calling on Him in prayer, God said He would show us "great and mighty things *which you do not know*" (Jer. 33:3 NKJV; emphasis added). He will show us things that are not on any Web site or any humanly produced information source.

I explained that we are then listening to the only One who always speaks absolute truth, who is pure and holy, who is always honest and never prejudiced, and who never makes a mistake in what He tells us because He alone knows the future and what wisdom or direction we need.

At a recent national committee meeting, the young marketing manager of one of the world's largest mission organizations said to me, "You must stay on this committee. You have such a loud voice." Taken aback, I tried to explain that it was from projecting to audiences for so long. But he countered, "No, no. We know *how* to communicate it, but you know *what* to say."

Puzzled, I spent many hours trying to figure out what he meant. Then it dawned on me: It was what I had heard from God in the countless hours of listening in my prayer closet that they were anxious to hear.

Why did that young executive think this senior citizen had something to say? Because more than fifty years ago, I learned that it is much more important to communicate vertically—with God in heaven—than to communicate on a horizontal level to people.

Perhaps I (and most of us) will never catch up with the increasingly sophisticated methods of modern communication. We may never be computer technicians, but he was voicing the desperate need for truthful, reliable, God-given content in communicating.

Our listening to God will never be replaced!

How Do We Communicate Vertically?

I believe that God initiates all prayer. Although there are many ways of praying, there are three special ways in which He is the instigator of our prayers.

These three ways of listening to God will be studied in this section: (1) listening to God through the Bible, (2) listening to God when He puts His thoughts directly into our minds, and (3) listening to God when we aren't even asking.

Of course, circumstances and needs prompt many of our prayer requests, and God surely listens to those. *But in these three methods we get our prayer content directly from the Father in heaven, assuring us that what we are praying for is fielded to us directly from His omniscient mind.*

In this chapter, we will study about God's telling us what to pray about from His Word.

Listening to God Through His Word

When we were on the brink of another knowledge explosion as people invaded outer space, there was great apprehension and even fear in America. The Russians had beaten us to outer space with their Sputnik launching with astronaut Yuri Gregarian in it!

Preparing to speak to my church ladies that day in 1961, I was kneeling in prayer early in the morning, asking God to give me what He wanted them to hear that day. But nothing came. Heaven seemed closed to me. Exasperated, I finally got up from my knees and went out to get the morning newspaper. The headlines screamed, "Russians Conquer Outer Space." President Eisenhower's front-page speech tried to calm and assure us. (Today having seen their Mir spaceship flounder, we see it differently. But then it was panic.)

Shaken, I picked up my Bible. (I already had lived through World War II with husband, Chris, as a bomber pilot, not knowing from day to day if I was a bride or a widow, since military v-mail took a couple of weeks.) That morning, God answered my prayer by saying to me to turn to Colossians 1. I did, and in verses 16 to 17, I read about Jesus, into whose kingdom we Christians have been transferred at salvation: "For by Him [Jesus] all things were created, both in the heavens and on earth, visible and invisible, whether thrones or dominions or rulers or authorities—all things have been created by Him and for Him. And He is before all things, and in Him all things hold together."

God then calmed my heart with, *Evelyn, it is not who conquers outer space but who created it and who holds it all together that counts.* I had my answer for that day—and for all future days—from God speaking to me out of His Word, the Bible.

We smile at that outdated happening now with our incredible photography of what may be the edge of space and what perhaps, they say, may be the beginning of the universe—along with our actual exploration of the moon by humans. But no matter how our technology advances, and no matter if we learn to travel easily to and populate other planets, we still will only be thinking God's thoughts *after Him.* He not only created and holds together everything we ever may discover, but also His omniscient mind figured it all out in the first place—whenever that was! Every law of physics that we haven't discovered yet, every physical law that may be different in various parts of the universe, every moral and spiritual law by which He runs humankind are His alone to reveal to us at His discretion—and in His time.

The secret is to keep as up-to-date on the content of *what* we say as it is to keep up-to-date on the new methods of *how* we say it.

How about you? *If things get out of hand on our Planet Earth with perhaps yet undiscovered forms of destruction or conquering of our country, where will you go for answers for yourself personally—and to help others?* Have you learned where to go to get the wisdom you may need in the future for your peace of mind transcending it all? God has it all for us—in His Word.

How Do We Get This Wisdom from God?

When I prayed, "Lord, change me—not my kids, not my husband," I meant it. But I didn't have any idea *how* God wanted to change me. So when asking Him in prayer, "Lord, how do I change?" He let me see His answer in James 1:5:

> If any of you lacks wisdom, let him ask of God, who gives to all liberally and without reproach (NKJV)

"If any of you lacks wisdom." The first ingredient in finding wisdom is acknowledging we don't have it. At a dinner party after a large seminar in the South, a recent college graduate was trying to look clever. "How smart are you?" he asked looking me right in the eye with a little smirk on his face. "If you don't tell us, I will—because I know." That's the best way I could think of to ruin a beautiful party. So I looked right back at him and said, "OK, I'll tell you how smart I am." His grin widened. "I'm smart enough to know I don't know, but (pointing toward heaven) I'm also smart enough to know Who does know. And I'm smart enough to listen to Him."

"Let him ask." I took God literally and spent fourteen months with only my Bible and God, seeking His wisdom for how He wanted me to change. I have the Bibles I have marked as God spoke to me since I was eighteen years old. And what had been true all those years exploded into a deluge of God's speaking to me those fourteen months.

God never coerces us. It is when we approach His holy Word with expectation, eagerly waiting to hear His voice through it, that we get His awesome, omniscient answers for our need.

"Of God." God never told us seeking human knowledge is wrong. But wisdom is not knowledge in itself. *Wisdom is information we apply that produces our character and our lifestyle.* The only safe source for something that vital is God Himself.

I call my United Prayer Ministry board my "prayer-and-advisory" board. Since 1973, they have given to me the scriptures God has given them for the ministry and me. And I have listened to them! My Bibles are dotted with their names by those verses. Sometimes I give them an assignment to seek advice from God, to listen in the Bible, and then to call me or to share at board meetings what He said. I take their answers from God.

My family also does the same thing. Their names also are here and there in my Bibles—beside a scripture God has given them for a specific time or need in my life. This has been especially true when I am overseas, and these verses are a very precious source of direction, security, and comfort to me. Just as I was leaving on every overseas ministry trip, I would call my mother from the last city in the United States to tell her goodbye. Her last words to me every time were, "Don't forget Ephesians 3:20!" And I would go with the assurance God was going to do those things "exceeding abundantly above all we could ask or think," which He always did because He had given it to Mother for me out of His Word.

"Who gives to all liberally." My Bibles, since I was eighteen, have gotten progressively more and more marked up. Now as I date and record what He says so liberally and what I say back to Him in the margin, I can barely squeeze in another word.

At a National Prayer Committee meeting in Washington, D.C., Glenn Sheppard, recently returned from an Asian country where He saw God do incredible miracles in answer to prayer, glanced at my open Bible and quipped, "That's the messiest Bible I ever have seen!" His grin was partly awe and partly a "good-for-you" smile.

At the National Day of Prayer on Capitol Hill in Washington, sponsored by our National Prayer Committee, a Jewish rabbi was to read from the Old Testament. Just before the program started with members of Congress present, a page came dashing over to Vonette Bright and me. "The rabbi doesn't have a Bible along. Could he please borrow one of yours?" Vonette said she didn't dare. Her notes were in hers, and she was on right after him. Well, it was my turn soon after her, but we knew the situation was desperate. Although I, too, had my notes in my Bible, I handed it over.

When the rabbi quickly leafed through some of my dog-eared, tear-stained Bible full of Post-It notes where no more conversations with God would fit, he turned around to catch my eye. Giving me a thumbs-up and a "way-to-go" grin, he turned to Isaiah, stood up, and read first in English and then in Hebrew God's Word from His prophet Isaiah to us. Vonette grabbed my hand and said, "Let's pray." And we whispered, asking God to speak to him through that Bible as He had to both of us through the years.

When our National Prayer Committee was young and had just a few of us back in the seventies, how precious it was as sometimes we would spend whole days with our Bibles open and praying what God was saying for each other. *I keep thinking what we may have lost by having to do so much modern horizontal communicating to keep up these days.*

"And without reproach." The only time God is displeased with us for asking is when He chides or thunders, *Don't ask! I already told you that! Where? In My written Word!* Of course, in that written Word it shockingly says in Proverbs 28:9, "He who turns his ear away from listening to the law, even his prayer is an abomination." So God expects us to ask—and to listen to Him.

But God has never said to me, *Are you back again? I gave you some wisdom yesterday!*

No, He can't wait to give us the next step when we've used what He gave the day before or the hour before. Sometimes I almost apologize for taking up so much of His time as I constantly bombard Him with questions and cries for help as I write. But my finite mind cannot comprehend the fact that His infinite mind can field all the questions from the whole world at the same time. *So He, unlike us, can give His undivided attention to each person reading His Word at once—and He does! What a God!*

The other day while checking something in one of those old marked-up Bibles, I suddenly clutched it to my breast and squeezed it while love for it swept over me and a couple warm tears trickled down my cheeks. *What an incredible treasure from God!*

What's So Great About the Bible?

The Bible is the only book on Planet Earth whose Author is always present while we are reading it. Most people clamor to get a best-selling author's autograph. *God is the Author of the world's all-time bestseller.* According to the December 29, 1999, issue of *USA Today*, the world's bestsellers are:

THE BIBLE	2 BILLION COPIES
Quotations from the Works of Mao Tse-tung	800 million copies
American Spelling Book by Noah Webster	100 million copies
The Guinness Book of Records	81 million copies
The McGuffey Readers	60 million copies

And our overwhelmingly top bestselling Author not only takes the time to speak to us individually through His Word, but He also stays around long enough to discuss it with us.

I had been reading a lovely children's Bible storybook to our seven-year-old grandson James. "Would you like one of these Bible books for Christmas?" I asked. "No, Grandma, I want a *real* Bible. You know, one that has Romans and Corinthians and all that stuff in it!" (He got his Bible for Christmas.)

Are we becoming a generation of spiritually poor Christians because we have substituted putting a few verses on an overhead screen in place of *physically* handling our Bibles? Touching, holding, writing in it, dating, and underlining what God says makes it the most precious possession I own.

When to Stop Reading

Reading the Bible will only become prayer when we stop reading and interact with the Author, God. That communicating with Him is prayer. It is not ceasing to read the Bible, but knowing when to stop to pray and apply it.

It was just three weeks before I was to go to South Africa to minister for a month during their violent terrorism just before apartheid rule was broken. Everyone seemed apprehensive about my going into that political upheaval, and some family members were sure I would not come back alive. I knew God had told me both blacks and whites should attend the prayer seminars together, and even my Sally, who had handled my traveling to many war-torn countries, would not order new books for our inventory, saying, "What's the use when Evelyn isn't even coming back?"

In the midst of their fears, I was reading the first chapter of Revelation. Suddenly, tears filled my eyes. My heart seemed to skip a beat. There it was—God speaking to me through His written Word.

I had just read John's overwhelming description of the glorified Christ and John falling as a dead man at His feet. And then Jesus laid His hand on John and said, "Do not be afraid; I am the first and the last, and the living One; and I was dead, and behold, I am alive forevermore, and I have the keys of death and Hades" (Rev. 1:17–18).

Tears ran down my face as I cried, "Oh, dear Jesus, would You lay your hand on me?" And I knew He had. I had the positive assurance from Him that even with the terrorism, *He was the One who had the keys of my death.*

It was awesome to see the blacks and whites already on the same telephone prayer chains, and even greater to see that the whole body of Christ could, and did, worship and study together in love. And I was safe!

Expect the Unexpected

God's Word in 2 Timothy 3:16 (KJV) tells us four things that Scripture is good for:

All scripture is given by inspiration of God, and is profitable for *doctrine*, for *reproof*, for *correction*, for *instruction in righteousness*. (emphasis added)

God has given all of them abundantly to me through the years. Always open to His speaking while I read the Bible, *I have come to expect the unexpected.*

"*Doctrine.*" I expected to learn doctrine when I studied the Bible, but it is an unexpected thrill when God suddenly shows me a new-to-me truth. It was never a surprise when over and over He confirmed in my heart what I already believed. But it was totally unexpected when God would stop me on something I had been taught that wasn't exactly the way He had said it.

"*Reproof.*" Although I am always aware that there are things in my life that are not pleasing to God, I never am expecting it when He stops me while reading the Bible. And His calling the attitudes, priorities, reactions in me that violate His holiness *sin* sends me to my knees begging, "Oh, Father, please forgive me!"

"*Correction.*" This means God is telling us to turn around in our thinking or actions, so it usually is coupled with one of the others. It is in prayer that I submit and make commitments to His unexpected advice. However, it is in my actions that I apply what He has said—and am corrected!

"*Instruction in righteousness.*" As I look back, I am amazed to see that God has called me to new ministry opportunities through stopping me when I was reading devotionally. He has revealed what He wanted me to do according to His plan for me, not mine.

The first major instruction for ministry in my life came when I was reading Revelation 3:8 devotionally one morning as a pastor's wife in Rockford, Illinois. A large two-year national campaign planning to pray for and evangelize the United States had asked me to find out in six months' time exactly what happens when women pray. Not having a clue how to conduct such an experiment, I was stalling—until God stopped me on His words, "Behold, I have set before you an open door." I knew I had my answer. I went to prayer, promising God I would obey His call. Then I immediately phoned headquarters and accepted the task.

What I thought was a six-month task turned out to be a lifelong calling from God all around the world. I shudder to think what I would have missed if I hadn't been willing to listen to God as He spoke so powerfully to me and to respond to His words.

The next ministry opening came when I had left all the praying in that church and moved with my husband to St. Paul, Minnesota. While reading devotionally, 1 Timothy 4:6 suddenly almost jumped off the page at me: "In pointing out these things to the brethren, you will be a good servant of Christ Jesus." Knowing I deeply wanted to be a good servant of Christ, I looked in the previous verses to see what "these things" were. The very first verse of chapter 4 explained it: "But the Spirit explicitly says that in later times some will fall away from the faith, paying attention to deceitful spirits and doctrines of demons." This was not studying doctrine *about* demons; it was the doctrine *of* demons!

I certainly was not expecting that calling. Actually I was totally unaware that the problem even existed, much less that God would expect me to do something about it. *But I prayed a deep prayer of submission that morning, telling God I would do it—whatever it was.*

To my surprise, I started getting invitations to speak on the subject from Christian schools, several colleges, and many youth group leaders—all concerned about the experimenting with séances, levitation, calling forth Mary Worth in school mirrors, Ouija boards, and unbelievable supernatural things among their Christian youth. I never learned where those invitations came from. Most of them were strangers to me. And I certainly had not told them! But it was God calling me through His written Word to teach the next generation about dabbling in those supernatural things He calls an "abomination" (Deut. 18:12 KJV). And seeing the students' repentance evidenced by bonfires burning their paraphernalia and even destroying their satanic music made it all worthwhile to have listened, although reluctantly at first, to God in His Word.

Then it was time for another unexpected calling. I was feeling sorry for myself because all the wonderful "What Happens When Women Pray" life had been left behind in Rockford, Illinois—or so I thought. While still busy putting out the occult brushfires, once again I was reading devotionally. This time it was when Paul wrote to young Timothy telling him to "stir up the gift of God which is in you" (2 Tim. 1:6 NKJV). God firmly admonished me. Confused, I foolishly asked Him, "What gift?" His pronouncement startled me. "Prayer, of course!"

Somehow I had thought that original experimenting was all there was to the call. Then a church in White Bear Lake, Minnesota, called and wanted me to teach a six-week series on prayer. It soon became obvious it was a prayer seminar, so we renamed it "What Happens When Women Pray."

In the midst of the last almost thirty years of prayer ministry around the world, God added another call through His Word. While reading the account of Jesus calling Saul on the Damascus road "to bear My name before the Gentiles, and kings, and the sons of Israel" (Acts 9:15), I suddenly felt an overwhelming call of God. We already were averaging 25 percent of attendees in my seminars here and abroad praying to make sure Jesus was their Savior and Lord. But this was something more. My recorded prayer in the margin of my Bible says, "6/7/89 Oh Jesus, I want to tell the whole world of *You*. Bring back *Jesus* to our churches. Please, Lord!"

That was nineteen months before I received the call from Lorry Lutz to become the North American director of the AD2000 Christian Women United, designed to reach the world with prayer and Jesus by the end of the year 2000. God had prepared me with a special burden for the task. He knew I would soon be writing the curriculum *A Study Guide for Evangelism Praying* for the women around the world. All because He spoke directly to me—while I was reading His Word.

Dear reader, what might you be missing if you are not reading His Word—not to see how much you can read in a day or a year, not to study it for your students—but just for yourself? Just for being open to the sovereign God of heaven calling you to help Him fulfill His plan for this earth?

For Me Personally

All of God's speaking to me through His words, giving me the content of my prayers has not been only for ministry to other people. *The vast majority of them have been for me personally.* How I would love to share all the thousands of them with you. (When writing my book *Lord, Change Me!*, I spent a whole month cutting down from the ones I had selected—when the editor and I decided that book should cover other topics too! See that book for those we did leave in.) Here is just a little speck:

When I turned seventy, my body was getting tired from a full-time international ministry. But my birthday prayer from God was Philippians 2:13: "For it is God who is at work in you, both to will and to work for His good pleasure." It was God telling me that *I* was not doing it anyway and that He would continue giving everything I needed for the next year. With stunned tears in my eyes, God told me that He was just using me. He was doing 100 percent of the work. "Thank You, Lord," I humbly and gratefully prayed. He kept His promise, and I found it incredibly true—as I launched the North America Women's track for AD2000 and wrote its international curriculum that year.

The next year I felt so very alone. My support team for our AD2000 track was gone—Sally Hanson, our secretary/treasurer, to Arizona and Kathryn Grant, my co-chair, to minister in Japan. Reminding the Lord that they did the things I cannot do, God sent me to Philippians 4:13 for my birthday verse early: "'I can do all things through Him who strengthens me." It was exactly twenty-five years to the day when I had started His *What Happens When Women Pray* project. Assuring me with the "I" pronoun, I knew I could do it.

But God quickly added that I must build it on last year's birthday verse of Philippians 2:13 of His doing all the work. An amazing confidence swept over me. I could do it simply because it was God doing it in me. A new resolve tightened in my stomach area. *Yes, I can do it—and I did—because He is actually doing it in me!*

Arriving in Japan the first time, I was terrified. I didn't have a clue how to reach the Asian mind. I had brushed up on bowing as you hand your calling card—never across the table but walking around it, etc. But the night before the first seminar I panicked. I felt like my body was literally shaking. Upon my opening my Bible where I was reading devotionally, God powerfully said to me in Psalm 16:8: "Because He [God] is at my right hand, I will not be shaken."

Taking Him at His word, I stood up to speak with my translator from America, Chiko Templeman, standing on my left side. Then I said that, although they could only see two people, actually there were three on that stage. Chiko, myself, and the God of the universe, whom the night before had promised to be on my right hand. And He would tell me what to say, I would say it, and Chiko would translate it for them into Japanese. Immediately the audience was at attention. And God miraculously moved in our midst. I repeated that introduction every time on our whole tour, and at the end the pastors and missionaries who had invited me asked, "How did you ever figure out the Asian mind like that?" "I didn't," I said. "God told me—when I was reading Psalm 16:8."

Retreats and Seminars

We have a little exercise for hearing God speak to us through His Word that we practice in seminars and retreats with amazing results. Virtually no one earnestly seeking to have God speak ever has been disappointed. Sending them out in absolute silence to read (unless they have something more important than God has to say to that person), I assign the same portion to everybody.

The formula for the exercise is simple. After asking God to remove all our preconceived ideas and to show us His relevant and true words for that day or specific need, I send them off alone to do the following:

Read until God speaks. How will He speak? By His making something stand out on the page, by our feeling a little "uh, oh" at some specific words, by God's bringing the exact comfort or wisdom we needed right then, or perhaps by God's thundering at the words that reveal a sin in our lives.

Stop. This may be the most important part of the formula. We tend to give ourselves brownie points for reading on and on (and at other times there are reasons for doing that). But actually we can only really deal with God on one point at a time. So we stop for a very important next step.

Pray. We then interact with the Bible's Author's, who has just spoken to us—God. This is asking God questions, having Him give us understanding, and most important, making a promise to Him to obey what He has said.

Write God a letter. We ask the participants to write a letter to God, confirming what He has said to us and what we have promised Him, addressing it to themselves. The committee then mails it back to the writer in about a month for a personal checkup to see if it was merely an emotional promise or a genuine, life-changing commitment.

Still in silence, they return and gather in small groups to share with each other what God said to each of them. When I say "go," the noise almost lifts the ceiling. I do not know if it is staying silent for an hour or, as I believe it is, their exploding at God having actually spoken to them personally through His written Word, many for the very first time!

Gary Smalley had come out of seminary to be our church's associate pastor, and he had asked me to run this kind of a fall kick-off retreat for the paid and volunteer Christian education staff. We laugh now at how, with all of his new degrees, he wanted to work out an outline of what they were to look for. "That would wreck the whole thing," I said firmly.

At that retreat I assigned Galatians 5:1–6:10. Then I explained that they would not get any instructions from us but were to listen to God telling them each something of His plans for the Christian education department in the coming year. When we came back together, we made a large circle, knelt, and each prayed sharing what God had said. Soon we were all weeping, and my senior pastor husband and Gary, kneeling side by side at a davenport, were sobbing. *God had told us all the same thing. "Let the Holy Spirit do more leading in the education department of this church!"* Wow!

I also have seen many marriages healed at retreats as husbands and wives have read and prayed separately what He said to them each while alone with the Lord. Then they have come back to pray together sharing what God told each of them needed to change in their own lives. God gives infallible instructions from His Word!

Our United Prayer Ministry's annual board prayer retreat in June 1991 turned out to be awesome. What God had planned through His speaking none of us could have imagined. It was an incredible step in His sovereign, amazing plan.

We were reading about Jesus telling the cost of being His disciple in Luke 14:25–35, stopping most of us on verse 27: "Whoever does not carry his own cross and come after Me cannot be My disciple."

As we gathered back to share with each other what God had said, Karalee, our board secretary, wept and prayed these words: "Count the cost, and then seek the lost!" I recorded them in my Bible that day.

Just three years later, Karalee's husband, Paul, was crushed to death in an accident—between two trucks. In church the Sunday after he was crushed, as the pastor read the prophecy about Jesus from Isaiah 53, which God spoke to Karalee in verse 5: "But He was pierced through for our transgressions, He was crushed for our iniquities."

God revealed to Karalee that it was His will for His Son to be crushed—so that He could save the world through His death. He had not been out of control. It was God saying this scripture was for her—as she was left with a family to raise alone. I have watched Karalee through it all sitting serenely in board meetings, visible peace on her face while we all wrestled and prayed.

God kept His promise for her family. Her three children's hearts turned to serving the Lord in different stages of preparation. One daughter already has traveled to China with a Christian music and drama team and is now in Youth with a Mission's School of the Bible. At the same time, Karalee, with grit and faith in God, has finished a master's degree in counseling and psychological services. She now is a part of a very fine Christian counseling service. Her Christmas letter, after saying she will do whatever the Lord leads her to do in service to Him—until Jesus' coming back or being called home—concluded with: "In the meantime He has given us His Word and His Holy Spirit to guide us through this earthly life."

At that Luke 14 retreat in 1991, I prayed confirming that God had said the same thing to me that day also. But it was just another step in that scriptural portion for me. In 1988, I already had recorded in the margin of my Bible by Luke 14:27, "No matter what the cost, I will finish what God would have me to do—*win the lost.*"

Even before that, however, while reading in Luke 14 in 1982, God had stopped me on verse 33: "So therefore, no one of you can be My disciple who does not give up all his own possessions." It was just days before I was to leave for my first trip to India. We had waited for ten years for grandbabies. Our daughter Nancy had just had Cyndi, and Jan was overdue waiting for Jenna. I cried to the Lord, "Does this mean I have to give up my grandbabies too?" He said yes.

I wept. The grief was so deep—until I read further. God stopped me—on 15:7, where Jesus said, "I tell you there will be more joy in heaven over one sinner who repents than over ninety-nine righteous persons who need no repentance." My prayer changed to "Oh, God, exchange the joy of holding new grandbabies to the joy of seeing one sinner come to Jesus in India!" I wrote to both those wee ones from India, "God answered Grandma's prayer. Thousands are accepting Jesus at our meetings in India!"

Have I found the Bible to be sufficient for all the traveling alone overseas, all the lost babies—and the ones who lived to bring eight wonderful grandchildren into my life?

Have I found God's Word capable of answering all my questions during my own and my family's debilitating diseases; surgeries, including my husband's for cancer; and some much too personal to share? Have I found it adequate to supply all my needs? Oh yes. *God's Word is not only adequate, but also surprisingly, thrillingly, overwhelmingly abundant!*

How can you get what to pray about from God? Just take time to listen to what He says directly to you from what He already has written down in His incredible Word, the Bible—and start praying.

Reflection Questions

Examine your heart:

Take an honest inventory of your life this past week. How many hours were spent listening to other humans on TV, radio, your computer, at school, the theater, chatting, reading, being instructed?

[_____hours].

How many hours did you spend listening to God in the Bible and in prayer?

[_____hours].

What percentage of your wisdom did you get from humans?

[__%].

From God?

[_____%]

Does your answer seem to suggest a better balance in horizontal versus vertical communicating might be wise?

Scripture:

Read Romans 11:33–36 in your own Bible if possible. In what ways is God, the world's all-time best selling author, superior and thus more trustworthy to produce your wisdom for living than any human? Think of some of the awesome divine input in your life you may be missing by your percentage of horizontal (with people) rather than vertical (with God) communicating.

For you to do:

Since Romans 12 begins with a "therefore," it is referring back to what you just read in chapter 11. Because of who God just told you He is, read chapter 12 expectantly to see what God will say to you personally. Stop immediately when you feel He has, and interact with Him in prayer about it. Write God a letter, recording where He stopped you, why you think He did, and what you promised Him you will change in your thinking and actions because of what He said to you.

"Dear Heavenly Father: _____

_____

_____."

For you to pray:

"My holy, holy God, I bow humbly before You in deep adoration of who You are. Thank You for teaching me the importance of listening to Your infinite wisdom instead of only human input. I promise to keep listening to You in the Bible, praying and applying what You say every day and until I, too, prove that Your Word is not only sufficient, but surprisingly, thrillingly and overwhelmingly abundant. In Jesus' precious name, amen."

CHAPTER 9

Listening to God's Thoughts to Us

ONE OF THE MOST amazing aspects of prayer God taught us that He does when we pray is that *He frequently answers our prayer requests by putting His thoughts directly into our minds.*

When we are praying, God incredibly responds to our requests by this method. How thrilling it is when God answers our questions or requests by answering, not with written or audible words, but by putting His thoughts into our minds.

It is not some weird process for the spiritually elite; it is God's gift to every Christian willing to be still long enough to give Him time to answer. This wonderful method has grown and grown as my intercessors and I, and those I teach, have practiced this together.

God's putting His thoughts into our minds like this usually takes place when we are already praying. God responds to what we have asked of Him.

On our first trip to Israel, I was deeply in prayer in the Garden of Gethsemane. An infection had kept me from hiking there with the tour group, so they sent me on ahead by taxi. Sitting under an old olive tree during my hour's wait, my heart broke as I read Luke's account of Jesus being arrested—in that very garden. I wept at His being beaten, mocked, spit upon, forced to carry his cross, jeered at, nailed to that cross, and then dying in agony—all for me. I bowed deeply, grieving in prayer until I thought I could not stand it. "Oh, God," I shuddered, "how could this be?"

179

Suddenly there was a voice. It was God's! *But there's victory over this place!* I almost thought I heard it ringing like iron striking iron, resounding among the trees. But it was God's thoughts to my heart—reverberating as clearly as if it had been audibly shouted. It immediately lifted my sorrow and turned my weeping into joy. And I knew my Jesus was not there, or dead—but risen and reigning supreme at the right hand of the Father. *The Father whose thoughts had just penetrated my grieving soul!*

God's Thoughts?

For years, I wondered if this prayer process really was scriptural. I knew it worked for me, but I'm a stickler for having a biblical basis for what I think—and much more for what I teach. But in October 1992, His words in Psalm 139:17–18 almost jumped off the page as I read them:

> How precious also are Thy thoughts to me, O God! How vast is the sum
> of them! If I should count them, they would outnumber the sand.

I read it over and over, carefully examining the wording and asking God to show me the accuracy and truth of what I was seeing. Yes, the psalmist definitely had said it was precious that *God's thoughts were coming to the psalmist,* not simply that God's thoughts were precious. So I knew God's thoughts coming to me also could be precious.

Here are some insights on God's thoughts:

"How precious." Listening silently for His response when I have come to Him with a question or a need is one of the most precious sides of my prayer life. My heart leaps at His voice as I have waited, expectantly, for an answer to my request. A spontaneous thrill wells up within me, and I feel wrapped in His holy presence every time it happens. *God is speaking to me!*

"Thy thoughts." Knowing humans never could comprehend His mind, God explained His thoughts to Isaiah to record for us: "'For My thoughts are not your thoughts, neither are your ways My ways,' declares the LORD. 'For as the heavens are higher than the earth, so are My ways higher than your ways, and My thoughts than your thoughts'" (Isa. 55:8–9).

The actual thoughts of God are far above our understanding, infinitely higher and greater than any thoughts we could think up in our own finite minds. Yet He showers them freely upon us when we ask.

"To me." That the God of heaven would bother to take His time to speak to me, a mere human, instead of enjoying and giving full attention to the angels of heaven who are adoring and praising Him is beyond my understanding. How could He stoop to listen and then take the time to field the answer to me—right when I am asking? "Oh, God, there is no way to understand Your love, Your caring, Your interest in me! But thanks, dearest Father!"

"How vast is the sum of them." How could the God who has all the wisdom and knowledge of the universe lavish them on me? "Oh, God, I bow humbly at your feet, so unworthy. Yet so grateful!"

"When I consider Thy heavens, the work of Thy fingers, the moon and the stars which Thou hast ordained; what is man that Thou dost take thought of Him?" (Ps. 8:3).

With six billion people on Planet Earth, how could this God—who keeps track of every hair on every head with everybody losing and growing so many new ones each day—take time to respond to our asking Him questions? But that's how much He cares for you and me! But I have found that not only is He willing, but also He is actually eager, even anxious, to give me His thoughts.

"They would outnumber the sand." We've vacationed every summer for fifty years in the sand dunes on the shores of Lake Michigan, hiking the vast sand beaches, climbing the huge sand dunes, and occasionally getting our boat hung up on a shifting sand bar. I feel with the psalmist that all of God's thoughts to me through all these years far exceed even that much of the world's sand. Trying to number them for this book, I threw up my hands and cried, "I can't, Lord. There are no human words to describe the gargantuan number of what You have said to me."

Right When I Need Them Most

Everything was set for my prayer training in the restricted states of India, but I could not get a visa. Everything was tried by that country's organizers and our organizers, with much fervent prayer by both groups. Time had almost run out when, in desperation, I pleaded with God for help. Suddenly two surprising words shot into my mind from Him: *Call Chicago!* I searched for Chicago's India consulate office phone number, dialed, and was confronted with the question, "Why would you want to go *there?*"—as if it were the most undesirable place in the world. "To teach prayer," I meekly replied. Never questioning what *kind* of prayer, he immediately said, "I'll get you in!" And the Chicago-issued visa arrived just hours before my plane left.

We tried in vain to add the New Delhi permission for more than a week while I ministered there, knowing that it was advisable to get it. But lines ended with the person in front of me and every door slamming before we ever got to present my case. So I flew to that restricted state using my Chicago visa. Interrogating me under glaring lights when I finally got off the plane, the officials decided to let me stay, restricting me to just their capital city. It was only when a doctor called New Delhi trying to get permission for me to come to her house outside the city limits that the person yelled over the phone, "What's she doing *there?* That's illegal! Who gave her a visa?" "No, it's not illegal. It was your Chicago office in America, sir." Since there was only one plane a week and all the roads out had been bombed in a recent uprising, I had to stay. Once I dashed to my hostess reporting a man with a gun behind a bush outside my window. "We were not going to tell you," she said softly. "That's your police protection!" *But God wanted me there!*

All but one of their restricted states sent women leaders to learn evangelism praying, sleeping on the floor and eating their native food. They took the books, videos, and tapes back home to start prayer ministries where I never could get a visa to go—all because God answered my prayer of desperation by putting that far-out thought in my mind: *Call Chicago!*

Not All Are That Serious

All real needs are not that dramatic. Our AD2000 Christian Women United had taken over the Wheaton College campus for a long weekend last summer. My co-chair, Kathryn, was still in Japan, and Mary Lance Sisk, who was to kick off her new *Love Your Neighbor* material, suddenly was ordered into surgery for a seriously corroded ceratoid artery. Frantically trying to reschedule speakers with arrival and departure flights, timings, etc., I absolutely could not get to a store to buy a desperately needed speaking dress. (I had gone down several sizes on orders of my cardiologist, and nothing fit!) And I had told God so in prayer.

I had taken a few minutes out to read God's Word and to pray to replenish my empty emotional reservoir, when suddenly God said perhaps the most shocking words He ever has put in my mind: *Shut your Bible and go to the David Edwins store!*

I laid aside my Bible and drove to a store I'd never been in. Then the real surprise came. The window display was filled with summer dresses, all with appliqués of lighthouses (our theme was lighting your environment with Jesus, as part of Mission America's Lighthouse Movement). And in my best color! I went inside and immediately found the two that would get me through the weekend in style. *All because God replaced the reading of His Word with His thought to me—to fill my urgent need.*

When Speaking

At a retreat in Minnesota's northern lakes district, I had carefully worked out each session's speaking topic. Just as I was ready to get up to speak, God suddenly put a powerful command into my mind. *Change your topic to praying in My will.* Stunned, I stumbled up to the platform mentally laying aside my prepared speech, while I tried to form at least a three-point general outline in my mind. But God hadn't intended to leave me stranded when obeying His abrupt thought to me. He brought every point and every scripture in the order He wanted—while He moved mightily in the crowd.

But what I couldn't have known was that following me was a testimony by a young woman broken by what had happened in her life. The crowd reached out to her in immediate empathy, understanding God's teaching on His incredible attitude toward it from His Word I had just taught. Then God poured out His power on that retreat—melting, transforming, and uniting us all. No carefully prepared message ever could have done what God did by putting those simple words in my mind. "Thanks, God—for that surprising thought!"

For years, God and I have had a running agreement about His and my words when I speak. I have promised Him I'll stay open to His putting His thoughts into my mind during a speaking session—even if it isn't in my carefully prepared notes. I'll be flexible!

In my opening prayers before beginning to teach, I usually renew that agreement. In front of those who expect to hear from me, I clearly ask God to put into my mind only those thoughts He wants me to say. Then I trust Him for the grace to be able to ignore all my prepared notes that I had thought were so important.

And He takes me up on that promise almost every time I stand in front of an audience. The best part, however, is that almost always some attendee will come to me and say of the whole day's teaching, "That one thing was a life-changing point for me. It's just what I needed." And I hadn't even thought of it! But God had! *And He, not I, knows the answer to the needs of every person in the audience. My part is to listen— and to obey.*

His Thoughts Just for Me

My first recollection of God's thoughts coming directly when I was bewildered and sad was when we lost our third pregnancy. After a miscarriage and a full-term stillborn, I was now in the hospital losing the battle to keep the third baby—when we were so anxious to start a family since my husband had been in the air force in World War II so many years. So, lying there, in prayer I was questioning God with my puzzled, "Why?"

Then God put His answer into my mind—as clearly as if He had written it on the hospital wall. *It's Romans 8:28!* That was all. God knew He didn't have to quote it. I knew it by heart and hung on to that promise through those dark hours: "We know that God causes all things to work together for good to those who love God, to those who are called according to His purpose."

I not only had His immediate answer, but I also understood that with those three children, my dad an invalid, and my father-in-law suddenly dying and leaving a small brother and sister we were partially responsible for, I never could have gone back to college and Chris to seminary to prepare for God's calling on our lives. But I also had my "philosophy of life" that has never failed until this day—that God is working out everything for my good. All because of God's thoughts to me!

I still frequently ask Him where He wants me to read devotionally each day, not necessarily following some preconceived reading plan. Through the years He has put the name of a book of the Bible, a place on a page, or some specific written word of His. And they always turn out to be incredible insight into what is going on, or will be, in my life right then.

This book would fill ten volumes if I were to list every time God put His thoughts directly into my mind when I was asking. It is one of the major ways He has taught me not to lean on my own understanding. "Trust in the LORD with all your heart, and lean not on your own understanding. In all your ways acknowledge Him, and He shall direct your paths" (Prov. 3:5–6 NKJV).

His Thoughts to Me for Others

When I write, I record what God has said, not just for me personally, but also what He wants said to others through me. Every book, tape, or message I have produced has not been thought up by myself, but has originated from God Himself. I know that I don't know, so I beg Him to tell me only His thoughts for every subject in every book. And I wait in prayer for each thought from Him. *That's why the pencil copy of every point comes in my prayer closet.* Then I go to my computer (or old electric typewriter when I first started) and put it in its final form. *But it is all directly from Him.*

When I can't think of the correct word to type, the tendency is to scan back and forth in my brain like a computer screen, searching for it. But I've learned the fantastic secret of waiting for God's thoughts, and a feeling of relief breaks out in the pit of my stomach when I remember to put it into practice. Deliberately relaxing, I ask God to put His exact words into my mind. The smile spreads to my face when I type in His Word, His thoughts to me, on my computer!

I have a sign over my computer that says, "Come, Holy Spirit, Breathe on me." God the Father, God the Son, and God the Holy Spirit are one—the triune Godhead. One of the jobs of the Holy Spirit is to recall what God or Jesus has said to us previously (see John 14:26). But this is a different step. This is God putting *new thoughts* from Him into our minds—when we ask.

Teaching Silence in Prayer Groups

The "silent periods" of our 6S prayer method somehow seem less important than the others like "subject by subject," "short prayers," "simple prayers," "specific requests noted and dated," and "small groups usually are best." Those were things we could *do*. But *not doing*? That was harder to grasp—and to practice.

Pray-ers start shuffling their feet, flipping in their Bibles, or looking through their notes when there's a lull in the praying. Nervous little coughs or clearing of throats spread as if they were contagious. Somehow we have been programmed in our culture to think we are not doing anything if we are silent. *However, the silent times between audible prayer requests are God's times to speak.* His time to get us back on track with His priorities for us to pray about. His time to tell us a request that never entered our heads. Or He may desperately want to give us an immediate answer to that for which we just had been begging.

But We Must Listen

But this fantastic process of God putting His thoughts directly into our minds does not work if we are not listening.

How easy it is to come to Him with our requests and then jump up from our knees and dash off so fast God can hardly catch us. But it is in the waiting in silence, disciplining our minds not to hop to the next thought or our bodies to the next activity, that we hear *Him* speak.

Also we have found it is easier to talk *at* God than to listen to Him. This is much better than not praying at all, but it falls so short of the riches of heaven He has ready to pour out to us when we give Him a chance.

Also learning the wonderful art of having a two-way conversation *with* Him is very good and is a great part of what prayer really is. But learning to have the patience and grace not to say anything after we have asked for an answer is absolutely awesome. We suddenly are hearing the mind of God. *We are listening, uninterrupted, to the God of the Universe, the eternal God of the past, the present, and the future.*

Not Just Pondering

We must constantly stay alert to what we think is praying when it is only pondering. Unless God is putting His thoughts into the process some way, the thoughts will be only our own. "I have spread out My hands all day long to a rebellious people, who walk in the way which is not good, following their own thoughts" (Isa. 65:2).

Pondering is mulling something over and over in our minds, rehearsing, cogitating, and rethinking our own thoughts and solutions. This process is good. My father, a state highway contractor for many years, had his whole day figured out before he got out of bed—because he had thoroughly pondered every step of the upcoming day. But it was only two years before he died that he accepted Jesus and discovered the best of that process—letting God add His thoughts to the pondering. As an invalid, my father sat through many days with his Bible open, letting God both speak through it and give His thoughts to him. *Pondering turns into prayer only when we include God's thoughts with ours.*

Four Sources of Wisdom

Not every thought that pops into our heads is from God. The Book of James warns us that not all wisdom is from above, from God, but has three other possible sources. A life full of bitter jealousy and selfish ambition produces disorder and every evil thing, in contrast to God's wisdom, which produces purity, peace, gentleness, is reasonable, full of mercy and good fruits, unwavering, and without hypocrisy. James says,

> This wisdom does not descend from above [from God], but is *earthly* [from other people], *sensual* [from within our fleshly selves], *demonic* [from Satan's kingdom through demons] (James 3:15 NKJV; emphasis added).

These three false sources of wisdom are constantly vying to have input in us that will control our lives. The Bible warns us about all of these other sources other than God to which we listen and get false advice for living—producing what we do.

Earthly wisdom. This is the constant, unrelenting barrage of communicated suggestions that pellet us from every direction, trying to change us into a composite of their messages. Romans 12:2 warns us not to be *conformed* to this world, but to be transformed into God's will for us. Peter tells us to "gird up the loins of your mind" so you will not live according to your former lusts before you became a Christian—which are bombarding you from every side.

As a former college psychology professor and I were waiting for the convention's autograph line to begin, we were chatting about the books each of us had spoken on during that convention. "You won't like my book, Evelyn," he said. When I asked him why, he said, "Because I have better answers and solutions in this book than the Bible has." "You're right! I won't like your book!" I retorted firmly.

My heart broke as I watched attendees going home with both books—one desperately trying to say only what is truth from God, and the other proudly displaying a man's human improvement on God. What kind of arrogance, I wondered, would produce that book when God is much more than a trillion times smarter than all the humans put together. I wondered how much prayer had gone into writing that so-called Christian book.

"See to it that no one takes you captive through philosophy and empty deception, according to the tradition of men, according to the elementary principles of the world, rather than according to Christ" (Col. 2:8).

Sensual wisdom. The thoughts that come from our fleshly selves are not very beautiful according to Jesus in Mark 7:21–23: "For from within, out of the heart of men, proceed evil thoughts, adulteries, fornications, murders, thefts, covetousness, wickedness, deceit, lasciviousness, an evil eye, blasphemy, pride, foolishness" (KJV). Jesus did not think much of sensual wisdom. No matter how great we think our own wisdom for running our lives is, we may be only deceiving ourselves. It is shocking that Proverbs 12:15 says that "the way of a fool is right in his own eyes."

Demonic wisdom. The Bible warns in 1 Timothy 4:1: "The Spirit explicitly says that in later times some will fall away from the faith, paying attention to deceitful spirits and doctrines of demons." In our "What Happens When Women Pray" seminars, one of the prerequisites we teach to having prayer power is, *Make sure it is God to whom you have drawn nigh.* Satan is a liar and the father of lies, the deceiver.

God's wisdom. But then there is that absolutely true, always dependable, for-our own-good wisdom from God. It is given to us in myriad ways, but God's putting His divine thoughts directly into our minds—when we ask Him—is definitely one of the best!

Is there an answer to this bewildering morass of voices? Yes. *Test it by the Bible.* God will never put any thought in your mind that is contrary to His printed instructions. Advice from the other three is only as good as *their* source. If their wisdom is from God and true to His Word, then it is safe. But all other unbiblical advice is to be shunned. It can be very dangerous.

God's Reasons

God has put His thoughts into my mind in every kind of experience I have gone through in my long walk with Him, and they are as varied as the circumstances prompting them.

As a pastor's wife with small children, I was producing Sunday-school material weekly, speaking on program committees' assigned topics, teaching an evangelism Bible study every week, and fulfilling all the then-demanded duties of a pastor's wife to attend every meeting any-body else might be expected to attend. My refuge was running to God to hear His voice. It would be like being back in the Garden of Eden walking hand in hand with Him—before Adam and Eve's sin broke that beautiful communion.

There was a song God used when my life seemed to be closing in. I would sink onto the piano bench, and the stress would melt away as I softly played and sang:

I come to the garden alone, while the dew is still on the roses;
And the voice I hear, falling on my ear; the Son of God discloses.
And He walks with me, and He talks with me, and He tells me I am His own.
And the joy we share as we tarry there, none other has ever known.[1]

Last night, those feelings engulfed me again as I waited in silence while God kept pouring into my mind more and more of what He wanted me to say in this chapter—reminding me of so many of *His thoughts to me*. Suddenly it was there again. I sang that song over and over in my mind.

God was so close, I felt I almost could reach out and put my hand in His. So close His thoughts just naturally flowed into me. So close I kept wiping warm, sweet, grateful tears. God's thoughts—to me!

Reflection Questions

Examine your life:

Do you basically pray *at* God, or have you learned the incredible thrill of having Him put His thoughts into your mind and heart in answer to your prayers? Have you been limiting God in your prayer life by not listening because you thought He finished communicating to us when His words in the Bible were all penned?

Scripture:

Turn in your Bible to the 139th Psalm. Read verses 1–5, noting God's knowing *your thoughts* even before they are words on your tongue. Did this surprise you? As you now read verses 17 and 18a, note that there are "also" *God's thoughts to us*. How frequently have you taken time to stop and listen for His divine thought while praying? Rarely? Usually? So often that God's thoughts to you outnumber the sands of the sea? Do you cringe or rebel at, or just ignore, the ones you don't like, loving and accepting only the comforting ones? How "precious" have His thoughts become to you?

For you to do:

List the reasons why this awesome privilege may not be operating fully in your life:

_____

_____

Now think something you sincerely want to know or need. Ask God to bring His thoughts about it to your mind. Now in absolute silence wait *listening*—disciplining your mind not to hop to the next thought and your body to the next activity. Be aware that His answer may not be timed to the way you asked, so keep the process going daily as He unfolds His perfect will in His perfect time and His perfect way.

For you to pray:

"Holy, holy God, forgive me for not listening enough, uninterrupted, to You the eternal God of the Universe—and for perhaps not recognizing Your voice. Thank You that You are anxious to give me Your omniscient thoughts. I long for this precious relationship with You. I promise I will do my part. In Jesus' precious name, amen."

CHAPTER 10

Listening to God When We Are Not Even Asking

ANOTHER WONDERFUL method of listening to God is when we are not even asking. Suddenly, He surprises us with something to pray for seemingly out of nowhere. *Without any preparation, He puts into our minds His new request for us to pray.*

An Assignment from God

In most of our praying we are approaching God, often trying to overcome His seeming reluctance about something. Not in this case. *Without any Bible reading or questions from us, He just unceremoniously drops one of His prayer needs on us.* Unlike a parent urgently praying after hearing his or her child has just been in an accident, this kind of urgency in prayer is from God without our knowing why—and usually without any explanation from Him.

God in some way initiates all prayers, but in this kind it is so obvious that He did. *This is an assignment from God directly to one of His children.* The request rarely is for the benefit of the pray-er—until they rejoice at God's answer. But to realize that God had picked us out specifically to pray for something He wanted and then answered our praying truly is overwhelming. When this happens to me, my whole being cries out, "Oh, God, I am not worthy. But thank You, heavenly Father, for the privilege."

Although there are many methods God uses to communicate with us, this is one of the most exciting because *it involves His breaking into the normal routine of our lives with something more important to Him than we already were doing.* It usually is startling because, as pray-ers, we probably do not have any idea that this intercession is needed, much less that we are needed to be part of God's whole process. Of course, He could do it all by Himself, but God graciously has given us the privilege of helping Him run Planet Earth through our prayers—especially those He specifically gives to each of us.

Is This Still for Today?

The Bible is full of examples of God abruptly breaking into a life with an assignment—Moses, Abraham, Joshua, the Old Testament prophets, Peter, Saul on the Damascus road, and the list goes on.

But those were back then—and this is now. *Does God still break into our routine lives, and even into our routine praying, to give us an assignment or command?* A letter from China to our United Prayer Ministry board showed us God still speaks like that:

I am nineteen years old. I believed in God about a year ago. Thank God He guided me to listen to your station. Your programs are very helpful. *When I prayed one night, I heard a faint voice say to me that I should listen to Trans World Radio and obtain knowledge and truth.* As I turned on the radio I heard "My Prayer Program." I knew then that praying was more than confessing sins. It is praising and thanking God, and we should pray for non-believers.

I, too, still hear God's voice. After returning from a trip to India where I had seen so much prostitution, I was completely devastated. These are published estimates: About one hundred and fifty thousand prostitutes work that area, the single largest profession for working women. It is reported that 25 percent have been abducted and sold, with 8 percent of these by their fathers after being forced into incestuous relationships, and another 6 percent sold by their husbands. Physically they are dumped into extremely deplorable, decrepit old buildings, victims of every varmint and human predator. Perhaps 15 percent have been dedicated to the goddess Yellamma (goddess of fertility) to become temple priestesses. The thing that hurt me the most was how so many lamented that it starts with little girls about eight years old, despite government intervention.

Back home in my comfortable bed, over and over God would wake me with a start in the middle of the night telling me to pray for those little girls. My pillow would already be wet with tears as I cried out to God with a broken heart for them. I could hardly stand it. God kept reminding me of my four little granddaughters.

As I prayed night after night for them, I finally cried out, "Oh, Lord Jesus, come quickly and take them out of their misery."

But His quick response to my heart was, *If I do, their eternal end will be worse than now—unless you rescue them with My salvation!*

This was one of the most horrifying messages I ever have received from Jesus. I'm still praying—for all the local women who were trained to pray for and reach them when I can't.

Barb, then a mortician and one of the most powerful pray-ers I have ever met, told me as she sat in our monthly board meeting munching her croissant and fruit salad, "Suddenly God dropped on my head like a brick an urgent prayer request to pray for my mother's salvation." She questioned God, "Here? Now?" And God said, *Right here! Right now!*

Barb continued, "I started shaking all over and lost track of the board meeting as I frantically prayed silently for my mother." Her mother was Jewish, and we all had prayed too. But for years, Barb had fervently implored God and urged her mother to accept her Messiah—always being met with impenetrable resistance.

In just a few days, however, her mother announced firmly to Barb that she wanted to attend the conference being held at the local Hebrew mission, a Christian place that no faithful Jew would ever go!

Almost in shock, Barb drove her there and sat in amazement as her mother prayed to receive Jeshua—Jesus—as her personal Lord and Savior. Six months later, on Mother's Day, she went to be with her new-found Messiah in heaven.

God's Plan for Earth

God has an overall plan for Planet Earth. And while no human can understand what He is planning, He calls on His children one by one to pray to bring it about.

> O LORD, Thou art my God; I will exalt Thee, I will give thanks to Thy name; for Thou hast worked wonders, plans formed long ago, with perfect faithfulness (Isa. 25:1).

Prayer is one of the main ways God communicates and completes His plan for Planet Earth. I don't understand why God needs us, but in His sovereign will, He has so decreed it. One of the greatest things God taught us is that He wants, even needs, us to pray for what He wants to accomplish down here. Our getting what to pray for directly from God helps keep our plans from being the evil plans Jeremiah wrote about: "But they will say, 'It's hopeless! For we are going to follow our own plans, and each of us will act according to the stubbornness of his evil heart'" (Jer. 18:12).

Occasionally God gives one of His huge assignments—one He intends to use to change a whole segment of society, a ministry for Him, or a Christian leader. *He has planned the far-reaching results of these abrupt announcements to us before He calls us to pray.* These usually are extremely strong promptings to prayer for something I did not have an inkling needed to be prayed about. These may seem relatively insignificant at the time, but I have found they can be a part of God's movements on earth.

In April 1994 as I was praying, suddenly God interrupted with a command: *Pray for Promise Keepers to be more evangelistic—to concentrate more on winning people to Jesus.*

Startled, I wanted to question the command, since that wonderful emerging movement certainly was one of God's answers to our twenty years of praying for America. I was thrilled with what they were doing, and I already was praying much for them.

But this call to prayer was different. I felt myself bowing under the weight of it. Several months of agonizing praying kept me almost sleepless some nights. That burden persisted daily for many months then settled down to just deep intercession for them for the next couple of years.

Little by little, reports of increased evangelistic activities in their rallies and among the men when they got back to their homes kept surfacing. I was thrilled. But the burden was still there.

At a committee meeting in Colorado Springs, my plane was late and I missed the introduction of a new member. Someone informed me that he was Gordon England, the Evangelism Director of Promise Keepers. My heart soared. That night we all had dinner at Dick Eastman's house, and I was seated next to Gordon. Opening the conversation, I asked, "Did you know you are an answer to my prayer?" Curious, he asked how. "Well, in April 1994, God powerfully called me to pray for Promise Keepers to become more evangelistic, and I've been praying it ever since. And they called you to direct their evangelism."

Startled, he countered, "When did you say you started praying that prayer?" When I repeated April 1994, he drew in his breath. "That was the same year they called me to be their evangelism director—the very next October."

God also distinctly called me to pray for Steve Douglass while he was in Harvard School of Business following graduation from Massachusetts Institute of Technology. He had grown up in our church, and I was his pastor's wife. We were including Steve in our regular praying for the young people of our church during those "What Happens When Women Pray" years, and he was keeping track of us when visiting home.

But suddenly one day God almost shouted at me, *Pray for Steve.* Flooding into my mind were things that had shocked us pray-ers, such as—if your roommate hangs his necktie on the outside doorknob, he is entertaining a girl, and you are not to come in. So I started in earnest, begging God to protect him, keeping him from the temptations pressing in on him from every side.

God was preserving Steve because He had great plans for him—as the assistant to the founder of one of the world's largest evangelistic organizations, Campus Crusade for Christ, which just reached their billionth person for Jesus. No wonder Satan was nervous and God was enlisting special prayer for Steve.

It was four and a half years after starting to pray for Promise Keepers to be more evangelistic that Gordon, Steve, and I were riding to the Colorado Springs airport in the same car. They started comparing stories. "You mean she prayed for you, too?" Gordon quipped in pretended horror. And Steve, with a big grin responded, "Yes, for me too!" "We didn't have a chance!" they both chimed in with mock groaning.

What a privilege God gave me. Yes, the price was high as I prayed and wrestled for several years, often in tears, for those two—one whom I knew; the other I didn't. But God did.

I started being a serious intercessor as soon as I accepted Jesus at age nine, concentrating mostly on the unsaved neighbors and friends we brought to our church for the preacher to explain Jesus to them. As I look back at more than sixty-nine years of God's teaching me how to pray, I am in awe at how He has had His plan for incredible things all worked out (before the foundations of the earth), and then used the prayers of His weak and feeble saints to bring them to pass. God is sovereign, and He could just manipulate these things and people around at His every whim, but He often chooses to assign believers to pray for it first!

Responding to God

These calls from God to pray do not become prayer until we respond to the One sending the request—*and actually start praying about it.*

These prayers then fulfill all the facets of Paul's admonition in Ephesians 6:18 to pray for all the saints. Saints, according to the Bible, are ordinary people who were redeemed when they accepted Jesus as Savior and Lord. Ephesians was written "to the saints who are at Ephesus, and who are faithful in Christ Jesus" (Eph. 1:1). And these saints are to pray for all the other saints in these ways:

The National Prayer Committee was choosing a new director for our annual National Day of Prayer, held on Capitol Hill every first day of May. We prayed for many months seeking God's choice for such an important job. Since Congress had passed it into law, many members of Congress attended, and at least one spoke, representing the rest. Leaders and intercessors from across the nation came to pray. We needed God's choice.

As we each prayed fervently at home and together at our national committee meetings, God seemed to give to each of us the same name: Shirley Dobson. We were thrilled. But we were even more thrilled when, after her own heart-searching praying for God to show her if it was His will for her, she knew it was. Months and months of intense prayer from us, and her, had gone into that invitation and acceptance.

But that was not my only praying for Shirley Dobson. God already had given me Shirley as my special prayer assignment. It was one of those important ones God gives me when I'm not even asking.

Shirley's and my planes were departing from Washington, D.C., at the same time after one of our meetings, so we shared a taxi. Suddenly Shirley reached out and took hold of my hand. "Let's be prayer partners," she said almost impulsively. Immediately eagerly agreeing, I added, "But I already have been praying for you for six months." Surprised, she asked about it, and I told her of the call from God to pray and how it had been fervent, wrestling praying that came when God stopped me cold and gave me a prayer assignment. We parted at the airport—promising to pray. But my promise had been made six months before!

Praying, Not Talking

Keeping my praying for her in my own heart and not talking about it, I just kept praying.

Not knowing that much about her ministry, I could not have known what or why God asked me to pray. But I obeyed anyway. I understood her responsibility a little as all of us on the National Prayer Committee, sponsoring the National Day of Prayer, struggled together with her over issues such as "Which religion's prayers do we pray as a democracy?" and "Praying in the name of Jesus." We bombarded heaven with her for God's answers.

This kind of praying is not for the pray-er to influence or to persuade another person by counseling or preaching. No, it is letting God answer our prayers while we keep silent and pray. Otherwise, *we* would be steering them, *not* God.

However, God may have had lots of people praying for Shirley. Perhaps He had called hundreds of others to pray especially for Shirley too. We will never know. But we do know when He powerfully lays a prayer burden on our hearts! *And the wonderful thing about God is that He always makes us feel that the weight of the request and magnitude of the burden is ours alone!*

A young pastor's wife stopped me after a seminar to tell me about her secret praying. "I pick out a need absolutely nobody else knows about, and I pray really hard for it. Then," she said, "when God answers, I know it was my prayers that did it."

I sensed she was struggling with her self-worth in that overwhelming position for the first time. *But God does show her, and us, our worth to Him—by answering our prayers.* What a wise, understanding God we serve!

A friend told me how God kept prompting her to pray and to write a note to a new person at her church whom she had only just met. She put it off as long as she could, until God impressed upon her to write Isaiah 41:10: "Do not fear, for I am with you; do not anxiously look about you, for I am your God. I will strengthen you, surely I will help you, surely I will uphold you with My righteous right hand."

The woman responded graciously to the note, thanking my friend and saying, "I have no idea why God would prompt you to write this." Six months later, my friend received a phone call from this woman, asking her to pray. The woman's son had hanged himself. She shared how God had prepared her through the scripture my friend had sent. Although at the time she had no idea why God wanted that scripture sent to her, she committed it to memory and it had comforted her through her son's death.

God needs us to pray!

How Long Do We Pray?

When God answers, He lets us go back to more ordinary praying—until He assigns again!

This is what God usually does with all prayers—those sudden, unexpected ones from Him and those family needs, ministry problems, or whatever God emphatically calls us to pray for. *He knows there is no way we could stay praying with that same intensity for years and years, so He turns the agonizing prayers into persevering prayer as long as the need persists.* This same progression usually is in all of our important praying for family, friends, church family, pastors, coworkers, student colleagues, political leaders, and others. *And He turns our struggling in prayer into praise—when the answer comes!*

Sometimes the answer comes almost immediately, and the praise can begin at once.

However, there are times when we persevere in prayer through the years for a lost loved one, a wayward child, or something equally devastating. The intensity might come and go those years, but through it all we keep on praying.

Then there are those circumstances in which we must hang on to

God in faith, believing that He will answer, even if we have to learn about it in heaven.

Others Praying for Me

Many parents tell of suddenly feeling their child is in danger and needs prayer. Sometimes they call it a *premonition*. This very well could be from God calling on them to pray. But it certainly is wise to pray!

I am so grateful for all those to whom God says, *Pray for Evelyn. Right now!* And they do. And I will never know who most of them are. But I wish I could tell each one of them how deeply grateful I am. Grateful that they were willing to interrupt their personal time to give God, and me, some of it! Now I can only say thanks to them and to God! Will I get the chance to thank them in person in heaven? Or won't I need to—and won't they need it? We will both be giving God all the glory!

However, I am very grateful when I pick up the phone and someone says, "God told me to call you and pray for you!" It always is when the stress is overwhelming, the problem has not found a solution, and I almost feel I cannot go on. Then that friend, or stranger, on the other end of the line calls in the God of heaven into my distress. And the tension melts and trickles and then flows from me like a river. I am refreshed, renewed, revitalized!

One of the most awesome times God asked somebody to pray for me was when a woman from one thousand miles away called and asked me why God woke her to pray urgently for my family right then. As far as I knew, my children, their spouses, and my grandchildren were enjoying a winter retreat at their cabin. But a winter thaw caused the ice on the chimney to melt, collect at the bottom, and then refreeze, completely blocking the escape of all carbon monoxide gas. At the same time God woke this woman to pray, our son-in-law said a voice woke him, saying, *Go outside.* He stumbled out the door, and the oxygen revived him enough to evacuate the rest of the family—except three-year-old Jennifer. As they were getting in the car to rush to the hospital, there she was sitting in the car. The snow was three feet deep and over her head, making it impossible for any toddler to walk through. Stunned, her daddy asked her how she got out of the cabin in the deep snow. Nobody questioned when she answered, "An angel carried me, Daddy."

Why God called on a woman who had only seen me as the teacher of a prayer seminar she attended instead of calling on me, I will never know. But I will be forever grateful that she was one of those who was able to discern God's voice and was willing to pray fervently when God called on her for a specific need.

Incredible Answers to Prayer

The apostle Paul urges us:

> With all prayer and petition pray at all times in the Spirit, and with this in view, be on the alert with all perseverance and petition for all the saints (Eph. 6:18).

"Be on the alert." The most astounding times this happens is when a complete stranger calls or writes a note telling me God just stopped them and said, *Pray for Evelyn Christenson.* And they usually ask me, "Why am I praying?" And when I tell them the immediate circumstance that desperately needed prayer, there usually is a long, surprised silence—as they try to fathom that God counted them worthy to entrust them with a need in one of His children. Immediately we are fast friends!

Just two months after major colon surgery, I was bringing a short message in a Mission America meeting in Arizona. The postsurgery weakness was overwhelming and had not been helped by the long plane ride. When I stepped into the church, their prayer committee met me. "Please come to our prayer room. We want to show you our prayer map." There on the wall was a huge map with a pin for every person they were especially targeting with prayer. And there was my pin stuck right in Minnesota! Then they said they knew of my physical need, and God had told them to set aside that whole day to pray for me. I could hardly speak, I was so humbled and stunned. How could people I'd never met be so kind—and, as it turned out, so powerful in their praying for me?

A special thrill comes when a loved one, friend, colleague, or coworker calls to tell me that, as they were sensing I desperately needed encouragement and support, God stopped them in their tracks and said, *Pray for Evelyn!* The cooling effect of God's hand on my feverish forehead as they pray slowly dispels the frustration. I am changed by their prayers because they stopped to pray when God called on them.

I have worked incredibly close to Kathryn Grant as my co-chair of our national AD2000 Christian Women United. Since Kathryn not only knows, but also "keeps alert" to my needs, I can hear her soothing voice praying for me over the phone as we have labored usually long distance or even across the Pacific Ocean. Also, one of my greatest privileges has been to deeply intercede for her through foreign mission stints, surgeries, and even as a representative to the United Nations—when God stopped me and said, *Pray for Kathryn!*

"Perseverance and petition for all the saints." Virtually all of my coworkers have phoned or written me that at a particular time God laid my need heavily on their hearts. They all are extremely busy leaders with ministries of their own—yet they stop to pray for me. This is one of the greatest privileges of working with those who belong to the body of Christ!

The word *petition* in Ephesians 6:18 refers to a specific request, not just a general prayer. This is what makes the prayers of colleagues—and loved ones—unique.

On one occasion there was deep hassling and sifting from Satan (see Luke 22:31) as I struggled with a coworker to keep a point in our curriculum, *A Study Guide for Evangelism Praying*, biblically grounded.

Without my having shared the problem with either of them, both Mary Lance Sisk and Bobbye Byerly called and announced, "God has said to pray powerful spiritual warfare prayers for you!" And they did. God could not have given them a more specific petition than that—without even knowing about it!

Then they prayed the persisting in prayer of Ephesians 6:18 until God solved it—which He did—almost miraculously!

I just got another incredible illustration for this chapter! Being past my publisher's deadline for this book, as I was hurrying to finish this chapter, a huge problem that had been annoying for weeks finally surfaced. Last Thursday night, my computer software crashed—taking with it chapters in various stages of completion and editing, leaving me with only copies on paper. *I called my telephone prayer chains and told everybody who called me to pray like they'd never prayed before!*

After typing this one back into the computer, I worked on it several hours—only to have the computer once again not file it where it could be found. I finally dropped my head and cried out, "Lord, I cannot do it! There is no time to get the computer fixed. *Please* get the material back into it, and make the deadline!"

But our son, Kurt, who has his Ph.D. in computer science, came to my rescue. Working almost two days, he finally found what was causing the glitches in the software. But before he had, an incredible thing happened to me. Peace! Indescribable peace! I wondered for a minute if I had just gone numb, not able to feel any longer. (I've been working an average of fourteen hours a day for weeks on this book, so I thought it might be possible.)

But then I knew. *It was all that prayer!* Prayer from people I asked, but also prayer from those all over who are praying for this book—perhaps not even knowing why they are praying. But God has put them all together—and He sent His incredible answer! (If you are reading this book, you will know my computer and I made it!)

"Oh, heavenly Father, I am not worthy—but I am oh, so grateful!"

We May Never Know

There are times we never will know why God interrupted our lives to tell us to pray for someone someplace.

I remember God's waking me from a sound sleep by piercing my foggy mind with His incredibly urgent, *Pray for so-and-so in that city!* God named the person and the city, and that was all. Startled wide awake, I prayed for most of the rest of the night. It was a distant relative I didn't even know had gone to a convention in that city. Once in a while I worried about it later, and a few times I wanted to ask about it—but I never did. That was God's end of it. Mine was just to pray—when God told me. But it is an incredible privilege to pray—because God knows that He can call on me any time of day or night, and I will pray—right then. *He doesn't have to tell me why.*

Whose Voice?

One of the most dramatic examples in the Bible of God's speaking so shockingly was to Peter. When God was ready to send Jewish Peter to the Gentiles, it took strong interrupting of his way of thinking on God's part. So God sent a vision with a voice explaining that nothing He had created was unclean. Strong-willed Peter argued with God at first. In fact, it took three times to finally convince him.

When the voice in Acts 10:13 came to Peter in a vision, he responded to it as "Lord" and questioned eating unclean things in the vision. But then Peter identified the voice giving him instructions about going down to the waiting men as "the Spirit." Are these two different voices? No. *This is the triune God at work.* The Spirit is the Spirit of God, delivering the Father's message.

Cornelius already was a devout man who prayed with all his household. They just didn't know about Jesus yet. But he also obeyed the voice of the angel God sent to him in a vision and sent for Peter.

When Saul heard a voice on the Damascus road as he was en route to persecute the Christians in that city, that voice identified itself as "Jesus," another member of the Trinity (Acts 26:15). And Saul (whose name had been changed to Paul) told King Agrippa that "I did not prove disobedient to the heavenly vision, but kept declaring" (v. 19) the salvation in Jesus to the Jews and the Gentiles.

When God was preparing Ananias to send for Saul, newly blinded and called by Jesus, Ananias also heard a voice in a vision and responded, "Behold, here am I, Lord" (Acts 9:10). Ananias was afraid because of how much harm this Saul was doing to the Christians, but when God said, Go! Ananias went!

My children often have quipped, "If Mother is sure God said it, that's it. She will do it. We might just as well not bother talking about it."

Sometimes it is as simple as obeying when I thought I was doing something better too—such as putting down my Bible and going to David Edwin's store because He had the exact dresses I needed for our 1999 Wheaton national conference. But I've learned never to question God when He gives me instructions like that. *He doesn't waste His time just chatting with us.* When He breaks into my self-absorption, I know He means business. And I obey!

God is longing to get our attention. Are we listening?

Not Obeying?

What if Peter had not obeyed? His obedience was a part of God's opening up the whole Gentile world to Jesus' gospel. What if Ananias had been too afraid of Saul to obey God's voice? What if Saul on the Damascus road had stubbornly rejected Jesus' voice to go to Jews, Gentiles, and kings? What if Cornelius had not responded and had still been missing what he was missing—Jesus? What if *we* don't obey?

The first time I can remember God's calling that definitely was when, after we had moved into our new church building in Rockford, Illinois, had doubled our membership in four years, and the church was busy with activity every day and night of the week. But, with no advanced notice or our ever having discussed it between us, God suddenly stopped three of us women in the new lower auditorium. The burden was so strong and the urgency so great that we threw our arms around each other and sobbed. All three of us were hearing simultaneously from God, *Pray for the church every week.*

Our response was instantaneous. We never questioned it. God said it, and we did it—for almost four years until our "What Happens When Women Pray" experimenting in prayer started. (Jesus taught that when a steward is faithful and does a good job, he is not sent on vacation or sabbatical or given early retirement. He is given the next bigger task by his master.)

This was not figuring out the needs and visions for the church, but responding to a direct command from God to pray for it. We left the prayer topics and results to God. Our only responsibility was to pray. And we did!

But trying to stay faithful and keep on obeying was one of the hardest things I ever have done. Somebody interrupted every Thursday afternoon meeting—a husband home for a late lunch, an off-schedule repair man coming in the middle of our praying, sick children, sick us, changed children's piano lessons, or sports practices or games. Satan didn't miss a trick trying to wear down our resistance, but we persevered until the bigger "What Happens When Women Pray" experimenting took over.

What if we had not prayed? What if we had been too busy with our around-the-clock family, church, and ministry responsibilities? *Would God have given us the privilege of a lifetime prayer ministry if we hadn't done even that first assignment?*

Entrusted

The most important word to me in this whole process is *entrusted*. God entrusted one of His problems to our weekly praying every time He broke into our routine to ask us to pray specifically for one of His needs. I really cannot understand this. He could snap His divine fingers, and it would be done. *But God has graciously chosen to let us be part of His running Planet Earth—by entrusting us with what He desires and plans!*

This is a compliment from God, because He knows whom He can trust. He knows which ones of us will accept His assignment to pray with childlike faith—and do it.

Jeanne, at the time editor of our board's newspaper, wrote me the following note:

About 11:00 one morning, God impressed me strongly to pray for my friend Karen. As I prayed, I began to weep. All through the day I prayed and wept with no idea of what was going on. That evening, I just stayed in bed, praying and weeping softly. I couldn't go to sleep. Around 1:00 A.M., the phone rang. Karen's brother, Ted, had committed suicide. He had been in the car in the garage all day, and no one found him until his wife came home from a women's meeting that night. God alone knew how desperately Karen needed my prayers that day.

Part of the "praying without ceasing" teaching of *What Happens When Women Pray* is not that we, like monks, will try to be praying twenty-four hours a day. *It is just staying open to God all day and all night, just in case He decides He needs to call on us to pray.* Not just begrudgingly giving Him some of our much-needed rest or time on a project, but eagerly awaiting His voice.

People often complain to me that God never speaks to them. Could it be that when He did speak to them in the past, perhaps over and over, they never responded? Did they continually reject the responsibility of His assignment, and He gave up, knowing it was useless to keep speaking?

What might you be missing?

Out of the Blue

One Saturday morning last April while I was praying, the words "Lo, I am with you always" shot into my mind like an arrow from Jesus. Recalling them as His words in His Great Commission in Matthew 28, I was very grateful and thanked Him—although I was a little puzzled as to why He had interrupted my praying with those words.

The next day He abruptly added the words, *I'll be with you now—and when you die I'll be there holding your hand. And then I'll be with you forever in eternity.* I questioned why again. But the next morning, I was surprised when I spent the day in the hospital emergency room while they tried to figure out what my heart was doing. (Only one-third of it is working muscle and pumps only about a third of my blood to my body.) But I had complete peace all day.

Three weeks to the day later, my husband landed in the same emergency room with atrial fibrillation that would not stabilize. As I sat by him, I was praying over those words, "Lo, I am with you always." I thanked the Lord that He would be with Chris always too. Then I prayed, "Lord, those words seemed to come right out of the blue."

No, God answered clearly. *Right out of the green!*

At first, I didn't understand what God seemed to be saying to me. "What did you say, sir?" I questioned.

Immediately coming to my mind was that spot on the page of my Bible in Revelation 4:2–3 in which the apostle John describes heaven: "Behold, a throne was standing in heaven, and One sitting on the throne . . . and there was a rainbow around the throne . . . *like an emerald in appearance*" (emphasis added).

Green! Right out of the throne room of God with its gigantic green rainbow of precious emerald around His throne!

Those sudden, powerful words of assignments or instructions do not come from somewhere in outer space—*out of the blue.* No! They come from *out of the green*—right from God!

Reflection Questions

Examine your life:

Is being available to God twenty-four hours a day for *His* unexpected prayer assignments a part of your current lifestyle—or have your prayers only been what *you* wanted from God? How frequently have you experienced God entrusting you personally with a need when you were not even asking and then the thrill of seeing it come to pass—because you prayed?

Scripture:

Commit to memory the short, succinct instruction for 1 Thessalonians 5:17: "Pray without ceasing." Knowing no human being could pray verbally around the clock forever, do you see this as an impossible biblical command or just an unrealistic suggestion you have a right to ignore? Or what, if anything, do you think God is saying He wants to teach you about his incredibly powerful prayer privilege?

For you to do:

Recall some time, if possible, when you felt you received a surprising and perhaps urgent burden from God to pray for someone or something. Honestly admit what you did about it:

    [] Not believed God does that since Bible times?

    [] Not recognized it as from God?

    [] Ignored because preoccupied with more important things?

    [] Just counseled the recipient about their need instead of praying?

[] Begrudgingly prayed a short passing prayer?

[] Prayed fervently and persistently?

Since understanding 1 Thessalonians 5:17 as being committed to staying available to God around the clock, record what changes in your day and night lifestyle you are now willing to make:

DAYS:_____

NIGHTS:_____

For you to pray:

"Oh, dear Father in heaven, I am overwhelmed that You are waiting to ask me to pray about your needs down here on earth. I am so unworthy, Lord. But my heart is exploding with anticipation at Your entrusting me with some of them. Lord, please don't look further for anybody else instead of me. I promise You I will pray in faith—regardless if I don't know why or see an answer from You—even until I get to heaven! In Jesus' precious name, amen."

PART FOUR

What God Is Doing In the New Millennium

CHAPTER 11

What Have Christians Done with Jesus?

ONE OF THE MOST precious praying experiences that can happen to a Christian is praying *with* Jesus. To be in His presence sharing His love, His compassion, and His burdens is a rare gift from Jesus to His followers. But to feel His hurting heart is even more awesome.

For more than two weeks, I kept waking in the night weeping and praying about *what we have done with Jesus.* But I was not praying *at* Jesus or *to* Him; I seemed to be praying *with* Him. His heart, too, seemed to be breaking with mine as He was sighing sorrowfully, *What have they done with Me?*

That praying we were doing was not over what humans had done when they mocked Him and spit upon Him and killed Him on a cross. Peter had explained that in the first sermon to the emerging church after Pentecost:

"Therefore let all the house of Israel know for certain that God has made Him both Lord and Christ—this Jesus whom you crucified." Now when they had heard this, they were pierced to the heart, and said to Peter and the rest of the apostles, "Brethren, what shall we do?" And Peter said to them, "Repent, and let each of you be baptized in the name of Jesus Christ for the forgiveness of your sins." (Acts 2:36–38)

My praying with Jesus was not even about what those who have rejected Him as Savior have done to Him through the centuries—reducing His name to a swear word.

But what that praying with Jesus was about is the question He is asking today: *What have Christians done with Jesus?*

This question has given birth to some of the most urgent praying God has taught us to do in this thirty-year current prayer movement.

Have We Regressed Back to Before Jesus' Coming?

I watched with alarm as a scattered trend decades ago developed into widespread acceptance among many Christians: *praying and preaching without mentioning the name of Jesus.* For years, I have fervently prayed whenever I saw this happening. I was praying, I'm sure, with Jesus our intercessor in heaven as He, too, sees us doing this and prays for us.

I counted five consecutive Sunday morning services in a fine church in which people prayed from the pulpit, the talented pastor preached, and the choir sang great hymns such as "God of Our Fathers"—without anyone's ever once naming the name of Jesus. I gave up counting and multiplied my prayers!

My denominational executive friend in Canada sadly said to me, "Evelyn, I'm playing racquetball to befriend a man of a pagan religion, but I can't take him to my church." When I questioned why not, he replied, "We have marvelous sermons about Abraham, Moses, and David. But at the door my friend warmly thanks my pastor for reinforcing what he thoroughly believes from our Bible about the Old Testament characters. But he never has had to confront the name of Jesus as the only way to God." I grieved with him and wondered how many of our churches have regressed back to before Jesus to make those of pagan religions feel comfortable.

Paul in Acts 13:32–33 says, "And we preach to you the good news of the promise made to the fathers, that God has fulfilled this promise to our children in that He raised up Jesus, as it is also written in the second Psalm, 'Thou art My Son, today I have begotten Thee.'"

At a national retreat last fall, the wife of the president of one of America's fine denominations told me her heart was breaking. Her husband, she told me, was speaking in one of their denomination's churches one recent Sunday morning. "But," she sighed, "he was astounded as the pastor told him not to speak of Jesus as the only way to God because that offended people in his church!" Have we become so tolerant of human hang-ups that we have forgotten Jesus' own words:

No one comes to the Father, but through Me (John 14:6).

Jesus Is Not Just Another God

It is easy for Christians to talk in general about God. All religions have a name they call their particular "supernatural being" that they created for themselves to worship. So there is no uniqueness in our talking openly about a "god." That word is nonthreatening, is politically correct, does not embarrass anyone, and makes us tolerant of all the other people who are trying to come to God in their own way. *But the confrontation comes when we specifically use the name "Jesus."* He marks the difference in a "god" to whom people are *trying* to draw nigh and the only real God to whom we *can* draw nigh—through Jesus.

Of course there are other "gods," but they all are of Satan's kingdom. Satan is called "the god of this world" in 2 Corinthians 4:4.

Pregnant out of wedlock, the Virgin Mary faced not just embarrassment, but being socially ostracized and perhaps being stoned to death. I've often wondered, *What would have happened if she had aborted Jesus?* How about us? Have we tried to hide or ignore Him—or substituted the more general name "God" when we are too embarrassed at the name of Jesus?

How hurt Jesus must be that Christians—for whom He suffered and died—are too embarrassed to say His name. Hurt that we mistakenly take it for granted that everybody must know we are talking about *Him* when we are ashamed to mention Jesus' name. Hurt that we frequently pray on and on quoting words of every Bible character except Jesus. Hurt that we name our prayer rooms after Old Testament heroes but almost never after Jesus. Hurt—and bewildered—that we have lost the *joy* that comes from His name: "Until now you have asked for nothing *in My name*; ask, and you will receive, that your *joy* may be made full" (John 16:24; emphasis added).

One of the greatest legacies Jesus left His followers was His joy, which is available to us by the simple praying in His name. *Jesus' name—all that He was and is and is to come!*

While ill one recent Sunday morning, I had looked until I found a church service being televised. I was astounded to discover this popular preacher was interviewing an expert on the topic: "Since they [another religion] and Christians make up three billion people—half the people on earth—all we have to do to have world peace is for the two religions to get together." Holding up the book explaining this solution, he said he was proud to be in it. Then they announced a national convention to bring together both sides and teach us all how to bring world peace. The reasoning was that, since the two religions have so much in common in all the Old Testament prophets, and since they believe in Jesus as *one of the prophets*, there really is no problem in reconciling the two. I dropped my head in my hands and shuddered an agonizing cry as I prayed, "Oh, God, what have those Christian leaders done with Jesus?"

That prayer has prompted much praying since then as I have begged God to show our own Christian preachers and teachers the truth about oneness. The truth that it is only our Jesus who, through His blood, has made all of us who believe on Him *one in Him*. As the apostle Paul explained:

> But now in Christ Jesus you who formerly were far off have been brought near by the blood of Christ. For He Himself is our peace, who made both

groups into one, and broke down the barrier of the dividing wall, by abolishing in His flesh the enmity . . . that in Himself He might make the two into one new man, thus establishing peace, and might reconcile them both in one body to God through the cross, by it having put to death the enmity. (Eph. 2:13–16)

The truth is that Jesus is the only real reconciliation there ever can be on earth. Wars, peace summits, organizations, marches, and laws never have and never will bring oneness. Only Jesus!

In our prayer seminars, thousands of women have voiced the same burden for the church they attend. Their hearts are breaking with mine—and with Jesus'—for our Christian leaders to search the Scriptures as to Jesus' name, not what fits with the theological boxes into which we have crammed Him.

It is not that there are no churches lifting up Jesus. There are some absolutely great ones! It is so wonderful to be privileged to teach and worship in them. Jesus is there—Lord! But many have become enmeshed in their programs and plans—without Jesus as their priority. These are the churches Jesus is weeping over.

For twenty years I have prayed, "Bring *Jesus* back to our churches. Please, Lord!" And we have all prayed together, "Lord, show our preachers and teachers—and all of us—the difference between us the body of Jesus and His mission field."

The theme for the Protestant Women of the Chapel's all-Europe convention was "The Shepherd." It was thrilling for me to teach many of the things the Father intended the Good Shepherd, Jesus, to be and to do. The most important, of course, was that, although many historical shepherds had given their lives for their sheep, it was not God the Father who did that. It was the *Good* Shepherd, Jesus, who not only gave His life to redeem humankind, but also uniquely took it up again—to become the only *risen* Savior of the world!

What an awesome privilege we have to be able to pray on this side of the cross, the tomb, and Easter morning. We are eligible for all the power of the name of the glorified Savior of the world.

"God" Is Not a Substitute for "Jesus"

In our praying, the Father has taught us that "God" is not a substitute for the name of Jesus, although it is true that Jesus is God and part of the triune Godhead, as proclaimed in John 1:1: "In the beginning was the Word [Jesus], and the Word was with God, and the Word *was* God" (emphasis added).

I cringe when I hear someone pray, "Father, we thank Thee for dying on the cross for us." Jesus talked *to* the Father *from* the cross, asking why He had forsaken His Son. Had the Father (along with His Spirit) died on the cross, what would have happened? There would have been an instantaneous explosion of chaos in the universe, with everything in outer space veering out of its orbit and crashing into each other with no divine power supernaturally in control.

Although it is true that Jesus is God and a part of the triune Godhead, their names are not to be used interchangeably. *God the Father sent His Son to earth.* Jesus' prayer life was praying *to* the Father, always in obedience to the Father's will, including dying on the cross. Jesus' high priestly prayer to the Father in John 17:11 gives us an awesome picture of their oneness: "Holy Father, keep them in Thy name, the name which Thou hast given Me, that they may be one, even as We are."

"Holy Spirit" Is Not a Substitute for "Jesus"

A current trend among theological circles is that some people are replacing Jesus almost completely with the Holy Spirit.

The New Testament teaches the awesome roles of the Holy Spirit. He played a huge part in *Jesus' life here on earth*—descending on Him after Jesus' baptism, sending Him to the wilderness to be tempted by Satan, and on through His earthly life. The Holy Spirit also calls *believers* into ministry, sends them, empowers them, gives them boldness, comforts them, teaches them, recalls what Jesus taught them—and much more. Then He convicts *sinners* whom those believers are trying to win to Jesus. We cannot save a soul!

All three members of the Trinity—God the Father, God the Son, and God the Holy Spirit—always have been and always will be! The Trinity is in perfect oneness with separate functions, completing the fullness of the Godhead. All three were operating in perfect unity in the mystery of the divine Trinity in those first Christians.

Here are a few biblical concepts about the beautiful and perfect relationship of God, Jesus, and the Holy Spirit:

Jesus. In John 16:7–14, Jesus explained that it would be good for Him to go because *He, Jesus, would send the Holy Spirit*. Then He described some of the roles the Holy Spirit would have in their lives—ending with *the Holy Spirit glorifying Himself, Jesus*. What a precious relationship! Jesus explained more of that relationship in John 14:25–26: "These things I have spoken to you, while abiding with you. But the Helper, *the Holy Spirit*, whom the *Father* will send *in My name*, He will teach you all things, and bring to your remembrance all that *I [Jesus]* said to you" (emphasis added).

God. Then in the Gospel of Luke, *Jesus* commanded that they would wait for the power promised by *His Father*, who was *the Holy Spirit* (see Luke 24:49).

Holy Spirit. The Father and Jesus both had promised the *Holy Spirit*. "*He [Jesus]* commanded them not to leave Jerusalem, but to wait for what the *Father* had promised" (Acts 1:4; emphasis added).

God the Father, God the Son, and God the Holy Spirit—the

Godhead! All are incredibly one in a mystery no human could ever understand, yet powerfully operating flawlessly in their roles with each other toward us!

And while benefiting from the all-important roles of all the members of the Trinity—the believers preached Jesus!

After Saul was called by Jesus on the Damascus road and his eyesight was restored by Ananias, he joined the disciples and "immediately he began to proclaim Jesus in the synagogues, saying, 'He is the Son of God'" (Acts 9:20).

Before telling His followers to wait for the Holy Spirit in Luke 24, Jesus told them that "repentance for forgiveness of sins should be proclaimed *in His name* to all the nations, beginning from Jerusalem" (v. 47; emphasis added).

In His Great Commission in Matthew 28, Jesus told them to baptize in the name of the Trinity—Father, Son, and Holy Spirit. But Jesus taught them "to observe all that I have commanded you; and lo, I am with you always" (v. 19). Jesus promised to be with them always—even to the end of the age!

Then, in His last words to His followers before ascending back to the Father, Jesus said to them: "But you shall receive power when the Holy Spirit has come upon you, and *you shall be My witnesses* both in Jerusalem, and in all Judea and Samaria, and even to the remotest part of the earth" (Acts 1:8; emphasis added).

The Holy Spirit was absolutely necessary in His vital roles, *but believers were to be witnesses unto Jesus.*

Paul's prayer for the believers in Ephesus gives us a beautiful, balanced picture of how we, too, should pray for our personal relationship with all three members of the Godhead. (Here's a condensation. Please take time to read all of Ephesians 3:14–19.)

For this reason I bow my knees before the Father . . . that He would grant you . . . to be strengthened with power through His Spirit in the inner man . . . that Christ may dwell in your hearts . . . that you, being rooted and grounded in love, may be able . . . to know the love of Christ which surpasses knowledge, that you may be filled up with all the fullness of God. (Eph. 3:14–19; emphasis added)

Have We Replaced Jesus' Name?

It is amazing how many names we Christians have substituted for the name of Jesus. We do things in the name of our church, our denomination, our Christian organization, our national or local project, or even in our own name.

When reading the Book of Acts to see how much of what the first Christians did was in the name of Jesus, I was astounded. It was everything! I finally gave up my looking, because I could not find them doing anything in any name other than the name of Jesus. Here are a few examples:

Healing in His name. Peter with John, on their way to pray in the temple, said to a beggar who had been lame from his mother's womb, "I do not possess silver and gold, but what I do have I give to you. In the name of Jesus the Nazarene—walk!" (Acts 3:6). When the man was instantly healed and walked and leaped and praised God, the people ran together wondering where that power came from. So Peter answered, "On the basis of faith *in His name, it is the name of Jesus* which has strengthened this man whom you see and know" (v. 16; emphasis added). The number who believed then came to be about five thousand! Jesus' name!

In prison, Peter and John were commanded not to speak or teach in the name of Jesus—because there was so much power in it. But they promptly retorted: "Whether it is right in the sight of God to give heed to you rather than to God, you be the judge; for we cannot stop speaking what we have seen and heard" (Acts 4:19–20).

Praying in His name. How thrilling it is to read Jesus' own words about praying in His name: "And whatever you ask *in My name*, that will I do, that the Father may be glorified in the Son. If you ask Me anything *in My name*, I will do it" (John 14:13–14; emphasis added).

What an awesome privilege for us believers! Our names can accomplish nothing supernatural. But Jesus, the Son of God, has freely given us His name, which incorporates all He is, to use in prayer!

Praying for the salvation of lost souls. It was because of all authority having been given to Jesus that we go and make disciples of all nations for Him. How? Through His name! The Bible uses the words *believed, saved,* or *born again* to describe the salvation process. This is the most important prayer anyone ever will pray because it determines not only their life with Jesus here on earth but eternity with Him— because their sins have been forgiven.

There is *no other name under heaven* that has been given among men, by which we must be saved (Acts 4:12; emphasis added).

Praying against demons. Our granddaughter Jenna was playing an imp (demon) with other girls her age in the Easter presentation of their church seen annually by thirty thousand people. They were part of the scene of Jesus battling Satan to get the keys of death and Hades from him with real fire belching to depict hell. The first night, the teenagers were terrified to be part of battling Satan, and just before they went on, Jenna's sister, Crista, opened the door of their dressing room. And there they all were—dressed like demons—kneeling in a circle on the floor doing spiritual warfare praying! They knew where their authority against Satan came from. Jesus!

Even the demons know Jesus. A man in the synagogue possessed by the spirit of an unclean demon cried out with a loud voice, "Ha! What have we to do with You, Jesus of Nazareth? Have You come to destroy us? I know who You are—the Holy One of God!" (Luke 4:33–34). Jesus cast out the demon. Then Jesus stopped to heal Peter's mother-in-law of a high fever. And as he went on, "Demons also were coming out of many, crying out and saying, 'You are the Son of God!' And rebuking them, He would not allow them to speak, because they knew Him to be the Christ" (v. 41).

This is the Jesus those scattered Christians were preaching when there were great signs and miracles of demons being cast out, the lame walking, and the paralyzed healed. (See Acts 8:5–7 for one example.) This is the same Jesus living in us who has power over the evil world of Satan!

Our desire in our prayer training is to keep Jesus' name in its rightful, authoritative place. May we never replace Jesus' name with any other!

But Have We Let Jesus Replace Us?

The greatest compliment I ever receive is when someone approaches me after I speak at a conference or seminar and says, "You just disappeared. All I saw standing there was Jesus!"

This is an answer to years of praying the deep desire of my heart that Jesus, not I, will be seen. Praying to open a speaking session, I usually implore openly: "Lord, please let me disappear. May no one see a pink dress up here. *May we all see only Jesus!*" And God does answer that prayer. Frequently people in the audience will come to me in awe, telling me that they were not aware of me—just Jesus—as I spoke. What a precious privilege! *What God does when we pray!*

At our "Pray Minnesota" prayer rally, the staff person sitting next to me told me as I walked up to speak that she looked and I was not there. Rather than seeing me, it was as if she was seeing Jesus. Just before going up the last time, a worship team holding glistening royal gold banners with a name of Jesus on each led us in awesome, holy worship of Jesus. When the music stopped, we at first thought someone had forgotten to turn the tape. But it was intentional. The worshipers stood as if frozen, holding their Jesus banners.

In the awesome silence, little by little people began to weep in the audience. Then they started filing down to the front and kneeling in prayer in repentance and adoration of Jesus. Suddenly some were lying prostrate before Jesus—deeply repenting in reverence at His holy presence. I stood speechless, trying to discern how to finish the rally. Since the worship team was soon to take the banners to Jerusalem to say "Welcome Jesus to Jerusalem" for the next millennium, we prayed for the shining banners to be Jesus' light where they had rejected Him before. And the challenge we consecrated ourselves anew to fulfill was to take this holy Jesus, the Light, to our own cities and towns.

You Have Not Denied My Name

When writing chapter 3, I referred you to this chapter for the third of the three reasons no one has been able to shut the door of prayer that Jesus opened to me in 1967. That third reason was "because . . . you have not denied My name."

This was Jesus in heaven speaking to the apostle John on the isle of Patmos, commending the church at Philadelphia that no one could shut the door He, Jesus, had opened to them—because (1) "you have a little power," (2) "you have kept My word," and (3) "you have not denied My name" (Rev. 3:8).

I've just scratched the surface trying to write of the passion of my heart since the day I accepted Jesus at nine years of age. Since then I have given my entire life—including my prayer life—to Jesus. I'm constantly struggling to lose my life for His sake—and then experiencing His ecstatic joy in exchange for my human inadequacies. I tenaciously hang on to the name of Jesus, no matter what direction other Christians are going. I weep with Jesus over the slighting of the name that is above every name—the precious name of Jesus I learned to pray as a child.

However, many Christians are not aware that they are denying Jesus' name. Usually it is done in blissful ignorance.

There are times and ways we, perhaps unknowingly, deny Him. When we are building our own kingdoms in *our own names* instead of building the kingdom of God's dear Son in our service for Him—that is denying His name. When we *forget* His name while we are consumed by the name of our favorite football, basketball, or hockey team. We *ignore* His name when explaining a biblical truth that finds its culmination and current application because of Jesus' death, resurrection, and ascension. This is denying Jesus' name.

Here are some more possible innocent ways in which we Christians deny His name:

- When our music in the *car or home* does not include songs about Jesus.

- When our *bookshelves* are crammed with books, some good and some not so good, without being able to tell we are Christians.

- When all of our *periodicals and donor lists* we support are secular.

- When the *reading material on our nightstands* never include Jesus.

These are not deliberately denying Jesus. But He who sees all these sides of us is crying out, *What have you done with Me?*

Then there are those times when Christians deliberately deny Jesus' name. Not all Christians are anxious for people to see Jesus in them at all times—or even know they are Christians.

When we are embarrassed to admit we are Christians in certain social circles, or when it is a disadvantage to be honest about Jesus in business circles—that is denying Jesus. At those times when being a Christian may not be politically correct and we carefully avoid letting it be known, we are denying our Jesus. We have become like Peter.

After Peter bragged that, even if everybody else failed Jesus, he would never fall away, Jesus warned him, "Truly . . . this very night before the cock crows you shall deny Me three times" (Matt. 26:34). That night as Jesus was arrested and led away to Caiaphas the high priest, Peter followed at a distance and stayed in the courtyard while they held court to convict Jesus. When recognized, Peter progressed from denying he had been with Jesus to denying it with an oath. Then when confronted with the accusation, "Surely you too are one of them; for the way you talk gives you away," Peter began to curse and swear, "I do not know the man!" (vv. 73–74)

Of course, there are those to whom Jesus will say on Judgment Day:

I never knew you. Depart from Me (Matt. 7:23).

Christians today rarely sink to cursing and swearing in denying Jesus; they usually just shrink from openly living and sharing Him.

Jesus had very strong words for those who deny Him before people:

Everyone therefore who shall confess Me before men, I will also confess him before My Father who is in heaven. But whoever shall deny Me before men, I will also deny him before My Father who is in heaven (Matt. 10:32–33).

But this Jesus whom we deny is the same Jesus who invites us to be forgiven. Even Peter, when he went out and wept bitterly over his horrible denial of his Lord, was forgiven by Jesus.

This same Jesus not only invites us to let Him forgive us, but He also paid the price on the cross so that we could be forgiven. The One whose name we are embarrassed to speak shed His own blood for the forgiveness of *that* sin. What we are denying is what has made our forgiveness and salvation possible—Jesus and His death on the cross.

This is the same Jesus who then used Peter to preach the first sermon—

starting the Christian movement for the whole world until the end of time.

This is the same Jesus who forgives our denying Him when we pray repenting—and restores us to usefulness in His service too.

We Want to See Jesus

At a women's retreat in Florida, we did an exercise in which everyone went off alone in absolute silence, read a portion of Scripture, and prayed for God to change us through it. I had prayed much and thought God would have me assign a certain chapter for us to read. But as I was walking up to speak, the Lord very powerfully said to me, *Matthew 28!* A little concerned that this chapter about Easter morning and the Great Commission was too familiar, I still obeyed God, announced it, and sent them off to read and pray through Matthew 28.

Returning still in silence, we formed small groups of four to share. When I gave the signal to start speaking again, they almost exploded. Our own group included one of the officers of the organization. She just stood there stunned, her face actually glowing. "I saw Jesus!" she said. Later she led in prayer from the platform, and several said to me, "Did you see her face glowing?" Why? She had seen Jesus!

The rest had found Jesus in that chapter too—every side of Him imaginable. Lunchtime should have concluded their sharing, but I knew they had much yet to say. So with two and a half hours left of my teaching, I turned the roving mike over to them for the next hour and a half. The message became so clear as they shared one by one.

Some learned they should seek Jesus as the women did at the tomb, others stopped at encountering the risen Jesus, and some lingered just being with Him. Some stopped to worship Him as the women had done that first Easter morning, some were overwhelmed that all authority had been given to Jesus, and others saw they were to expect the world to refute His resurrection. Many felt His sending them, others promised to obey His Great Commission, and others clung to His promise to be with them always—even to the end of the age. It was awesome.

After the attendees had left, the officers had their usual annual meeting with their speaker to decide what to do next year. After many suggestions from each of them, they asked for my opinion. I said I wouldn't dare even venture a guess—because they already had their mandate from Jesus—directly to their members. They were to lead their followers deeper into Jesus this next year—the Jesus whom they all had just seen in Matthew 28!

The secret of keeping our public praying centered on Jesus is spending enough time with Him in private.

Praying in Jesus' name produces a joy that is humanly indescribable. (Review chapter 2 for the mind-boggling magnitude of what A.D. praying includes.) How foolish we are to shortchange ourselves when all of this *power* and *answered prayer* and *joy* have been available for two thousand years. But not only is it available, Jesus actually instructed us to pray in His name—that our joy might be full! Again here is Jesus telling us about it: "Until now you have asked for nothing in My name; ask, and you will receive, that your joy may be made full" (John 16:24).

We need to love that name, need to want to say that name, need to practice saying it, singing it, praying it—Jesus! That is what engulfs our beings with His joy.

Is There Hope?

Yes, there is hope! It seems that there is a widespread moving toward restoring Jesus in the prayer movement taking hold in our country. We see many indications of people searching for Jesus to become more meaningful in their lives.

There is a steady growth of signs that Jesus is not only being given His rightful place, but also again is being extolled. Many organizations and churches that have mostly based their teaching and doctrine on

Old Testament principles (without realizing what they were leaving out) suddenly are lifting up Jesus as the Redeemer, the Savior, and the coming King of kings. They now are majoring on the awesome results of His incarnation, death, resurrection, and ascension—with thrilling prayer answers.

God is increasingly answering the prayers that were prayed in the prayer movement thirty years ago! There has been a steady persisting in prayer as increasing thousands have faithfully prayed, and God has heard!

One large committee to which I have belonged for many years caused me deep concern by its almost constant emphasis on theology of what was before Jesus came to earth. I have prayed deeply and persistently—with Jesus—about what we were doing to Him. I was not alone in my praying. Others have shared how they, too, have been praying that prayer for several years. One said he dropped off the committee a couple of years for that reason.

But God does answer prayer! My heart almost exploded with joy at our last annual meeting. We have turned a dramatic corner! There was an absolute radiating of Jesus in our leaders as one by one they shared Him—not just a good scriptural lesson from another Bible character. The new plans, projects, and revamped objectives all centered on Jesus. It was the greatest meeting we ever had. One member reported of later hearing one leader's message—absolutely burning with fire to make Jesus known in ever deepening ways.

When it was my turn to share, I tried to contain my excitement. Overwhelmed and excited at God's answering so many years of praying, I said, "It seems to me that in America we have turned from a God-inspired human prayer movement to a divine moving of God—in Jesus' name!"

From a prayer *movement* to a *moving* of God! It is happening!

Reflection Questions

Examine your life:

Take a quick mental inventory of what music you play in your car, your home, or your workplace. Which books are on your nightstand—in your bookcases? What periodicals come in your mailbox? Which fundraising organizations have your support? What pictures are on your walls? Do you find it easier to talk about *God* in general than to identify with Jesus by name? Is Jesus pleased and smiling –or is He crying, "What have you done with *Me*"?

Scripture:

Turn to John 20 in your Bible. Pray asking Jesus to remove all your preconceived familiar ideas and to give you a fresh new vision of Himself. Read unit 1 until you feel perhaps a powerful or even a twinge of Him touching your heart. Stop and pray *to* Jesus or *with* Him if possible. Take time to stay in Jesus' presence, focusing on what He has revealed to you. (If you choose, finish the chapter now or continue using it this way until completed.)

For you to do:

Record where Jesus stopped you. In your own words, write down what your fresh glimpse of Him gave you. What was your response to Him?

For you to pray:

"Holy, holy Jesus—please forgive me for replacing Your name with my ministry's, my church's—with my own-name. Forgive me for being ashamed to say Your name when it was not politically or socially correct. Jesus, please replace my ego and my personal ambitions with *You!* Thanks for suffering and dying for me. Help me to love You so much that I will want to say that name, sing that name, pray in that name—Your name—JESUS—always, everywhere! Yes, in Your name I pray, amen."

CHAPTER 12

What We Are Doing with Jesus?

THAT THERE was "something more" that women could do for Jesus had been burning in my heart for years. Often I had cried out to God for a powerful army of Christian women to pray for and to reach the world for Jesus—longing to reverse so much of what many Christians were doing with Jesus.

The "something more" our world needed was Jesus. And the power to bring Him to our world was prayer.

On June 7, 1989, while reading about Jesus appearing to Saul on the Damascus road, suddenly I felt a powerful call to reach the lost who were without Jesus in the whole world. Exploding from my heart was the prayer, "Oh, Jesus, I want to tell the whole world about *You!*" Then in January of 1991 an invitation came to me from Lorry Lutz, director of the AD2000 Christian Women United, to be its North American women's coordinator—a direct answer to that prayer.

The AD2000 international movement was exactly what I had been praying for all those years. Christians all over the world were coming together with one goal and one timetable: to pray for and reach every man, woman, and child in the world with a culturally understandable gospel of Jesus by the year 2000. (Another year was added later, making it "AD2000 and Beyond" by the year 2001.)

Kathryn Grant had the same burden, and for several years when ministering we knelt together, asking God to let us be part of organizing America's women to do it. At our first AD2000 international directors' meeting that May, I asked for Kathryn to be my co-chair.

Perhaps you have missed hearing about this exciting movement. If so, this chapter will show you the women's part in God's awesome calling of millions of people worldwide to be a part of the whole international AD2000 movement He was raising up. Starting in the late eighties, God had been individually burdening leadership and laypeople all over the world with the same urgency to pray for and reach the whole world for Jesus by the year 2000. They were ready—and so were we!

Our women's "something more" was simply adding the praying for and sharing of Jesus (evangelism) to whatever God had called their organization or church to be doing. We were to be a *network*. Not organizing women, not taking them away from their current calling, but just adding that something more—evangelism.

However, becoming "something more" would take extraordinary prayer. *It would have to be God's empowering it and accomplishing it—in answer to a new and deeper dependence on Him in prayer.*

Our First Prayers

Suddenly the insurmountable task of attempting to call North America's Christian women together with a common cause loomed ominously. So again Kathryn and I started to pray. For months we prayed through lists of names of women in leadership, bombarding heaven and begging God for wisdom. He assured us of each of His choices, and when we telephoned them, everyone (except one) gasped and responded with, "I knew there was something more, but I didn't know what it was. Now I know. This is it!"

Sixty-four of us gathered for our first meeting in Washington, D.C., in May 1992, still uncertain what *it* possibly might be. We had been instructed to include as many different Christian theological persuasions and as much ethnic diversity as possible, which we did. But most of them never had met anybody from "that" church before. They were skeptical—and we were apprehensive!

Prayer Brought Surprising Reconciliation

Facing those already successful leaders, I admitted to them that I was not sure myself if this project was God's will. So I asked us all to kneel and pray silently, asking God if and how we should continue, and not to pray out loud until they individually got an answer from God. It took about twenty minutes of silence before there was a gushing of prayer, all affirmative. *Yes, God said we were to join together with our resources, support, prayer, and unity to reach our country for Jesus!*

Immediately the unseen barriers that had divided us melted. It was as if all of the ministries we had built were like sandcastles on the beach—and a huge wave had leveled them all. The ground suddenly was flat at the foot of the cross!

Much prayer for wisdom—along with plans to cooperate, to share materials, to build up one another, and to pray for each other—kept us busy until our parting prayer.

Then we divided two by two, each having just one prayer partner. People rarely allow leaders the privilege of admitting they have needs, and these women were no exception. So I asked one to share a personal need with her partner, then the partner to pray for her. They then were to exchange roles. Their eager response surprised me, since they were so diverse in theology and prayer methods. I glanced up from my praying in time to see two powerful leaders (each representing hundreds of thousands of followers) who had never communicated in any way with the other—weeping. With their arms encircling each other, the tears of joy were rolling down their faces. Women who had not really trusted each others' differences now loving each other—united as one in fulfilling Jesus' Great Commission to this day. God had performed our first miracle!

AD2000 North America Women's Track was born! *We were about to see what God would do with a network completely focused on Jesus and run on prayer!*

Building Our Network on Prayer

Many subsequent meetings with growing numbers at Kay Arthurs's Precept headquarters multiplied the joy. Hugs and squeals of delight are still the order of the day when our leaders meet. And the same love and oneness has spilled over to all of our women, not only in our country, but around the world as we have seen the unity of the body of Christ actually working.

Praying together produces unity. Planning, working, and having meetings together can produce wonderful oneness, *but there is a depth of love that comes only through prayer.*

Although we have been loosely knit organizationally, we have been tightly interwoven together in Jesus' oneness. Our long, deep times of prayer whenever we meet have become the most precious part of our relationship. We often are overwhelmed with awe as the presence of Jesus engulfs us. Tears flow, hearts exult, and songs of praise break forth. *What God does when women pray!*

People often ask Kathryn and me what the secret is of two women working together, always arriving at God's answer for our sometimes-differing views. *The answer is praying—with both of us desperately desiring God's will, not our own.* For twenty years, we have knelt in prayer in Kathryn's den and beseeched the Father for an answer or held hands and prayed quick SOS prayers in a prison. We have struggled over never-ending needs and decisions for our women's prayer and evangelism network and prayed long-distance between Kathryn living in Florida, North Carolina, Japan, or Singapore and me in Minnesota. But God always transcended the miles with oneness in passion and purpose—uniting us in Jesus' awesome love—to share Him.

Our other original officer, secretary-treasurer Sally Hanson, joined us in prayer, with her special prayer partner Jeanne Wagner, constantly holding up her end of the heavy administrative load—and us. JoAnne Jankowski, our legal adviser and officer, has been one of our most faithful pray-ers. Our hearts, like the 120 in the upper room after Jesus ascended, truly were in one accord.

For these whole nine years, without a break, my own personal United Prayer Ministry Board has prayed through every AD2000 need and decision for me. At monthly board meetings, they took notes as I shared in depth every facet of our network and then prayed for me until the next meeting. Three times a week, our telephone prayer chains called for specific requests and prayed fervently until the answer came from God. Every month, eighty handpicked intercessors on our prayer calendar were mailed detailed ongoing or anticipated needs. Faithful, persistent, consistent, fervent pray-ers!

National and Regional Conference Praying

There are special kinds of prayer that have produced the power of God we have seen in our conferences.

Prayer by women. All of the women involved in organizing prayer conferences pray constantly between regional and national conferences. Each location, theme, speaker, workshop, and musician is decided through much prayer by our officers, and the chair and her committees constantly seek God's guidance and will as they labor for the year preceding the meetings.

Before our 1995 "Women in Evangelism I" conference on the Wheaton (Illinois) College campus in July, our praying was special— begging God for an outpouring of His Spirit. That college was in the midst of the revival that had spread from Texas that spring, and each night, students had waited for hours in line to confess their sins and deposit garbage bags full of paraphernalia from sinful lifestyles. God was sweeping through the campus. I remember vividly how many of us agonized in prayer, begging God to keep the revival going at Wheaton—or to ignite it again when we got there in July.

Barbara Blanchard, our national board's prayer chair, is a Wheaton alumna and checked into a room on campus, spending ten days interceding for an outpouring of God for us. And God answered! The director of the Billy Graham School of Evangelism told us that we had the greatest power of the Holy Spirit of any meetings ever held there. Why? Because of the prayer—deep, agonizing, beseeching prayer!

Prayer for each convention. Each convention has had its own praying as its directors have enlisted powerful local intercessors. Our chairpersons have been selected because of their absolute belief in the necessity of prayer and their ability to organize and sustain it. And they have done it!

Preconference prayer the day before each event. Women pay to come a day early to attend and pray. Barbara, our prayer chair, reported about her pre-prayer day at our second Wheaton conference in 1999: "There was ecstasy, exuberance, somber meditation, conviction, and commitment—resulting in prayer and praise. We experienced the breaking down of cultural and denominational barriers and the warmth of love and acceptance." One commented, "The most moving part of the conference was the deep prayer offered then and also throughout the weekend on site by nearly twenty men."

As a result of all that prayer, women reported to us: "The preconference prayer set a tone of excitement and anticipation. My eyes and ears were opened to understand."

Others said, "It was a God-thing. I can't even put into words what happened. It was incredible, amazing!" "We came to understand the power of prayer. Everything was bathed in prayer!"

Still another commented, "I didn't expect the Lord to speak so clearly to me. Now I don't want to stand before my God with a list of empty excuses as to why I did not obey Him!"

Praise God with us for what He did when we prayed!

What Prayer Produces

Our conventions have been designed to bring Jesus' compassion for the lost to the individual women, with God sending them back to their own sphere of influence—to put into practice what He said to them. The miracles God has brought about as women have streamed home to start praying and witnessing for Jesus are awesome.

Individuals. Our Wheaton '99 Conference was carefully built around Mary Lance Sisk's *Love Your Neighbor* teaching and book. But a few days before it was to begin, she had carotid artery surgery. We thought everything had fallen apart. As we desperately prayed and scrambled to work out a new program format, the Lord kept saying, *Just Jesus!* to both of us.

Looking back, we are amazed at how little time was actually spent on books and procedures—and how much of our time focused on Jesus. His passion for the lost, His love, His sacrifice, His authority, His power, His commands, and His promises—from one speaker after another, all these became ours. The most incredible thing is that such a large percentage of the individual attendees eagerly accepted, *not our human persuasion*, but *God's call* to pray for, to love, and to share Jesus with their neighbors and friends. Everything we had hoped for and prayed for was there!

Entire churches. Barb Blanchard's own city was deeply impacted by the forty-two women from her church who attended the Wheaton '99 Conference. Here are a few things from Barb that are happening:

Group witnessing began at the Chicago airport on the return trip. Fervor in outreach with boldness has increased. Many unexpected opportunities to "splash living water" [from Esther Burrough's message] have arisen among motorcyclists, boaters, apartment dwellers, the poor and homeless, immigrants, and in the workplace. Prayer triplets have formed, prayer walking has commenced, neighborhood events have been held, the city has been mapped, and commitments have been made. Thirteen women are beginning to lead neighborhood studies. A teacher who was saved in August began a prayer fellowship at a local high school. Fifteen enthusiastic faculty and staff have begun to pray, share, and help start a student prayer group. New Bible studies have begun in two inner-city elementary schools. One has adopted the theme "Love Your School." Empowered by the Holy Spirit at Wheaton, one woman has been able to share spiritual truth every day since her return! So far she is discipling the two who have received Christ. The whole church has been trained in prayer and evangelism.

A refugee from the Congo had been abused, had two children, ran away from her home in Africa, and ended up in this church. When she came to our Wheaton '99 Conference on evangelism praying, she said the Holy Spirit ignited her with a fire to make Jesus known everywhere she goes. Her mother back in the Congo had been an evangelist, and God kindled the gift of evangelism in her at Wheaton. She is very interested in the immigrant community and is now leading a Bible study for twenty-two women, many of whom she led to Jesus. Astoundingly, the man with the usual Congo custody of her two children ended up a refugee in the same city—and, as the church marshaled prayer, she got her children back. Now she is planning to go to Bible school here and then go back to bring Jesus to her own people.

Small-town groups. The following note is from a group that is still praying with great results: "Thank you for the way you have ministered to me. Wheaton '95 was a pivotal time in my life. God wants us to move with Him—not to wait for the organized church."

Triplet Prayer Groups

My dream since 1984 has been to see whole neighborhoods, cities, nations, and even the whole world teeming with Christians praying in their small triplet groups—and then, while loving them with deeds of kindness, reaching them with Jesus' salvation!

The triplet method of pre-evangelism prayer is the basic praying we are teaching. As I mentioned in chapter 5, the triplet prayer method consists of three Christians each choosing three non-Christians they know or love and praying together a minimum of fifteen minutes once a week for the salvation of their collective nine. The secret is accountability and accessibility—with no large outlay of finances or programming.

When I was training the pray-ers for Billy Graham and Luis Palau's Mission England I, Brian Mills traveled with us, signing up pray-ers for their triplet program to pray for the lost before the crusades. They had started them two months before I arrived, and I would ask how many (having prayed at the most two months) had already seen at least one from their triplet accept Jesus. Never fewer than 25 percent raised their hands. Ninety thousand Christians prayed in triplets for a year before their evangelistic campaigns. And both evangelists reported that they had the greatest results in souls they had ever had—at least to that time!

Billy Graham's *Decision* magazine reported that before Billy and Luis even got there, many triplets saw all nine for whom they were praying accept Jesus. Prayer triplets work!

Esme Bowers, international coordinator for AD2000 in South Africa, reported that in 1997 she organized prayer triplets for a group of fifteen people in a small East London church and watched their faces light up. At the end of the month, the pastor phoned to say that he had ten new converts to be baptized that Sunday from the prayer triplets. Ten months later, he phoned to report that he now has seventy new members as a result of the prayer triplets that they adopted as their program. He hadn't baptized anyone in the previous ten years!

Esme said about her church in 1998, "I trained thirty-five people during a ten-week course with the *Study Guide for Evangelism Praying*. At the end of the ten-week course, thirty converts had come to know the Lord as a result of the prayer triplets. Six months later, I asked them to report to me any new converts. At least sixty-one had come to know the Lord through the triplets. Eight of the people were formerly Muslims. Women come to me in church to say they can see people's hearts softening." Esme now has more than fifteen hundred prayer triplets and has taught eighty-five seminars based on the *Study Guide for Evangelism Praying* since 1995. The power of prayer triplets!

New Plateau of Praying

When assigned the task in 1991 of producing prayer training material for all the AD2000 women around the world, I literally wrote it in my prayer closet—writing down what God knew was needed for this new plateau of praying for the nineties. This was to be switching our emphasis from the usual praying for our own needs to praying for the spiritually lost. Without remuneration and giving it all free to be used by our women internationally, I wrote to those who would use my A *Study Guide for Evangelism Praying*:

> The overwhelming desire of my heart is for whole nations to be filled with triplets of Christians—praying, loving, caring, witnessing—until the entire world is teeming with new believers in Jesus. This curriculum contains the heart of what God has taught me through a whole lifetime of ministry, and I have seen Him do great

and mighty things as I personally have taught these scriptural precepts to hundreds of thousands. This is the heart of the Gospel of
Jesus condensed into these few pages.[1]

Evangelism praying was also Paul's heart's desire after Jesus called
him on the Damascus road. As he shared in Romans 10:1:

My heart's desire and *prayer* for them is *for their salvation*. (emphasis
added)

I deliberately kept the curriculum simple so everybody around the
world could understand it, yet profound enough to include all the essen-
tials from the Bible needed to reach the world with salvation in Jesus.
We kept it short and inexpensive, condensing it in outline form into
just a small book. Then I promised that if they would follow its biblical
instructions step by step, they would have the indescribable joy of
watching the power of God reach those for whom they have prayed
with new life in Jesus Christ. Reports from around the world continue
to pour in as to the power of this kind of praying as they are doing it on
every continent. Here are the six simple study guide sections:

1. Why Evangelize? Jim Weidmann, executive director of the United
States' annual National Day of Prayer, while attending his first
National Committee meeting with us, said to me, "I'm a 'why' man. All
these evangelism organizations are just teaching methods. None is
telling *why* we should do it." "Except ours," I responded.

I had wondered at God's clear instruction to have our study guide open
with, "Why evangelize?" *Why* bring Jesus to the whole world? Of course
there is the well-known Great Commission of Jesus (which has not been
accomplished in almost two thousand years). But God wanted to challenge us Christians with the sobering thoughts that Jesus had done His
part on the cross—that He had left the reaching of the world to us—and

that Jesus said the end cannot come until we finish that task (see Matt. 24:14) because all nations will be represented in heaven (see Rev. 5:8–9).

God also wanted to bring us pray-ers back to the fact that the Bible really says that all people who have not accepted Jesus, even from other religions, are condemned already and need to be evangelized (see John 3:18). This is to alert us to the false doctrine of tolerance that is gaining ground today. Even more devastating, God wanted to reinforce the Bible's teaching that the future of those without belief in Jesus is an everlasting place of torment and banishment (see Rev. 20:15).

Our prayer life will change dramatically when we understand that, biblically, everyone who is not a believer in Jesus belongs to the domain of darkness and needs to be transferred to the kingdom of light through the forgiveness of his or her sins (see Acts 26:15–18). And Jesus came as light so that no one needs to remain in that spiritual darkness (see John 12:46). What really motivates us to change our praying is God's provision for all those still in spiritual darkness and the indescribable, abundant life available to them, with Jesus living in them here and eternal life in heaven with Him!

2. Our Personal Preparation. Some of the most important teaching that has not become obsolete since *What Happens When Women Pray* is that there are personal lifestyle requirements in order for our prayers to be answered by God. (See chapter 2 for the two classes of sins, which never become obsolete.) It has been amazing how many want to pray for others to be saved, only to discover they do not know Jesus personally either.

3. God's Power for Reaching the World. There has been much emphasis on winning people to Jesus through projects and programs, but Jesus warned His followers that they should not try to reach the world until they had received power of the Holy Spirit (see Luke 24:48–49). Understanding that the Holy Spirit works mightily in us to give us boldness and courage and that He alone can convict a sinner (see 1 Thess. 1:5) drastically changes our praying for and reaching the lost for Jesus.

4. How to Pray for the Lost. God has shown us that pre-evangelism praying is absolutely necessary because the reason we frequently see so few souls saved in proportion to our financial and organizational efforts is because we have failed to involve God in their lives through prayer first. The triplet prayer method is so effective because it stresses accountability and accessibility. Jesus taught that the devil snatches the gospel seed as fast as we can sow it, and Paul shows us that Satan has blinders on the minds of the unbelieving so that they cannot even see the light of the gospel of the glory of Christ. Only prayer in the authority of the name and blood of Jesus is effective in overcoming these spiritual obstacles.

5. How to Pray for Each Other. Surprisingly, pray-ers find that once they start praying for the lost in earnest, as one said, "All hell breaks loose." Praying for each other while we are reaching the lost is imperative because Satan does not want to relinquish those in his kingdom of darkness. It is startling to see that the New Testament attributes directly to Satan many of the problems Christians encounter—especially in evangelism praying and witnessing. But the Bible's emphasis on the wonderful promises of victory in the subtle ways Satan tries to thwart us is our hope and reason for praying for each other in this battle (see Eph. 6:8).

6. How to Reach People for Jesus. Juliet Thomas has organized triplet praying in every major city in India, but she asked me to include in the study guide *how those praying women could then lead those for whom they are praying to Jesus.* This kind of prayer task is not finished until they have had a definite opportunity to accept Jesus. Another step is praying for the new convert and sharing brief follow-up steps as they, too, become not just converts, but intercessors.

But There Is Still More

Mary Lance Sisk sat in front of me while I taught a prayer seminar in Charlotte, North Carolina. Suddenly both of us were aware of what felt like a strong electric current flowing between us. At that moment, she knew she was called to work with me in the goal of reaching the lost for Jesus—and I knew it at the same time!

God has given Mary Lance Sisk a wonderful method of prayer walking and loving your neighbors to Jesus called *Love Your Neighbor*. It adds another wonderful prayer method and puts feet to our evangelism praying while sharing tangible ways to love our neighbors.

Mary's book *Love Your Neighbor* encourages building relationships, gathering others to pray, opening your home, having compassion for and loving your neighbors, and bringing them to Jesus. It is a powerful method of neighborhood evangelism. We are so excited to see how God had this all planned for one to complement the other.

She and her husband, Bob, are leaders in the amazing prayer movement in Charlotte, and the "Love Your Neighbor" concept is exploding around our country. It has been translated for international use to be used in the same network as the study guide. Isn't God awesome?

Prayer, Care, Share

A very important part of our praying and sharing Jesus is caring. Bringing Jesus' love in as many different ways as there are spheres of influence of our women has opened doors and hearts to the gospel, along with *Love Your Neighbor*. Here are just a few:

Inner cities. Our board member Helen Harris hosted wonderful inner-city block parties during our conventions in Miami, Atlanta, Wheaton, and Bakersfield, California. She works with local churches and Christian organizations that have gathered donated clothing, children's games, a nurses' station for health checkups, and food. The children and adults who gather around first to listen to a local pastor preach Jesus and then enjoy the party. Breaking into groups of three or four led by counselors, her women knock on doors, inviting people to the block party or lingering on porches, sharing Jesus. A drill team or a choir may perform. Back at the convention, Helen and her women excitedly share with all of us how many accepted Jesus and other fantastic stories. It is one of the highlights of our convention!

Helen says she learned to pray with and disciple her neighbors after reading *What Happens When Women Pray* in the seventies, when she and her young family lived in inner-city Los Angeles, a community in which a large percentage of the children were on drugs, pregnant, and in gangs. Many of the fathers were in prison. She started teaching prayer to a group of desperate mothers, hosted Friendship Bible Coffees, and shared Christ with Campus Crusade's *Four Spiritual Laws*—a perfect example of what we were doing as a network! As she shared her story with us at our 1995 Wheaton Conference, she had a whole row of lovely, well-dressed, and educated young ladies stand. "These are those children from that community for whom we prayed so diligently—and introduced to Jesus!" said Helen as a thunderous applause broke forth. She still reaches that community with birthday cakes for the children, unconditional love, sacrifice—and Jesus.

Retirement homes. The president of a large retirement home network related to me how her life was turned around when she read *What Happens When Women Pray*. Through many years, she has seen the incredible results of putting prayer into her facilities. Senior citizens need our love and attention, but most of all they need our Jesus—now and for the eternity they are facing.

Hospitals. Our daughter Jan told me when I was writing the study guide not to leave out 1 John 5:13: "These things have I written to you who believe in the name of the Son of God, in order that you may know that you have eternal life." As the critical-care doctor of her hospital, Jan said the one thing most dying people want to know is where they are going. Is there eternal hope? Can I be sure? "I always leave 1 John 5:13 on their dying lips—after I have brought them Jesus!"

Airports. Stewardess Marilyn Wallberg has formed *Fly from Your Knees* with two other flight attendants from other airlines who met at our Wheaton '99 Conference. They are committed to praying every Tuesday morning for their airlines and their neighbors—fellow flight attendants with whom they work. Others are joining them.

Prisons. Ministering in prisons, says Fran Howard, is frightening because of the multiplying of the conditions that produce our bulging prison population. As one abused child becomes old enough to reproduce, several more just like him or her are born—to multiply again and again the abusive lifestyle. The addicts bring up addicted children. The molested become the molester—until they get Jesus. What drug programs fail to do, God sometimes does overnight. Jesus provides victory to those who bring their own praying to Satan with them—into his domain in many prisons. Then these released prisoners return to reach others with the freedom they found in Jesus while still incarcerated.

Curriculum Around the World

I'm frequently asked, "Did God ever answer the prayer of 'Jesus, I want to tell the whole world about You' that you prayed in 1989?"

Perhaps the greatest way was that my assigned task as part of the AD2000 international leadership team was to write the evangelism prayer curriculum, which has been translated into forty-seven languages (that we know of), plus multiple tribal ones. We have given it free and let groups keep any profit from sales to finance their own evangelism outreach. In Russia, they give one copy to each church, and the women copy it to share with others. They even have sent two copies to the North Pole.

Violet Metegha, regional representative for French-speaking Africa until her death in 1998, traveled to twelve countries, gathering women from all denominations and backgrounds to train with them. After Violet's visit, a group of women started sharing the gospel in another village. It ended with a march of more than two hundred women in a third city—with many accepting Jesus.

Lorry Lutz estimates that hundreds of thousands of women have studied the booklet in their own language and are praying in triplets for unsaved friends and relatives and for an unreached people group. Iqbal Massy has started more than one thousand triplets with a goal of five thousand more. Juliet Thomas has triplets organized and operational in every major city in India. Directors from other continents report similar praises.

The *Study Guide for Evangelism Praying* is the AD2000 women's evangelism curriculum across the globe. Although for seventeen years God has given me the privilege of teaching on almost every continents with an average of 25 percent accepting Jesus, He knew that no one person ever could begin to make an impact on the billions who need Jesus globally. *So He answered my prayer by using that little book to help others win the lost right around them to Jesus—without me!*

North America: A Mission Field?

Before our first meeting, Kathryn (a missionary for twenty years in Japan) and I (having ministered around the world for then ten years) struggled with the popular concept that North America was only to be the sending and supporting country in global missions, not a mission field itself. As we prayed deeply about it, I still can hear God's clear, firm words to my heart: *Evelyn, your country needs Jesus as badly as any country in the world!* Kathryn received the same assurance from Him.

None of us in our network has stopped reaching the whole world for Jesus just as we had before—praying, supporting, and still going. But we have now learned that the United States is one of the top three largest mission fields in the world.

Dee Eastman, wife and coworker of Dick, president of Every

Home for Christ, shared these statistics with us at our 1998 Atlanta Convention:

Our nation is a mosaic of Americans representing five hundred ethnic groups who communicate in 686 languages and dialects. Forty-two million Americans speak little or no English. The fastest-growing religion in America is Islam with twenty-five thousand converts each year with the majority coming from Catholic, Protestant, and Jewish backgrounds. Our own American Indians after two hundred years are still 94 percent unevangelized, and the Zunis and Hopis with six thousand each are considered two of the most unreached tribal groups in the world.

God has brought the world to our doorstep! North America is a huge unreached mission field—and a vital part of the world Jesus told us to reach for Him.

Following Jesus' Evangelism Plan

Why did Jesus tell His followers to wait in Jerusalem after He ascended? To wait for the Holy Spirit certainly was the main reason. But could it also have been that He knew that at the end of the ten days of praying, that city would be teeming with two to three million people celebrating Pentecost?

There were two categories of people who, according to the Acts 2 account, needed to hear of Jesus in their own tongue. The first group consisted of the Jews living in Jerusalem who heard in their own language to which they were *born* (see Acts 2:5–10). Although Jesus spoke Aramaic and Hebrew, He evidently never spoke to those from every nation under heaven in their own languages. The second group of people included the visitors, Roman Jews, proselytes, Cretans, and Arabs—who also heard in their own language. Those visitors were among the three thousand saved after that first sermon by Peter who returned to their homelands—with Jesus *in* them—to start evangelizing the world!

So it is with America today. Tom Phillips, President/CEO of International Students, Inc., reports that there are 601,000 future leaders of our world who currently are studying in our nation from nearly two hundred countries worldwide. Then the converts are communicating with relatives and acquaintances in their homelands, which are frequently closed mission fields. If we reach those students with Jesus, they will be able to share the gospel where we cannot. Most graduates go back to become leaders with their professional degrees—and if we pray and reach them with the light of Jesus, they take Jesus *with* them and spread His light. Our Jerusalem!

Did you know that the largest Christian church is in South Korea and that the world's largest Buddhist temple is in Los Angeles? Juliet Thomas from India excitedly said to me, "Oh, you have the 10/40 Window right in America!"

Are we forgetting that Jesus commanded His followers to go to the uttermost parts of the earth—beginning at their own Jerusalem?

But Don't Go without Power

When Jesus was ready to ascend to heaven, His followers must have been exploding with eagerness to go tell everybody about Him. But He sternly warned them, "You are to stay in the city until you are clothed with power from on high" (Luke 24:49).

In 1997, God gave me the same warning Jesus gave His disciples as He kept taking me back to Ezekiel 37, assuring me that there would be a great army of women reaching out to the lost. But He showed me many Christians today are like those in 2 Timothy 3:5, who are "holding to a form of godliness, although they have denied its power."

Yes, there is a rattling of the dry bones out there, but they have no breath [literally, "Spirit"] *in them,* God spoke to my heart. *Be careful that you don't mobilize a bunch of breathless bodies. Don't mobilize an army of walking zombies!*

This is one of our most urgent prayer requests for our AD2000 network—praying for God to send the power of His Holy Spirit into everything we do.

A Network Rudder?

How do you run a network? How do you steer without usurping the rights God has given to each organization and church? I puzzled over and prayed about that with every decision. Two years into the AD2000 network, God unexpectedly gave me the answer when I had asked Him to direct where I should read in the Bible that morning. *The Book of Esther,* He flashed into my mind.

"Oh, no," I countered. "I never want to hear that introduction 'Here she is for such a day as this!' ever again. I can't stand it!" God said it three times. I obeyed.

However, this time it was different. When Esther was to be used by God to save her people, Mordecai sent word to her: "Do not imagine that you in the king's palace can escape any more than all the Jews," God showed me that being a leader does not make me everybody's boss. Instead, He clearly told me I was a *rudder*—the piece on the back of a ship that is hidden beneath the waterline, useless if it splashes around at the surface to be seen. Down where it is dark and cold, the rudder is always straining, never wavering, against the current in order to steer the big ship. I wept deeply.

God also showed me that a *rigid* rudder is useless. It must be flexible, controlled by a powerful hand of one wise enough to see and correct when the ship goes off course. That hand is God! And our leader is Jesus. He said, "And do not be called leaders; for One is your leader, that is Christ" (Matt. 23:10).

I had my answer to running a network. *Never waver. Stay true to what you have been called to do. Steer. And pray!* Most days I have prayed a minimum of two hours—for the Lord to change me first and then to steer me in how He wants me to direct in every thrilling or overwhelming situation. Not bossing—but living the deep passion of my heart to put the telling of Jesus *first* into everything else we are doing. *Not sharing some piece of Jesus' ministry, but the whole gospel—His death, His redeeming blood, His resurrection, and His beckoning a lost world to come have their sins forgiven.*

I feel I have disappointed God many times as I missed doing what I was struggling so hard to do. But always working at letting God pilot me, being brave, never compromising, and never flinching has paid off in leaders and laypeople alike grasping the vision of returning Jesus to our churches. Jane Hanson, the international president of Aglow, herself steering about six hundred thousand women, threw her arms around me as tears rolled down her cheeks. "Evelyn, I've put evangelism into all of our Aglow praying!"

I'll never forget the day Judy Mbugua, our AD2000 Women's Track international president from Kenya, completely surprised me. She is the powerful president of all-Africa's PACWA organization—training women in reading, health care, and other skills. "Evelyn," Judy wept as she hugged me and said, "I want you to know I've put evangelism in all of PACWA!"

When There Are Differences

For thirty years, I never have had a problem working with all denominations and races—because we always have just studied the Bible's straightforward teachings on prayer and practiced them accordingly. But in this network, God occasionally has expected me to stand firm on a biblical principle. *What does the leader do and what does she pray in a network where all are equal—but she is responsible for its reputation and scriptural stand?*

After much prayer about my own attitude, God confirmed what I had been trying to do. *I can still love them dearly personally but at the same time not condone what they are doing or teaching.* Discussing this difficult side of leadership with Dr. Henry Blackaby, I asked what he thought of that solution. He seemed to be putting it slowly into his heart, and then he smiled warmly and said, "That's it, Evelyn! The love and unity is still there while you are fulfilling your responsibility."

My Own Preparation Prayers

Wisdom. How puzzled I was when a year before Lorry Lutz asked me to do the AD2000 task, God had clearly directed my 1990 birthday prayer for the next year to Solomon's request for wisdom: "So give Thy servant an understanding heart to judge Thy people and to discern between good and evil" (1 Kings 3:9). Before I even knew I would be tackling that decade-long task, I prayed, "Oh, God, I don't have enough wisdom! Give me *Your* wisdom like You gave Solomon!" But little did I dream how desperately I would need that wisdom in the whole coming decade.

Righteousness. As I mentioned previously, on January 1, 1991, God showed me out of Matthew's and Luke's first chapters that everyone He used in His Son's coming to earth the first Christmas already were righteous in His eyes—Zacharias, Elizabeth, Mary, and Joseph. "Oh, Father," I cried out in prayer, "make me righteous before You in 1991 so You can use me!" And that same month the ten-year invitation came from Lorry Lutz to be the North America director for AD2000 women. God was preparing me personally.

At the end of 1999 I wrote in my Bible beside Matthew 1: "Although I have not been able to *live* a totally righteous life these eight years, God knew my heart's desire to be righteous. But it takes so much of 1 John 1:7–10's confessing!"

Something New

As AD2000/Christian Women United is in the new millennium, God has brought much to pass for which we have prayed so fervently for many years. The AD2000 board of fifteen members is each taking responsibility for the various aspects of the network and doing a fantastic job!

God is shifting the awesome nine-year load from Kathryn's and my shoulders by providing finances for an office and an administrator. Our hearts are exploding with the awesome open doors and new opportunities. Answered prayer!

At our last 1999 board meeting, I was turning over the presidency to Kathryn Grant while I assumed the role of chairman of the board. Each of us thought the other was responsible for opening devotions—so neither of us had prepared ahead of time. So among Kathryn's first words as president were, "Just read us a psalm, please, Evelyn."

Immediately I said, "Psalm 73." It was where God had taken me the previous January after struggling with whether I should continue in my administrative duties of AD2000 Christian Women United. We had just completed exhausting Mission America and Love Your Neighbor meetings in San Francisco, alternating back and forth over the Bay. It was my seventy-seventh birthday, my heart was (and is) only pumping about one-third of my blood to my body—and I was tired. I was praying, asking God to give me His advice. Immediately He put in my mind to turn to Psalm 73:

> Nevertheless I am continually with Thee;
> Thou has taken hold of my right hand.
> With Thy counsel Thou wilt guide me,
> And afterward receive me to glory.
>
> Whom have I in heaven but Thee
> And besides Thee, I desire nothing on earth.
> My flesh and my heart may fail,
> But God is the strength of my heart and my portion forever.
>
> For, behold, those who are far from Thee will perish;
> Thou hast destroyed all those who are unfaithful to Thee.
>
> But as for me, the nearness of God is my good;
> I have made the LORD God my refuge,
> That I may tell of all Thy works (vv. 23–28).

Even if I could not perform all the administrative tasks the board now had picked up so incredibly well, my vision and burden for us to keep telling everybody of the awesome works of God—crowned with the sending of His Son to save the lost world—had not diminished. My passion would be there *forever*!

Still Our Prayer

Running our network on prayer has been a part of fulfilling one of the most explicit prayers Jesus told us to pray. As He went about proclaiming the gospel of the kingdom and healing the sick, Jesus saw the multitude. He felt compassion and deep sorrow for them because they were distressed and downcast like sheep without a shepherd.

So Jesus gave His disciples—and all of us who claim to be His disciples today—this powerful command to pray for the solution to their problem:

The harvest is plentiful, but the workers are few. Therefore beseech the Lord of the harvest to send out workers into His harvest (Matt. 9:37–38).

The harvest is lost souls. All the other things we do for Jesus should be the "means to the end" that open doors, prepare hearts, and make us eligible to share Jesus.

Jesus said, "The Son of Man has come to save that which was lost" (Matt. 18:11). Had He come *only* to feed the hungry and to heal the sick, He would have been a failure—for He left multitudes hungry and sick when He went back to heaven. But His purpose in coming was *to save those who are lost*.

Praying for and harvesting those precious souls for Jesus—in His love and unity—is the something more of praying we are doing in obedience to our Savior and Lord.

Reflection Questions

Examine your life:

Is there an uneasy gnawing inside you that there must be something more you, too, should be doing for Jesus—or even a burning reprimand from Him?

In Acts 1:8, did Jesus send His followers, and you, to be witnesses to Him *only* out to the world—or *both* there *and* in out hometowns? Which of these have you been neglecting?

Have you believed that all missionary work should be on the other side of an ocean—or something more you could add right in your sphere of influence?

Scripture:

Read Matthew 9:35–38 in you Bible. Is Jesus tugging at your heart to become one of the laborers so many have been praying for? Is He calling you to do something more in the harvest filed you, too, can see right around you? Stay in silence listening to Jesus deepening the "why" of His compassion for and sharing Himself with specific people He knows still are lost. Note any practical ideas on how to start that Jesus may be bringing to your mind right now.

For you to do:

Prayerfully form a prayer triplet with two other Christians. Record the three names of your triplet:

#1 Your name _____ #2 _____ #3 _____

Write down the three without Jesus you each promise God to pray together for weekly:

#1 _____ #2 _____ #3 _____

_____ _____ _____

_____ _____ _____

List your immediate ideas of how you might "care" with loving deeds and "share" Jesus' salvation with them.

CARE: _____

SHARE: _____

For you to pray:

"Holy, holy Jesus, I long for Your "something more" in my life. Forgive me for not feeling Your compassions for the *whole* harvest field—starting right at my house and workplace and school. Thank You that You came to save all of them. I promise You that I will begin to pray immediately for them by forming my triplet and prayer walking. Jesus, explode my joy as those who need You so desperately accept You as Savior and Lord. In Your precious name, Jesus, amen."

TO ORDER A *Study Guide for Evangelism Praying* and/or its companion book *A Time to Pray God's Way* by Evelyn Christensen and *Love Your Neighbor* by Mary Lance Sisk: Christian Women Unite, 1240 Iroquois Drive, Suite 510, Naperville, Illinois 50563. E-mail *JHintzCWU@aol.com.* Fax (630) 416-7732 Phone (630) 416-9770

CHAPTER 13

The Ultimate Prayer for the New Millennium

SINCE SATAN introduced sin to Planet Earth in the Garden of Eden, there have been two, and only two, spiritual kingdoms—Satan's kingdom of darkness and Jesus' kingdom of light. As the previous millennium's culture seemed to be sliding faster and faster into the kingdom of darkness, where is the kingdom of light? As teen shootings and suicides are escalating, where is the light? As our children are being led into a sewer of violence and glorification of filthy sex by the entertainment industry, where is the moral and spiritual light for the next millennium?

The light is already here. God has sent it to the world. The Light is Jesus!

The Light, Jesus, is the only solution to these evil lifestyles that come from the darkness in their hearts. Jesus came two thousand years ago to personally bring that transforming light to earth for those still in darkness. Jesus said:

I am the light of the world; he who follows Me shall not walk in the darkness, but shall have the light of life. (John 8:12)

So the real question is not, Where is the light? The question is, How can we Christians who have the light of Jesus *pray* so that this pervading darkness will be dispelled?

The ultimate prayer that will change our families, neighborhoods, workplaces, schools, and eventually our nation and the world into light instead of darkness is simple: *We must pray for each individual who does not already believe in Jesus to accept Him as personal Savior and Lord. Then the Light, Jesus, living in the new creations will spread His light throughout their own environments.*

Cassie Burnall gave her life for her Lord at Littleton, Colorado's, Columbine High School on April 20, 1999, when two students in black trench coats gunned down twelve of their peers and one teacher in premeditated slaughter before killing themselves. As a teen, Cassie had gradually turned into a violence-prone, suicidal young woman interested in witchcraft, drugs, and alcohol, even stashing away letters of how to murder her parents. Trying to rescue their daughter, her parents changed her school and strictly controlled her social life, finally letting her go to a church youth retreat. There Cassie found Jesus!

Her father explained on a television interview that when Cassie left for camp she was gloomy, with her head dropped down and not talking. "But," he said, "when she came back, her eyes were open and bright. She was bouncy and excited about what had happened to her. *It was like she was in a dark room and somebody turned the light on.*"

What was the light that turned on in Cassie? What prepared her for the eternity she unknowingly was facing? Jesus! Jesus said, "I have come as light into the world, that everyone who believes in Me may not remain in darkness" (John 12:46).

What changed Cassie so that she would bravely answer yes about her newfound faith—the answer that brought the final bullet blast into her body? Her Lord and Savior, Jesus Christ!

We must pray that all people who are still in the kingdom of darkness will accept Jesus as their Savior and Lord—and thus be transferred into Jesus' kingdom of light also. "For He [the Father] delivered us [Christians] from the domain of darkness, and transferred us to the kingdom of His beloved Son" (Col. 1:13).

What Actually Happened to This Light, Jesus?

One of the most poignant of the many prophecies about the Light, Jesus, coming is in Isaiah 9:2: "The people who walk in darkness will see a great light, those who live in a dark land, the light will shine on them."

In the fullness of time, that prophecy was fulfilled when God sent His only begotten Son as that light, and Jesus began His earthly ministry in that dark land beyond the Jordan. "From that time Jesus began to preach and say, 'Repent, for the kingdom of God is at hand'" (Matt. 4:17).

John's Gospel opens with Jesus, the Word, being with God in the beginning—and being God—and everything coming into being by Him. Then there is the amazing revelation of Jesus' coming to earth to enlighten people in that darkness: "In Him was life, and the life was the light of men. And the light shines in darkness, and the darkness did not comprehend it. . . . There was the true light which, coming into the world, enlightens every man" (John 1:4–5, 9).

But after He ministered only a little more than three years, his enemies *snuffed out* that Light on the cross. They killed it.

Then they *buried* it in a pitch-black tomb, where there was no light.

But on Easter morning, *the light shattered the darkness.* Jesus exploded out of the tomb—alive! Not resuscitated to die again but, unique in human history, resurrected as Lord!

Then, for forty days, Jesus kept appearing to His followers. *They had Him back!*

But then—puff! *The Light was gone.* Jesus, the Light of the World, led them out to Bethany and ascended to heaven right before their eyes. *Gone!*

Was there to be no more spiritual light for Planet Earth?

Where Is the Light Now?

Jesus already had said in John 12:35, "For a little while longer the light is among you." And in John 7:33, Jesus said, "For a little while longer I am with you, then I go to Him who sent me." So they should not have expected Him to remain physically as the Light of the World.

But Jesus also already had given them the solution to His not leaving the world without spiritual light:

You are the light of the world. (Matt. 5:14)

We Christians are to be the light of the world for Him—until the Light comes back as King of kings and Lord of lords to reign forever and forever.

How Can This Be?

There is a very simple solution. It was a mystery to all those who lived before Jesus, but now has been revealed to us, Jesus' followers. Paul explained it clearly in Colossians 1:25–27: "that I might fully carry out the preaching of the word of God, that is, the mystery which has been hidden from the past ages and generations; but has now been manifested to His saints . . . this mystery . . . is Christ *in* you, the hope of glory" (emphasis added).

Lighting the moral and spiritual darkness happens when Christians, with Jesus in them, shine Jesus' light to someone—who then accepts Jesus as Savior and Lord. Then with Jesus' light in that person, he or she radiates Jesus out to another person.

True Christian lighthouses are not people with radiant personalities, sparkling smiles, or warm-fuzzy, welcome-wagon friendliness. They are people who have *Jesus* living in them (see Col. 1:27), are shining *Jesus* into a dark and lost evil world by prayer and loving deeds (see Matt. 5:14–16), and are sharing *Jesus'* love and His desire to save them.

We can only become a *lighthouse* for Jesus when He is living in us. A real lighthouse is much more than simply displaying a decal or light bulb in a window of a house. It is:

> The Light, Jesus, *in* believers
> *In* the house, workplace or school
> Shining Jesus *out from* that place
> *Into* the neighborhood, workplace or school.

Lighthouses are only necessary when it is dark and dangerous—and when people are lost. For fifty summers, our family has deep-sea fished in Lake Michigan. When the blackness of a sudden storm descended (or we had failed to notice the falling darkness in our excitement of a good catch), we would anxiously scan the horizon for the blinking light from the Pentwater lighthouse to guide us safely in to shore.

True lighthouses contain and share the secret of guiding lost people out of the kingdom of darkness into Jesus' kingdom of light.

However, the Christian's lifestyle will determine whether others can see Jesus shining. Even though Jesus actually is living in a believer, living in sin will dirty up their lenses and keep Jesus' light from shining through. (This is why we must keep up-to-date confessing our sins so that God can keep us cleansed. See 1 John 1:8–9.)

Our family sometimes conducts our own church service when we all have gathered at the log cabin in northern Minnesota. One Sunday, our lesson was from Matthew 5:14–16: "You are the light of the world. . . . Nor do men light a lamp, and put it under the peck-measure, but on the lampstand, and it gives light to all who are in the house. Let your light shine before men in such a way that they may see your good works, and glorify your Father who is in heaven."

Not having a peck measure, we used a plastic pail. After our seven-year-old grandson sang "This Little Light of Mine" and we prayed, we passed the pail around. Then each of us told some sin that *could* be in us that would keep people from seeing Jesus' light shining from us while we put the plastic pail over our head. We all became very somber as one by one—from Grandma and Grandpa, parents, teenagers, grade-schoolers, and our preschooler—each named an ordinary wrong or naughty thing that *might* be in us.

Christians who are clean lighthouses for Jesus are desperately needed today as our country plummets morally and spiritually rapidly downward. *The Light of the world, Jesus, is our only hope!*

I almost gasped at the sight in front of me at a recent Atlanta Evangelism Conference. After Dr. Henry Blackaby gave the closing address, each of the women lit a candle and held it below the pew in front of her in the pitch-black sanctuary. Then I asked *only* those who would promise to let Jesus shine from them into their own homes, neighborhoods, schools, and workplaces to raise their candles to just below their chins. Suddenly that packed auditorium was glowing with a thousand faces radiating Jesus!

"For God, who said 'Light shall shine out of darkness,' is the One who has shone in our hearts to give the light of the knowledge of the glory of God in the face of Christ" (2 Cor. 4:6).

What Is the Ultimate Prayer of Our New Millennium?

God's Word reveals a surprising *reason* that we need to pray before we try to shine Jesus' light to them: "And even if our gospel is veiled, it is veiled to those who are perishing, in whose case the god of this world [Satan] has blinded the minds of the unbelieving, that they might not see the light of the gospel of the glory of Christ, who is the image of God (2 Cor. 4:3–4)."

It is possible for Christians to be shining Jesus and showing His love by wonderful deeds of kindness—and even sharing Jesus verbally in multiple ways—but, because Satan has blinders on the lost, non-Christians cannot even *see* the Light of Jesus we are radiating—not until God removes their blinders when we pray.

What is the ultimate praying we can do to dispel this horrible darkness? It is praying for all people who are still in darkness to accept Jesus, the Light. Then they won't be in darkness anymore.

As Jesus said in John 12:46, "I have come as light into the world, that everyone who believes in Me may not *remain* in darkness" (emphasis added).

Many people, in addition to Cassie's parents, were praying for Cassie before God broke through to her. God had to remove Satan's blinders on her mind—which He did! This is a supernatural battle. *One of the reasons our sharing Jesus so often fails is our lack of involving the supernatural God in their lives through prayer before we try to get them saved by our human efforts.* And all along they could not even see the Jesus we were radiating toward them.

The Ultimate Prayer for Eternity?

If we are truly sincere about wanting to bring the Light, Jesus, to Planet Earth, *we must see every family member, every neighbor, every colleague, every friend, every school chum, and every college roommate as condemned already if they are without Jesus!* In John 3:18, Jesus said:

> He who believes in Him [the Son of God, Himself] is not judged; he who does not believe has been judged already, because he has not believed in the name of the only begotten Son of God.

We also must realize where they are going eternally if we don't reach them with Jesus—to a Christless eternity in hell. "If anyone's name was not found written in the book of life, he was thrown into the lake of fire" (Rev. 20:15). Hell is that eternal place with no annihilation (see Mark 9:43–48) or reincarnation (see Heb. 9:27), that inescapable place (see Matt. 23:33), that place of fire and of weeping and gnashing of teeth (see Matt. 13:49–50), and that place of banishment from Jesus (see Matt. 7:21–23).

And we must keep praying the ultimate prayer for them—to accept Jesus.

Brett, our eight-year-old grandson, was sleeping over at our house. He had asked if he could have a copy of each of Grandma's books and headed for bed clutching an armload of them. He snuggled into his favorite spot, a down comforter and pillow right beside our bed, while I propped up on the bed and continued reading the popular *Left Behind* book.

Having just finished the children's version of that book, he suddenly looked up at me and asked, "Grandma, have you written anything about being left behind?"

"Actually, Brett, in that *A Time to Pray God's Way* book I did." We turned in his copy and found those actual words as I read to him about the look in Jesus' eyes when He came back to earth and looked right past me to the hungry people I was feeding and loving. How horrified I had been not to have Jesus' "well done," but instead His indescribable sadness at all those people I had fed but hadn't told about Jesus. "Brett, although it is good to do that, Grandma hasn't written about what to do *after* someone is left behind. *My books are about all of us getting everybody ready—not to be left behind!* That is what God wants you to do, too, Brett."

My last Sunday in Brazil I had spoken on "You have left your first love" from Revelation 2:4. After telling the church at Ephesus the good things they *were* doing, Jesus told them they had left their first love, and to repent and do the things from which they had fallen. I told them how, after I first accepted Jesus at age nine, week after week I would sit in church and grit my teeth and clench my fists in earnest prayer as the pastor gave the invitation to accept Jesus. These were *my* unsaved neighbors and loved ones we had brought so they would be saved. If positive thinking could have sent them down the aisle, they would not have had a chance.

At the end, the Brazilian pastor called for those to come to the front who would promise to pray for and reach others for Jesus. Although for twenty years my ministry has averaged 25 percent of our audiences praying to make sure Jesus was their Savior and Lord, as they surged forward, I started to weep. Still sitting on the platform, God clearly said to me, *Evelyn, how long has it been since you clenched your fists and gritted your teeth in prayer over a lost soul?*

Is everybody *you* love ready to die or to meet Jesus if He should come back today?

Are you praying that ultimate prayer for them—faithfully, fervently?

But What About Now?

How could people's accepting Jesus possibly change the environment of Planet Earth?

Each person who accepts Jesus is not only transferred into His kingdom of light but is also individually transformed into a new creation in Him.

> Therefore if any man is in Christ, he is a new creature; the old things passed away; behold, new things have come (2 Cor. 5:17).

Ephesians 2:1–6 explains the awesome transformation that takes place in each new believer in Jesus:

> And you were dead in your trespasses and sins, in which you formerly walked according to the course of this world, according to the prince of the power of the air [Satan], of the spirit that is now working in the sons of disobedience. Among them we too all formerly lived in the lusts of our flesh, indulging the desires of the flesh and of the mind, and were by nature children of wrath, even as the rest. But God, being rich in mercy, because of His great love with which He loved us, even when we were dead in our transgressions, made us alive together with Christ (by grace you have been saved), and raised us up with Him, and seated us with Him in the heavenly places, in Christ Jesus.

Old things of a godless lifestyle disappear—sometimes immediately, sometimes more gradually—as deeply entrenched addictions and sins are exchanged for the new abundant life in Jesus. "I came that they might have life, and might have it abundantly" (John 10:10).

Suddenly, through their new Savior Jesus they:

- have access to the Father with power in their intercessory prayers
- can receive wisdom from the omniscient God of the universe, who will give it to them liberally
- are no longer helpless about those they love who still need Jesus, but are able to pray for them in the name and authority of Jesus
- have an inheritance in heaven

The list is endless. But, best of all, everybody accepting Jesus will then have Him living in them, radiating out from them—transforming their sphere of influence!

Amazingly, all sins of the past are instantaneously forgiven at the moment of salvation. Although they may have to live with some of the consequences of past sins, they are free in Jesus! "Of Him all the prophets bear witness, that through His name everyone who believes in Him receives the forgiveness of sins" (Acts 10:43).

Also, they will never be alone again. No matter how abandoned by family and friends or left alone through a loved one's death or in calamity and sickness and imprisonment—the Lord promised in Hebrews 13:5, "I will never desert you, nor will I ever forsake you."

This New Millennium's Light

As the new millennium jumped hourly from time zone to time zone around the globe at midnight on December 31, 1999, people on every continent took turns gasping in awe and cheering at the exploding extravaganza of lights in their capital city as the year 2000 was born. The media covered scattered religious celebrations here and there, but basically it was the world welcoming in—what?

Did all those blazing lights really bring any new light to Planet Earth? Or are the same number of the world's people still in spiritual darkness?

Is it different now from when Jesus' birth abruptly ushered in A.D. from B.C.? Oh, our means of transportation and communication methods certainly have changed drastically. Our pace of life has increased greatly. Earth no longer exclusively holds on to its human occupants as they soar into outer space. Knowledge has inundated us. But where's the new light?

The Real Light of the World

Actually, the Light that came to dispel the darkness on Planet Earth came two thousand years ago when Jesus ushered in A.D. And He still is the only light powerful enough to overcome the darkness. Jesus!

That Light now is in heaven at the right hand of the Father. He is the Light Saul saw on the Damascus road—brighter than the desert's noonday sun.

He is the Light that the apostle John, while banished to the Isle of Patmos, turned to see as a voice spoke to him.

This is the Jesus we are bringing to the darkness of the earth! This is the risen and glorified Savior who left His light with us to light the earth!

A Goal to Be Like Jesus?

My life's goal since 1968 has been "to be conformed to the image of God's dear Son, Jesus," from Romans 8:29. Studying the New Testament revealed more and more characteristics of Jesus that I would strive, and sometimes struggle, to incorporate into my own life. There were many I expected and had loved for years, but there also were frequent surprises about who Jesus really was. But one day there was a jolting shock as I began reading the Book of Hebrews. These first words seemed more than I could handle:

God, after He spoke long ago to the fathers in the prophets in many portions and in many ways, in these last days has spoken to us in His Son, whom He appointed heir of all things, through whom He also made the world. And He [the Son] is the radiance of His [the Father's] glory and the exact representation of His nature (Heb. 1:1–3).

Jesus, the Son, is the *radiance* of the Father's glory! The glory Isaiah glimpsed as the seraphim cried one to the other, "Holy, holy, holy." The glory that had shone from Jesus on the Mount of Transfiguration. And *I* was striving to be like *that*?

Seeing that awesome dimension of Jesus, my heart cried to God, "Father, I am not worthy to want to be like Jesus. I cannot be like Jesus as You revealed Him in Your Word, the Bible. Father, He is exactly like You in all Your glory! I am not worthy!!"

As I began to question the goal that I had worked so hard to achieve through all these years, I almost felt I should say, "I'm sorry, Lord." But the Father immediately spoke firmly to my heart that He, the God who had written Hebrews 1:1–3, was also the God who had said in the same Bible that "to be conformed to the image of His Son" (Rom. 8:29) was His will for me—*and for all believers.*

My Jesus! Oh, yes, I want to be like Him so that I can radiate Him to a lost and hurting world.

But my ultimate goal is that, one by one, those to whom I shine Jesus will be drawn to His beauty and will accept Him as their personal Savior—until our neighborhoods, our cities, our nation, and the whole world are full of people who have Jesus living in them.

How Long Must Jesus Wait?

When John Glenn first orbited the earth February 20, 1962, the people of Perth, Australia, turned on their lights for him. From his tiny space capsule, he reported seeing a very bright light just south of the outline of a town in western Australia—Perth.

When Senator John Glenn orbited the earth as the oldest person in space October 31, 1998, Perth's residents again enacted the scene to honor him by turning on the lights of all the city office towers, stadiums, parking lots, and backyards. This time from 162 miles above the earth, he saw an absolutely brilliant blaze of light.

Almost two thousand years ago, the Light, Jesus, lifted off from earth through the clouds and ascended back to heaven, leaving His followers to be the light of the world.

Looking down through outer space from heaven, Jesus already has been waiting patiently almost two millennia to see earth finally ablaze with His light.

How many years is Jesus going to have to wait?

Which generation is going to complete Jesus' Great Commission to bring Him, the Light of the World, to those still in darkness?

Will you join me in praying for and reaching out to your friends, colleagues, and family members who are still in spiritual darkness? Will you radiate the Light, Jesus, into your home, neighborhood, workplace, or school until they—one by one—have Jesus living in them too and are shining His light to the ones next to them?

On and on—until Jesus can look down from heaven and see your home, neighborhood, city, state, our nation, and the world—ablaze with His light!

Reflection Questions

Examine your life:

As you begin the new millennium are you completely satisfied in our booming economy—or are you slightly fearful, very alarmed, or almost in despair at the downward moral spiraling of most of our culture?

Do you honestly see the future environment for yourself, your children, and your grandchildren as spiritually lighter or darker-with or without Jesus?

Do you believe the Bible that every family member, neighbor, colleague, or friend, without Jesus is still in Satan's kingdom of darkness?

Scripture:

In your Bible, read John 12:46 slowly and repeatedly. Now do the same with Matthew 5:14a. What is Jesus saying to you personally? Listen and interact with Him in silent prayer. In what way in this the new millennium's ultimate answer?

For you to do:

In your own words, write how Jesus showed you that *you* can dramatically change the environment around you—from Satan's kingdom of darkness to Jesus' kingdom of light. How will you then help complete Jesus' reason for coming to change the spiritual darkness on Planet Earth?

_____

_____

_____

_____

For you to pray:

"Oh, dear Jesus, I'm so sorry You have been waiting almost two thousand years to see Your light dispel the darkness on earth. I know You are the only Light powerful enough to conquer it. Forgive me for not radiating You all I could have. *I want to be a part of setting Planet Earth ablaze with You!* I promise to pray by name for those still in darkness around me. And, Father, I pray that You will remove the blinders Satan still has on them keeping them from even seeing Jesus that I'm shining to them. Then may they accept You, dear Jesus, and also radiate Your light—until our whole world is ablaze with You! In your awesome name, Jesus, amen."

Notes

Chapter 1: Who Is This God of Our Prayers?

1. George Barna, *The Second Coming of the Church* (Nashville: Word, 1997), 67–68

2. Ibid., 8.

Chapter 4: God's Divine Prayer Plans

1. Leith Anderson, *Leadership That Works* (Minneapolis: Bethany House, 1999), 150.

Chapter 8: Listening to God Through His Word

1. Don Clark, "Tidal Wave of Technology" *St. Paul Pioneer Press*, 12 July 1999, 1–2(E).

Chapter 9: Listening to God Through Prayer

1. C. Austin Miles, "In the Garden," (The Rodeheaven Co., 1940), in *Gospel Hymnal* (Chicago: Baptist Conference Press, 1950), 26.

Chapter 12: What We Are Doing with Jesus

1. Evelyn Christenson, *A Study Guide for Evangelism Praying* (Eugene, Ore.: Harvest House, 1996), foreword.